Christ Holy Church International
(1947-2002)

by Thomas Oduro

Lutheran University Press
Minneapolis, Minnesota

Christ Holy Church International (1947-2002)
by Thomas Oduro

Copyright 2007 Lutheran University Press. All rights reserved. Except for brief quotations in articles or reviews, no part of this book may be reproduced in any manner without prior permission from the publisher.

Encounters with World Christianity is published in partnership with Luther Seminary with funds from the Justice and Christian Community Program and the Global Mission Institute.
  The series editorial team is:
    Dr. Charles Amjad-Ali
      The Martin Luther King, Jr., Professor of Justice
        and Christian Community
      Director, Islamic Studies Program
    Dr. David Lose
      Academic Dean
    Dr. Frieder Ludwig
      Associate Professor of Mission & World Christianity
      Director, Global Mission Institute

Library of Congress Cataloging-in-Publication Data

Oduro, Thomas, 1955-
 Christ's Holy Church International : the story of an African Independent Church / Thomas Oduro.
   p. cm.
 Includes bibliographical references and index.
 ISBN-13: 978-1-932688-27-6 (alk. paper)
 ISBN-10: 1-932688-27-7 (alk. paper)
 1. Christ's Holy Church International. 2. Independent churches—Nigeria. 3. Igbo (African people)—Religion. 4. Nigeria—Religious life and customs. 5. Nigeria—Church history. I. Title.
  BR1463.N5O28 2007
  289.9'3—dc22
                    2007013530

Lutheran University Press, PO Box 390759, Minneapolis, MN 55439
Manufactured in the United States of America

This book is dedicated to:

My Parents: Emmanuel O. Dokyi & Agnes A. Akoto

Erwin and Lorraine Spruth

Most Rev. Dr. Daniel Okoh

My wife: Jemima

My children: Eric, Phyllis, Clement, Joel, Sabina, Rita

Board Members, Faculty, Staff and students of
Good News Theological College and Seminary

Leaders of African Instituted Churches

Leaders and members of Christ Holy Church International

All my friends and prayer partners

Table of Contents

Map of Nigeria 8
Introduction 9

Part One: Historical Antecedents

CHAPTER ONE: Overview of African Independent Churches 13
    The Popular-yet-Obscure Nature of Christ Holy Church International:
        A Paradoxical Concern 13
    Nature and Purpose of the work 14
    Definition of African Independent Churches 17
    Three Typologies of African Independent Churches 18
    Toward the Recognition of AICs 21
    The Emergence of AICs 28
    AIC Revivalism 37
    The Role of Women in West African Independent Churches 42

CHAPTER TWO: Nigeria, A Brief Introduction 45
    Demographic Data 45
    Politics and Governance 46
    Ethnic Groups 50

CHAPTER THREE: Christianity in Southern Nigeria 55
    Western Missionary Initiative Among the Igbos 57
    The Emergence of African Independent Churches in Nigeria 62
    African Independent Churches Among the Igbos 64

PART II: Leaders and Growth

CHAPTER FOUR: Christ Holy Church International, Early Beginnings ... 71
    Agnes Okoh 71

CHAPTER FIVE: Development of Leadership in Christ Holy Church
International 99
    Hezekiah D. Mbaegbu 99
    Enoch Okonkwo 100
    David Ozioma U. Nwaizuzu 102
    Marius Anyetei Okoh 102
    Samuel Ejiofor 110
    Gabriel Onuorah Chiemeka 111
    Daniel Chukwudumebi Okoh 112
    Conclusion 118

CHAPTER SIX: The Nature and Growth of Christ Holy Church
International 119
    The Nature of Christ Holy Church International 124
    Administration: Personnel and Finance 125
    Worship and Liturgy 128
    Uniqueness and Ecumenicity 128
    Major Factors of Growth 148
    Minor Factors of Growth 150
    Paradigms of Qualitative Growth in the Church 150
    Conclusion 155

PART III: Thelogy and Challenges

CHAPTER SEVEN: Theology and Theological Formulation in ...... Christ
Holy Church International 159
    The Statement of Faith 159
    Tools for the Formulation of Theology in Christ Holy
        Church International 178
    Conclusion 183

CHAPTER EIGHT: The Challenges of Ministering in Nigeria,
the Experience of Christ Holy Church International 184
    The Challenge of Being Accepted by Society 184
    The Challenge of Theological Education and Documentation 192
    The Cultural Dilemma 199
    Administrative Challenges 203
    Liturgical Challenges ....

The Challenge of Providing Social Services 208
The Challenge of Coping with Instability 210
The Challenge of Self-Sufficiency 214

CHAPTER NINE: Concluding Observations 215
The Unfinished Task 215
The Agnes Okoh Factor 216
The Contribution of Christ Holy Church International to
   the Study of African Independent Churches 218

Endnotes 221

Bibliography 247

NIGER
Sokoto
Kaura
Namoda
Nguru
Hadejia
Kano
Damaturu
Maiduguri
Potiskum
Bama
Rijau
Zaria
Kontagora
Kaduna
Bauchi
Gombe
Wawa
Jos
Minna
Kishi
Bida
Abuja
Yola
Ilorin
NIGERIA
Beli
Lokoja
Makurdi
Ibadan
Abeokuta
LAGOS
Benin
City
Enugu
Ikom
Warri
Owerri
CAMEROON
Port
Harcourt
Calabar
GULF OF GUINEA
AFRICA

Introduction

Christ Holy Church International (1947-2002): The Challenges of Christian Proclamation in a Nigerian Cultural Context

The phenomenon of African Independent Churches (AICs) in African Christianity has caused many scholars to research the causative factors of their growth and their contributions to African Christianity. The challenges that shape the formulation of theology and practices are more often than not overlooked. Many scholars have researched the already known ones, thus denying the reading public the privilege of expanding their knowledge of other AICs whose activities have added diverse dimensions to the quantitative and qualitative growth of Christianity in Africa.

This study explores and examines the history, beliefs, practices, and growth of Christ Holy Church International, an African Independent Church in Nigeria, founded by Agnes Okoh, an illiterate woman who, while returning from a market in 1943, heard a voice repeatedly saying "Matthew Ten." How Agnes Okoh, a marginalized woman and a widow, was able to found and lead an itinerant evangelistic team of 12 members in 1947 till it developed into a church with nearly 800 congregations in 2002 in a pluralistic, multi-cultural and multi-linguistic Nigeria is the focus of this book.

The ability of an African Independent Church to stay together without any schism for the past 55 years, the attainment of a modicum of self-sufficiency which enables them to provide sustainable care for nearly 1,500 pastors, the centrality of the Gospel, some innovative policies that are contextual yet evangelical—serving as vehicles of growth, the commitment to the study of the Bible, the manifestation of spiritual gifts, and a we-feeling that is reminiscent of the early church (recorded in the Acts of the Apostles) are some new insights this study contributes to the nature of African Christianity.

The work highlights the ministries of the unsung leaders and members of Christ Holy Church International who braved the storms of the Second World War, colonialism, the struggle for political independence, the Biafran war, numerous military administrations, religious unrests, poverty, cynicism, persecution, cultural impediments, theological and administrative limitations to build a community of faith which cherishes the proclamation of the Gospel in its entirety, love for one another, provision of free social services, leadership accountability, and a desire to be sensitive to the cultural diversities of her membership.

PART ONE

Historical Antecedents

CHAPTER 1

Overview of African Independent Churches

The Popular-yet-Obscure Nature of Christ Holy Church International: A Paradoxical Concern

Christ Holy Church International[1] is an African Independent Church (AIC) planted by Agnes Okoh, an illiterate Igbo[2] lady who began a prophetic-healing and evangelistic ministry after having had a strange religious experience while returning from market in 1943. The ministry has since grown from 12 members in 1947 to over a million baptized members in 2002 with close to 800 congregations in Nigeria. The church has recently established congregations in Ghana, another West African nation.

The religious experience of prophetess Agnes Okoh and the subsequent growth of the church give a clue to the mammoth expansion of the church in Africa, particularly the growth of African Independent Churches. Mission scholars in the West have labored to design Church growth methodologies which, to them, are very pragmatic and effective. Such methods, to all intents and purposes, do not have African churches in mind except for minor mention in some cases. Many African pastors and church leaders do not have access to books on Church growth. Where such books are even accessible the cost is too exorbitant for them to purchase. In fact, they hardly have the privilege of attending seminars, conferences and workshops on Church growth.

Leaders and members of Christ Holy Church International are no exception to the above. The causes and methodologies of the quantitative growth of Christ Holy Church International, therefore, is a subject that should excite Church growth scholars; it calls for a serious appraisal of some methods that tend to be contextual rather than normative, albeit fruitful. Whether the quantitative growth is matched qualitatively is another important point that will be examined later.

This work is a pioneering one because Christ Holy Church International, to all intents and purpose a big denomination, is not known to scholars who have written about AICs – not even Nigerian church historians.[3] The "hiddenness" of the church to scholars despite the fact that the church has congregations in 26 States out of the 36 States in Nigeria poses another problem with the authenticity of data on African Christianity. How could such a church escape the attention of church history writers and church growth pundits? How reliable, therefore, are the data and projections of missiologists on African Christianity, particularly, that of African Independent Churches, of which Christ Holy Church International is one?

Putting aside the questionable nature of data on African Christianity, the paradox of Christ Holy Church International being popular-yet-obscure still leaves other pertinent questions unanswered. How do pastors of Christ Holy Church International who do not have access to Concordances, Bible Dictionaries, Study Bibles and other basic study tools interpret the Bible? What is the basis of their hermeneutical principles? Do Western style seminaries with an emphasis on a good library, trained professors, students with post-secondary academic qualifications, and a curriculum that is considered "evangelical" matter in the growth and expansion of the church in Africa?

The gender and social status of Agnes Okoh are also issues which call for our attention. Why should people take the claims of "a divine call" by a woman who was illiterate in her own vernacular serious - let alone leaving everything to follow her? How was she able to establish a church and lead it? How did her illiteracy promote or affect the formulation of theological beliefs, evangelistic strategies, educational programs, mission statements and other policy statements of the church? How did an illiterate woman, who lived in a pluralistic religious society, claim to contextualize theology while at the same time claiming not to be syncretistic? How could an African woman, who under normal circumstances was marginalized, lead a church composed of both sexes? Finding answers to these and many other questions is imperative if one is to understand and examine the challenges of establishing an indigenous church in Nigeria.

Nature and Purpose of the work

Though there are several variations of the acronym "AICs" (much will be said about it later in this chapter), for the sake of uniformity "AICs" will be used in this work to mean African Independent Churches.

While researchers of African Independent Churches have, in the past, laid much emphasis on their vibrant liturgies, unprecedented growth, dynamic healing ministries, varied contextualization of Christian theology and unflinching belief in the activities of the Holy Spirit, not much attention has been given to the difficulties their leaders face in establishing their churches in multi-cultural and multi-lingual Africa.

Secondly, many AIC historiographers have not ventured writing about some other AICs apart from some already-known ones. Scholarly work by both Western and African scholars on AICs for over four decades has been about the same mega-AICs in West Africa viz, The Harrists, Celestial Church of God, Muzama Disco Christo Church, Cherubim and Seraphim Church, the Church of the Lord (Aladura), Brotherhood of the Cross and Star, and a few lesser known ones.[4] Leaders of the aforementioned churches are evidently the ones that attract the attention of many scholars. The attitude of over-researching already-known AICs and AIC leaders does not expose readers of African Christianity to the whole spectrum of the growth of the Church in Africa. Some of the prime movers are obviously left behind and some great events in African Christianity have been inadvertently sidelined by researchers for a long time.

This book will therefore have a two-fold purpose. The first is to write the history of Christ Holy Church International (1947-2002) focusing on the main events. In doing so, emphasis will be on the main people and the events that took place. The reason behind certain actions will be explored. The challenges of some members to convince people of the veracity of the call of Agnes and the genuineness of the miracles God used her to perform will be highlighted. The resultant persecutions the pioneers of the church endured will be another issue to be discussed. The task of formulating theologies that are normative for Christian doctrine and practices whilst at the same time being suitable and relevant to the context of the worshippers will be given a special treatment. Readers will follow the trend of the growth, the antecedents to growth, causative factors of growth and the task of managing growth in a multi-faceted Nigeria. All these factors will be put in the religious, social, political, economic, and philosophical context of Nigeria – particularly in Igboland. In telling the story, claims of some members about the active role of the Holy Spirit regarding the growth of the church will be highlighted and discussed.

The second purpose is to select and analyze some of the challenges and how leaders of Christ Holy Church coped with them, with their limited knowledge in theology, liturgy, missions, the Bible, cross-cultural evangelism and, some of the major languages in Nigeria. Some of the perceived challenges are: (1) establishing a church that has no historical paradigm with existing denominations, (2) ministering without having the privilege of seminary education, (3) supporting pastors and their families in a poverty-stricken country, (4) doing cross-cultural ministry without having access to any Christian mission tutelage, (5) proclaiming the Gospel during the Nigerian civil war, and (6) managing tribal, cultural, and linguistic diversity in the church.

These challenges will undoubtedly increase the knowledge of theologians, church planters and missiologists about the nature of indigenous ministries in Nigeria, and to a larger extent, Africa. The work will also challenge some theological faculties and mission scholars to take a second look at the applicability of some much-touted 'tested' theological, hermeneutical, Biblical, missiological and cross-cultural principles that claim worldwide adaptability, resulting in a qualitative and quantitative growth of the Body of Christ.

The findings of the research may either confirm or disprove earlier works on cross-cultural proclamation of the Gospel and principles of indigenous church planting. The writing of the history of Christ Holy Church International will in itself be an important contribution to what God is doing in other parts of the world and will thus draw attention to the ongoing ministry of the Holy Spirit in leading those who depend on Him. It will further confirm the important role of documenting narrative history as a means of studying the growth and challenges of indigenous church planting. It will also bring to the fore the contribution of women in African Christianity, through African Independent Churches, particularly from West Africa. Theologians and theological formulators may well find a new understanding of the necessity of the Church's contextualized ministries even if wrapped in traditional beliefs.

Making the experiences of Christ Holy Church International a paradigmatic study of all other indigenous churches in Africa is not the purpose of this dissertation albeit some Church historians, missionaries and theological faculties may find it useful in making decisions as to how to relate to African Independent Churches and understand the rationale of their ministries. I do not intend to subject the theology and liturgy of the church to any theological analysis. The objective is to write the history of the Church highlighting some important events and people. Any critical theological analysis could be done at a later time.

Definition of African Independent Churches

Since no scholarly work has been done on Christ Holy Church International, it will be helpful to lead the reader to some literary work on African Independent Churches, a group of Churches in Africa which Christ Holy Church fits.[5] Scholars who have written about AICs have taken various approaches. Some have written about AICs in particular regions[6] while others have written about the whole phenomenon on the continent.[7] Other scholars simply wrote about some specific AICs[8] while others concentrate on the biographies of some of the AIC leaders and their movements.[9]

Most of the early scholars who wrote about the AICs were Western missionaries. Some wrote out of curiosity, trying to find what the whole AIC phenomenon was about. Their curiosity was motivated by the spate of secession from Western mission-founded churches, the multiplication of AICs[10] and the AICs different outlook in theology, community and liturgy – outlooks that were different from the Western mission-founded churches. African scholars later developed interest in AICs and have written about them.

Harold Turner, an eminent researcher of African Independent Churches who also lectured for many years at the University of Nigeria, Nsukka,[11] has defined an African Independent Church as "a church which has been founded in Africa, by Africans and primarily for Africans."[12]

Much as I agree that African Independent Churches are founded by Africans, asserting that they are founded "primarily for Africans" is as inadequate as asserting that churches founded by Westerners in the west are founded primarily for Westerners. The place of birth of a church and the race of the founders do not necessarily determine the race and color of those who should be primary members of the church. The missiological activities of churches founded in the West amply testify to this fact.

I have, in this regard, defined African Independent Churches as, *congregations and or denominations planted, led, administered, supported, propagated, motivated and funded by Africans for the purpose of proclaiming the Gospel of Jesus Christ and worshipping the Triune God in the context and worldview of Africa and Africans.* The fact that African Independent Churches worship the Triune God in the context and worldview of Africa does not necessarily mean Africans are their primary targets of evangelization just as it cannot be said that Westerners are the primary targets of evangelization by churches founded in the west although there are many traces of western worldview and philosophy in the life of western-founded churches, even those in non-western lands.

Three Typologies of African Independent Churches

African Independent Churches have been categorized into various typologies, such as, "Ethiopian" and "Zionist" churches, "Prophet-Healing/ Spiritual" churches, and "Newer Pentecostal/Charismatic" churches.[13] Many scholars generally use three typologies – "African/Ethiopian" type, i.e. AICs which were founded on nationalistic and politically motivated grounds, "Prophet/Healing" type, i.e. AICs which emphasize prophecy and healing, and "Pentecostal/Charismatic" type, i.e. AICs that lay emphasis on Pentecostal features and the use of the gifts of the Spirit.[14]

Much as I respect the scholarship that resulted in the typologies, my own experience with AICs,[15] particularly those in West Africa, defies the veracity of the typologies. In fact some of the typologies are outmoded in certain parts of Africa. The African/Ethiopian type, for instance, is virtually non-existent in post-independent West Africa. With the exception of *African Church* in Lagos, Nigeria (founded in 1901), one can hardly identify an AIC which was founded with political motives in post-independent West Africa.

After decades of study of African Independent Churches it is evident to me that they have the following common traits: emphasis on dreams, divine revelation and visions. Healing, prophecy, Prayer, and exorcism are considered as essential ministries. Their worship setting is usually vibrant and lasts long. They make good use of African musical instruments, local gospel choruses, and some traditional lyrics that are usually accompanied by hand clapping and free dancing, even though they at times use Western musical instruments and sing some Western hymns and canticles. Since no particular ministry is not done exclusively by any particular African Independent Church, it is no longer proper to group AICs according to their ministry peculiarity, as for example, "Prophet/healing" type. With the exception of glossolalia, their ministries overlap tremendously. It is, therefore, proper to group them on how they perceive themselves rather than on a particular ministry that is most prevalent in their existence. In this regard, African Independent Churches can be grouped into three types: Conservative, Charismatic, and Reformed.

Conservative AICs

The Conservative African Independent Churches are those who hold on to the teachings and practices of their founders no matter the perception of the wider church or what the Bible says about such beliefs and practices. They are also highly ritualistic; having detailed rituals for most aspects of their religious life. Such AICs are founder-oriented. Their beliefs and practices are based on the fact that their founder has instructed them to do so, apparently after claiming to have had some dreams and seeing visions, at times to the disregard of what the Bible teaches.[16] This group of AICs cites divine revelations as the basis of their beliefs and practices. Thus, in most cases, their rituals, color of garments, design of garments, names of places, and religious paraphernalia, hymnody and the entire belief system are said to have been revealed by God, sometimes with angels acting as mediums. The claim that God revealed such beliefs and practices, and the great reverence for the teachings of their founders (usually deceased) make the thought of examining the Biblicity of their beliefs and practices a sheer foolhardy. Attempts at reforming such churches, either by the laity or second generation leadership, are, as a result, fiercely resisted. Local languages are usually their medium of communication. The validity of the existence of conservative African Independent Churches is based on the religious experience of their founders mediated by angels or other heavenly beings.

Charismatic AICs

Charismatic AICs constitute the second type even though some scholars prefer calling them Pentecostal/Charismatic churches.[17] This group has been aptly described in the following:

> Their founders are generally charismatic and younger men and women who are respected for their preaching and leadership abilities, and who are relatively well educated, though not necessarily in theology. These churches tend to be more sharply opposed to several traditional practices than is the case with prophet-healing churches, and they often ban alcohol and tobacco, the use of symbolic healing objects, and the wearing of uniforms. The membership tends to consist of younger, less economically deprived, and more formally educated people. They are often seen, particularly by the older AICs, as mounting a sustained attack on traditional African values.[18]

Charismatic AICs relish the use of English language as their first choice medium of communication. Western musical instruments are in most cases more preferable than the use of African musical instruments though the rhythms are usually African. Though AICs in nature, their administrative set up and ministries are not different from most Western Pentecostal/Charismatic churches. Some of their major theological emphasis are "speaking in tongues," "anointing of the Holy Spirit," "deliverance from evil powers" and "wealth." The cornerstones of Charismatic African Independent Churches are their collective ecclesial and Pneumatological experiences.

Reformed AICs

The third type is what I call the Reformed African Independent Churches. This type has more similarities with the Conservative type than the Charismatic type. They have, however, made some changes in their belief system as a result of either a new vision or revelation or an intense Bible study. Their theology is, more often than not, akin to Reformed theology though one finds some aspects of Catholicism and Pentecostalism in their theological beliefs. Like the Conservative type, the vernacular is the medium of communication in this type of churches. Most leaders of Reformed African Independent Churches usually have had a stint with the Conservative type but have seceded in protest of some beliefs and practices they considered as not Biblical coupled with their conservatism. Some of them are second or third generation leaders of what used to be a conservative AIC. They are usually well educated, open-minded, and teachable. Reformed African Independent Churches affirm the limitations of humanity and the struggle of Christians to fathom the Bible. While being aware of the need to conform to normative Christian doctrines and practices, they are, nevertheless, aware of the need to posit relevant and contextualized theology. They are careful neither to go to the extreme end of Western Christianity that is filled with Western culture nor attempt a total Africanization of the Gospel. This group, like the first type, believes in the revelation of God through visions and dreams. The medium or channel of the vision or dream is, however, considered as not important. What is important to them is the content of the revelation and its conformity to biblical standards. Christ Holy Church International, the subject-matter of this book, belongs to this type.

In revising the typologies of AICs, I agree with Allan Anderson that, "The outline is not presumed to be exhaustive or definitive, especially as the movements it encompasses are dynamic churches undergoing a constant process of change."[19] Nevertheless the importance of making clear cut typologies instead of perceiving them as one body cannot be ignored: "To distinguish between different types of AICs is necessary seeing that the opposite procedure of 'lumping them together' tends to obscure important historical forces which need to be well understood."[20] In this regard the mention of AICs in this work refers to the Conservative and Reformed ones since the Charismatic AICs do not consider themselves as AICs albeit by definition they are. They hardly co-exist with the other types of AICs.

Toward the Recognition of AICs

Trying to find the reasons behind the emergence and popularity of the AICs resulted, for instance, in the publication of Bengt Sundkler's *Bantu Prophets in South Africa*.[21] Sundkler concentrated on the dynamics of AICs, and their uniqueness in integrating culture and tradition in Bantu prophetism in areas such as leadership roles, women-in leadership, finances, worship and liturgy.

In documenting the histories and beliefs of African Independent Churches, some of the distinctive approaches of the AICs to Christian doctrine and practices that seemed "unorthodox" to normative Christianity but akin to the norms of African traditional religions caught the attention of some scholars and, therefore, created some doubts in their minds. These perceptions, as a result, reflected in the descriptive tags given to the AICs by some scholars; tags such as "sects," "separatist movements," "syncretistic movements" and many others. In Ghana, AICs were pejoratively called "spiritual churches."[22]

Other descriptive names given them were "African Independent Churches," "African Initiated Churches," "African Instituted Churches," and "African Indigenous Churches." All these names have the acronym "AIC." None of these names, on its own, wholly describes the historical and ministerial perspectives of the churches being discussed in this work although each of them is in a sense representative of an aspect of their history and nature yet inadequate on its own. It is ironic to note that leaders of AICs were not consulted by western mission scholars in the process of coining such names. Paul Makhubu, a South African AIC leader, states how insignificant such names mean to some of the AIC leaders: "People can call us what they want, judge us, and put us in pigeon holes if they wish. We exist and are growing fast."[23]

The desire for AICs to be recognized by Western mission-founded churches dates back to the last decade of the nineteenth century.

> After 1898 the first attempts to secure recognition from the mainline churches began. Sometimes this meant absorption...But usually it meant attempts to secure recognition, fellowship and legitimacy for autonomous AICs. In this it largely failed; mainline denominations were not yet prepared to treat them as fellow-members of the Body of Christ or to extend any kind of recognition. Throughout this period AICs were regarded as eccentric and their attempts to co-operate with historical or mission-related churches were cold-shouldered...[24]

This attitude was not limited to clergymen, some scholars found it difficult to recognize the AICs as churches of equal standing with the Western mission-founded churches. The attitude continued even in the early 1960s as is evident in a shrewd statement by Edgar Brookes in his Preface to the second edition to Bengt Sundkler's *Bantu prophets in South Africa* published in 1962: "There are elements in the life of some of the Bantu separatist churches which are not Christian in any normally accepted sense of the word – there are elements of true faith and vision. It is doubtful if any human being can wholly separate the wheat from the tares in this luxuriant field of religious activity…"[25] Not all critics were as diplomatic as Brookes. Professor Bolaji Idowu, a Methodist minister and an AIC cynic, said the following about them:

> The end product of this syncretism is a church whose characteristics are frothy, ecstatic ritual, seeing of visions, and dreaming of dreams, making predications and prescriptions, mass hysteria which gives birth to babbling of incoherent things as symptoms of possession by the Spirit. All these naturally make them popular with the mass who like neglected hungry sheep flock where they find promises of nourishment.[26]

These perceptions were in sharp contrast to how the Independent Churches perceived themselves. Ratovonarivo, an AIC leader in Madagascar, states a popular view among the AICs:

> For the sake of clarity in this paper, let us call the Protestant Churches which separated directly from the Catholic Churches, the 'First, or Original, or Ancient Independent Churches.' At any rate, the Church historians call them, together with the Catholic churches 'Established churches.' In this paper, 'Independent Churches' should be understood to mean those churches, which depend neither upon the Catholic churches, nor upon the first, original, and ancient Protestant the Established churches; although like all churches, the Independent churches accept the form and nature of the First or Original church.[27] [sic.].

To Ratovonarivo and other AIC leaders, their churches are not different in any way than other Protestant churches, be they evangelicals, puritans, fundamentals or whatever humanity has chosen to call them. Ratovonarivo's definition of African Independent Churches is based on what they read about the first church in the New Testament.

What might have confused scholars in this era was the dichotomy of comparing Western mission-founded churches to all others – i.e. the perception of all non-Western mission-founded Churches as African Independent Churches. The AICs, based on Ratovonarivo's definition, perceive a dichotomy of Churches in Africa and elsewhere – the oft-repeated Protestants and Catholics.

As a result of the different interests of scholars, the AIC phenomenon was initially received with mixed feelings. Some colonial administrators saw their popularity as potential time bombs of political insurrection. These perceptions, coupled with the AICs' own inability to articulate who they were and the theological reasons behind some of their activities which were considered contrary to national interests, resulted in their persecution by both non-AIC Christians and colonial politicians.[28]

In spite of the initial hesitation by some scholars to perceive AICs as part of Christianity, some scholars got closer to the African Independent Churches in an attempt to find out the reasons behind their beliefs and practices. Their findings reversed some of the oblique perceptions. The work of Turner, in this regard, needs special mention at this point. He wrote in an unbiased manner and attempted to explain the ministries of the AICs in a manner that unveiled the mysticism of their activities and rituals. He painstakingly worked on a typology that was neither derogatory nor judgmental.[29] He classified all religious movements in Africa (Islam, not included) into three categories: Neo-primal, Hebraist and Christian. Some religious movements in Africa who were initially identified by some scholars of the first phase as part of the Independent Churches were classified as Neo-Primal and Hebraist Religious Movements.

Turner defines Neo-Primal movements as:

> ...those new forms that have appeared as part of the reaction to the great changes occurring in African life in our period. Those who have felt the disturbing effects of contact with Western culture and religion, and have seen their own sanctions and unity being undermined, have sometimes sought to develop new forms of the old religions.[30]

Concerning the Hebraist, Turner says, "We use it to refer to those movements that have made radical break-through in favour of faith in the one God they find in the Old Testament, but which have not reached a Christian position."[31] The Neo-Primal and Hebraist movements are perhaps, the ones Philip Jenkins describes "movements far from any customary notion of Christianity."[32]

Under Christian category, Turner made two classifications. One he classifies as "missions and churches that have been developed from modern missionary work, together with the churches of white settlers and administrators."[33] This group is popularly known in Africa as "Western mission churches" or "mainline churches." Concerning the other group, after a long argument showing the limitations of earlier descriptions (such as, sects, syncretists, separatists, and independent) given to them by some scholars, he stated: "In summary phrase they may be described as 'independent churches of African origin', more briefly as 'independent African churches', or simply as 'independent churches.'"[34] This group of Churches is what is generally known as African Independent Churches – the locus of this literary review. Turner, thus, broke the dilemma of some scholars who hesitated to call the African Independent Churches "churches" since they perceived them as a different brand of believers in Christianity.

David Barrett was another scholar who wrote an important work on African Independent Churches. In his book, *Schism and Renewal in Africa,* Barrett in 1967 identified "...some five thousand distinct ecclesiastical and religious bodies in thirty-four African nations, with a total of almost seven million nominal adherents drawn predominantly from two hundred and ninety different tribes in all parts of the continent."[35] As the title of his book indicates, Barrett identifies the various causes of the emergence of African Independent Churches from the denominations founded by Western missionaries. He, therefore, gave credence to the term 'separatists.'[36]

Some scholarly works on AICs facilitated the understanding of their beliefs and practices.[37] Many scholars, as a result, recognized the tremendous growth patterns and the immerging contributions of African Independent Churches. An example of the effect of the new understanding of the AICs led Bengt Sundkler to make the following confession in the 1976 edition of his book:

> In the 1948 and 1961 editions of this study, we went so far as to suggest that the syncretistic sect becomes the bridge over which Africans are brought back to heathenism – a viewpoint which stresses the seriousness of the whole situation. Renewed contact in 1969 on the spot, with Zulu and Swazi churches have helped the author to understand better that he should have attempted to interpret the religious life of these groups *from their own viewpoint.*[38]

The AICs, it must be emphasized, did not earn this recognition passively. They worked towards it, although not with the intent of catching the attention of historiographers and other scholars. An example of the active part played by the AICs is about their growth.

AICs do not have mission schools and schools of evangelism, yet they have spread their faith far and wide, much to the admiration of many westerners and Africans. The numerical growth AICs has been hard to compute because many of them meet in countless houses located in many African towns and cities. The irony of popularity-yet-obscurity of Christ Holy Church International reinforces the belief that AIC growth data could be said to be lower than whatever figure church growth analysts put forward. Two words many scholars use to denote their growth are "mushrooming" and "proliferation." The use of any of these words is an admission of the difficulty of determining their growth data yet implicit of the fast rate of the growth. Nathaniel Ndiokwere, in this regard, perceives AICs as churches "springing up like fungus in all nooks and corners of Africa."[39] Because of their hiddenness, many AICs scholars find it difficult to compute the number of AIC adherents. It is generally agreed among scholars, nonetheless, that AICs grow at a very fast rate as the following statistics of AICs adherents show. Philip Jenkins notes that African Independent Churches "today claim an impressive 35 million members,.."[40] A different source reported in 2001 that AICs number 32 million.[41] If one is to take "today" in Jenkins' quote to be 2002 – the date his book was published – (taken for granted that each statistic is true on its own merit) one would be tempted to believe that AICs won 3 million adherents from 2001 to 2002 – an impressive growth rate in one year. Comparing a crowd of Easter pilgrims at two religious sites in St. Peter's Square at the Vatican, Rome, and at Moria in South Africa, respectively, Jenkins asserts: "Every Easter, more than a million ZCC[42] pilgrims gather for several days of celebrations at Zion City, the Church's chief shrine in South Africa. To put this in perspective, the crowd gathered at the ZCC's pilgrimage is larger than that which greets the pope in St. Peter's Square on Easter morning."[43] It is, therefore, no wonder that AICs are said to "currently constitute the fastest growing sector of Christianity in the world."[44]

The Church of Jesus Christ on Earth through the Prophet Simon Kimbangu, (*L'Eglise de Jésus-Christ sur Terre par son Envoyé Spécial Simon KIMBANGU*), an AIC founded in the Belgian Congo, now known as the Democratic Republic of Congo, for example, claims to have more than 8 million members worldwide.[45] The growth of AICs transcends the boundaries of Africa and not limited to Africans only.

Overview of African Independent Churches • 25

Lively AIC groups can be found, for example, in Amsterdam, London and Birmingham, Hamburg, Geneva and Zurich...Non-Africans have become members of these churches. Thus what started off as a church for Africans has now opened its doors to Europeans and others. Through this opening AICs are becoming not only global and international but also ecumenical and missionary.[46]

AIC congregations are scattered throughout numerous US cities, including Minneapolis and St. Paul, Minnesota.[47]

Growth was not the only factor that earned the AICs recognition. The AICs adopted an apologetic stance towards their critics. Many AIC leaders began defending their beliefs and practices, and vociferously critiquing their critics. Ndiokwere cites an example of a Vicar of the Church of the Lord (Aladura), an AIC in Benin City, Nigeria, cautioning his Roman Catholic critics to be circumspect before deriding AICs:

> What on earth is the Reverend gentleman doing while the Aladura Churches continue to win his members to their fold? Is it not his duty to strengthen their faith?...If what he termed 'mushroom', hand-clapping, band-beating, vision-seeing Churches could be daring enough to almost empty a Church, I would therefore appeal to the Catholic authorities in Nigeria to re-examine the ministerial priesthood...Priests should be warned to desist from self-defence action and from pointing accusing fingers at others, for much depends on them as good soul-winners for Christ. Moreover, they should be taught that greater soul-winning is neither done in the Church pulpit, nor in the sanctuary, nor in vicarages, but in the highways and hedges.[48]

Some leaders in Western mission-founded churches succinctly stated their understanding of the ministries of AIC and, thus, distanced themselves from AIC cynics. Nathaniel Ndiokwere quotes Dr. G. Ikeobi, organizer of Catholic prayer meetings in Onitsha, Nigeria, as saying:

> My view of these Aladura and 'Alleluia' Churches is that the God I call upon and worship wants me to get a feedback from them. To me, it is part of Christian charity and humanity to recognize the good in others especially when I have failed sometimes woefully to be good myself. These Churches are making the incarnation and adaptation we have failed to make. They are trying to bring God to the *life experiences* of the

people. They are not interested in saying and doing things that do not relate to the actual conditions of their hearers. In doing this, they may make mistakes, but my spirit tells me that if God spoke through an *ass* to a prophet in the past, He can today speak to me through them. So if some of the things we do do resemble their own, so much the better. Nobody has the monopoly of the Holy Spirit.[49]

A third factor that contributed to the recognition of AICs was an ecumenical effort made by the African Independent Churches in 1978 by organizing themselves into the Organization of African Instituted Churches (OAIC), an international ecumenical body, with Headquarters in Nairobi, Kenya. The Mennonite Board of Missions and other western-founded churches, had hitherto established a theological institute, Good News Training Institute, in 1971 in Accra, Ghana, to offer pastoral and theological education to the AIC corpus.[50]

The unprecedented growth of AICs, the work of some scholars, the ecumenical activities of the AICs and their apologetic approach to their critics and cynics made them a big force to reckon with in African Christianity.

The recognition of AICs, therefore, became a *sine qua non* in the history of Christianity. This recognition has been succinctly put by John Pobee & Gabriel Ositelu: "There is no way we can talk of world Christianity, much less Christianity in Africa, without taking account of this genre of AICs."[51] Much has, as a result, been written about their significance in Christianity. Pobee and Ositelu perceive their work as "African Initiatives in Christianity",[52] Allan Anderson sees the "initiatives" as a means of reforming African Christianity.[53] The significance of the AICs has similarly not escaped the attention of other scholars like Kwame Bediako who acknowledges AICs for "indicating the trend and direction of African Christianity."[54] To Andrew Walls, "they bring the elements of African religious consciousness into connexion with Christ."[55] Lamin Sanneh calls AICs "the signature tune of African Christianity."[56]

Unlike the early stages of their emergence when some scholars hesitated to call "churches," now they are considered as equally important as the Western mission founded churches. Pobee and Ositelu affirm that: "Mission-founded churches and AICs may differ from one another in ethos, style, theological emphasis, worship and spirituality; but they are siblings in God's family. Dare we disenfranchise or unchurch the other?"[57] With this recognition by scholars and church leaders, it was no wonder that two AICs, The Church of Jesus Christ on Earth by the Prophet Simon Kimbangu and The Church of the Lord (Aladura), were accepted as members of the World Council of Churches in 1969 and 1975 respectively.[58]

The acceptance of the AICs as "Christians" is, nevertheless, not a general phenomenon – particularly in Africa. Dean Gilliland has observed very fairly that "…there is more enthusiasm for African independent churches outside of Africa than inside."[59] Many African Christians who do not belong to the AICs, after comparing them to Western mission-founded churches, perceive the AICs as "imitators of Christianity"[60] who should not be taken seriously.

The Emergence of AICs

A 1971 gallery of 56 Africa Independent Church leaders under the title "Who's Who" shows a variety of AIC leaders with many backgrounds.[61] A common thing about most of them was that they were schismatics, i.e. they established their churches after having been either excommunicated from their churches for discarding their ecclesial traditions and norms or intentionally caused a rift in the church. They are, thus, perceived as disobedient to the authorities of their Western-founded denominations.

A brief history about the leaders in the magazine indicates that they defected from the Anglican Church, (also known as Church Missionary Society), Roman Catholic, Baptist Mid-Missions, Methodist church, Church of Christ, Baptist Missionary Society, Pentecostal Assemblies of Canada mission, Apostolic Church (Britain), Presbyterian Church, Dutch Reformed Church, Paris Evangelical Missionary Society, Salvation Army, London Missionary Society, and Rhenish Mission (Lutheran).

The list cuts across almost all churches planted by Western missionary societies. Prior to their secession from these churches they were holding various positions such as, priests, pastors, teacher-catechists, preachers, supervisors, chapel keepers, and evangelists. Others were laymen or women and communicants – virtually unnoticed by their church leaders.[62] In some cases large numbers of people followed the defectors. Matthew Ajuoga, a priest of the Anglican Church in Kenya, for instance, "left Anglican Church with 16,000 followers to form Church of Christ in Africa…"[63] When Maria Mtakatifu left the Catholic Church in 1960 to found the Maria Legio Church (Legion of Mary of Africa Church) "huge numbers of Catholics, estimated at 90,000 including many lapsed, converted to Maria Legio Church."[64] The causes of factors leading to such secessions are many, but for simplicity sake they have been grouped into two – latent and overt.[65]

Latent Causative Factors

The first causative factor was latent. It has three-fold aspects – education, philology, and Bible translation. As regards education, Fritz Raaflaub, one time President of the Swiss Evangelical Missionary Council, has noted: "In the work of the missions in Africa, school and church went hand in hand like twin sisters as if things had to be that way."[66] The mission schools afforded Africans the privilege to read and write the lingua franca of the countries of origin of the missionaries. This gave some Africans the privilege to be highly educated and the ability to rub minds with westerners.

Many African politicians who struggled for political independence were educated in the mission schools as Kwame Nkrumah, the first President of Ghana who wrestled political power from the hands of British colonial masters admits: "It is the missionaries who have really brought Africa to life. I and many others are everything we are because of their work and their help."[67]

John Baur, a Catholic historian, gives two objectives – ultimate and immediate - for the establishment of mission schools:

> The missionary objective was to enable the Africans to develop their own church: the Lutherans insisted that the converts should be able to read the Bible; the Anglicans wanted a self-reliant church as soon as possible; the Presbyterians and especially the Catholics aimed at spreading Christian civilization. So they all built schools; yet for them all the immediate purpose of the school was to convert as many as possible.[68]

If the ultimate objective of establishing mission schools was *to enable the Africans to develop their own church* then one can say that there was a prophetic motif in establishing mission schools. Later events that unfolded when Africans became *educated enough* to establish their own churches, as will be shown in this work, put a doubt on the ultimate motive of establishing mission schools, as Baur claims.

Western missionaries and some Africans who were gifted in linguistics devoted their time to study many African languages and reduced them into writing.[69] For instance Johann Gottlieb Christaller, a German missionaries among the Twi speakers in the Gold Coast, now Ghana "…plucked the language from the lips of pupils and of people he met in the street. Each day, in spite of the heat and in spite of mosquitoes, he burned the midnight oil at his desk."[70] As a result Christaller translated the Bible into Twi language in 1871, a hymn book, catechism, textbooks, documented 3000 proverbs, a 671 dictionary in Twi and an encyclopedia.[71] The work of philologists in Africa has enabled Africans to document their histories and rich heritages. Africans, have to some extent, avoided the pain of losing some valuable tradition through oral tradition.

The last aspect of the latent factors that caused the emergence of African Independent Churches is the translation of the Bible to local languages. "The translation of the Scriptures was often the first literature to appear in an African language. For many years, the primary objective of the mission schools was to enable people to read the Bible in their own language."[72] Translating the Bible into other languages, according to Kwame Bediako is akin to the doctrine of incarnation; it is a means "by which the fullest divine communication has reached beyond the forms of human words into the human form itself."[73]

Bible translators made the doctrine of incarnation simple and more meaningful to the simple-minded African who, without reading the Bible in his/her own vernacular, may not hear the voice of Jesus Christ. As a result of Western education and the translation of the Bible, many Africans were able to read the Bible as well as the Western missionaries. The Bible was, however, read by the missionaries and Africans with two different worldviews. According to Ogbu Kalu, "The missionaries read the Bible through the lenses of the Protestant emphasis on Word over Spirit and the Enlightenment desacralization of the universe. The Africans, on the other hand, read the Bible through their own traditionally 'charismatic' worldview…"[74]

Africans, while reading the Bible, found an affinity between their traditional religions and the Bible. In fact the Bible is replete with so many things that Africans know very well before coming into contact with Christianity. Some of the things in the Bible that are common to both Christianity and African traditional religion are: blood sacrifices, seeing visions and dreaming, building and use of altars, the importance of priests and shrines, undertaking of pilgrimages, defined domestic roles of husbands, wives, children, mode of training children, types of marriages – monogamy and polygamy, belief in and veneration of ancestors, the use of herbs and other natural elements as agents of healing, belief in miracles, the importance of fecundation in marriage, belief in angels as messengers of deities, dietary regulations as vehicles of holiness, rituals and many other concepts are all familiar with African traditional religion. All these are aspects of African traditional religions – concepts that have regulated the lives of many Africans for many years. Most of them were, however, suppressed in many of the churches established by the western missionaries.

Those who translated the Bible into African languages, in a sense, provided a means for the Africans to compare and contrast Christianity which was wrapped in Western philosophies and worldview and Christianity as inferred from the Biblical world. Bible translators, therefore, subverted the *cultural possessiveness of the Faith*, be it Anglo-Saxon culture, Germanic, American, Latino, or Zulu. In reference to Africans, translatability enabled them to appreciate the faith of their forefathers since the religion of the Hebrews is very much akin to that of African Traditional Religion.

Many Africans interpreted the Bible according to their own understanding, and questioned some of the policies[75] of the missionaries in light of what they read in the Bible. Some found Biblical legitimacy for some of their practices, such as polygamy and ancestral veneration.[76] These new-found revelations in the vernacular Bibles and the other latent factors already mentioned, prepared some Africans to challenge some western missionaries in a bid to rid Christianity of some Western cultural nuances, thus making it more meaningful and relevant to the African – leading to the establishment of African Independent Churches. The stage was thus set for overt maneuvers by some Africans to call for a church that will be more meaningful to them.

Overt Causative Factors

The second main causative factor leading to the emergence of African Independent Churches had a three-fold segment: African nationalism, religious paternalism, and cultural revivalism.

Colonial interests differed from one African country to another. For instance while colonialists in South Africa were bent on settling on the land, with no intention of returning to Europe, the interest of West African colonialists was more of economic, i.e. amassing of wealth through trading. These different interests determined how Africans were treated in their own regions and countries. There were, however, some humiliating treatment and perception of Africans that was common to the colonialists. African politicians commonly perceived the colonialists as usurpers of the powers, privileges, wealth and positions of Africans.

With the dignity of Africans hampered by some Europeans, many Africans did not make a distinction between the politician and the missionary since the churches were patronized by both European missionaries and politicians. Some African Christians, (in most cases those who came to Africa from the Diaspora and those who had their education in the West) in an attempt to hasten the fulfillment of the psalmist's prophecy in Psalm 68:31, *Envoys will come out of Egypt, Ethiopia will quickly stretch out her hands to God*[77] debunked the oft-believed idea of the West introducing Christianity to Africa. The Ethiopianists seceded from the missionary churches to plant their own. They thus earned the name "Ethiopian churches."[78]

> Andrew Walls argues in support of the motif of the Ethiopianists:
> Ethiopian stands for Africa indigenously Christian, Africa *primordially* Christian; for a Christianity that was established in Africa not only before the white people came, but before Islam came; for a Christianity that has been continuously in Africa for far longer than it has in Scotland, and infinitely longer than it has in the United States. African Christians today can assert their right to the *whole* history of Christianity in Africa, stretching back almost to the apostolic age.[79]

To some extent the term "Independent" can be applied to this group of churches since they extricated themselves from European domination. Apart from a change of leadership not much was done in the Ethiopian churches to reflect their Africanness. Their vituperations, however, awakened the minds of many Africans to question the motives of Western missionaries.

Religious paternalism was very evident in most Western mission-founded churches; it was similar to the tendencies that led to the formation of the Ethiopian movement - the only difference was that there were no political inclinations. Some western missionaries pushed many African Christians to the periphery of church leadership even though most of the Africans were at the fore-front of evangelization, teaching new converts and translating the Bible into African languages.[80]

The case of Samuel Ajaye Crowther, a recaptive slave of Yoruba origin who distinguished himself as a career missionary and was, therefore, ordained as the first African bishop of the Church Missionary Society in 1864, also serves as a good paradigm of the extent of Western missionary paternalism. Crowther was humiliated by some Western missionaries after stigmatizing his leadership qualities.[81]

The humiliation of Bishop Samuel Crowther and his replacement with a European bishop infuriated the Africans. Walls aptly observes: "...the refusal to appoint an African successor to Crowther, despite the manifest availability of outstanding African clergy, marks an important point in the history of African Independent Churches."[82] In a bid to rebuff the paternalism of the Europeans, the Africans founded the United Native Church in 1891, a church which served as a precursor to the formation of AICs in Nigeria.

When one considers the overt activities of Africans regarding Western missionary paternalism, particularly with the view of the leadership qualities of Africans who seceded from the mission churches to establish their own, one can not help but agree with Philip Jensen for perceiving Western missionary paternalism as "ignorant."[83]

Cultural revivalism was the last segment of the overt activities leading to the planting of African Independent Churches. It was the most pronounced and commonest. David Bosch identifies *the Gospel and Culture*, as one of the dominant missionary motifs in post-Enlightenment missionary activity. "The Enlightenment, however, together with the scientific and technological advances that followed in its wake, put the West at an unparalleled advantage over the rest of the world."[84] Western missionaries saw Africans as people still living in the pre-enlightenment age – a situation that needed to be reversed so as to have a share in the advantages of the enlightenment. Western culture, therefore, became a *de facto* lifestyle and was thus imposed on the non-western world without taking cognizance of the effects of the imposition. The missionaries, obviously, took the Gospel to Africa to *save* them from the depravity of sin. The Christian message of salvation, however, went hand in hand with Western civilization. Many Western missionaries sometimes believed that supplanting African cultures with that of the West would bring "the abundance of the good things that modern education, healing, and agriculture would provide for the deprived peoples of the world."[85] Bosch sums up the problems resulting from the cultural imposition of Western missionaries:

> The problem was that the advocates of mission were blind to their own enthnocentricism. They confused their middle-class ideals and values with the tenets of Christianity. Their views about morality, respectability, order, efficiency, individualism, professionalism, work, and technological progress, having been baptized long before, were without compunction exported to the ends of the earth. They were, therefore, predisposed not to appreciate the cultures of the people to whom they went –the unity of living and learning; the interdependence between individual, community, culture and indus-

try; the profundity of folk wisdom; the proprieties of traditional societies – all these were swept aside by a mentality shaped by the Enlightenment which tended to turn people into objects, reshaping the entire world into the image of the West, separating humans from nature and from one another, and developing them according to Western standards and suppositions.[86]

Supplanting African cultures and worldviews with that of Europe cut across every fiber of the African society – social set up, ethical innovations, philosophy, and religion. "Some of our customs and traditions, which are good, were said to be evil and heathen. People were told to abandon them without much teaching and explanation. Western culture was preached as being Christian and good."[87]

The result of the influence of the Enlightenment on Western missions in Africa caused some Western missionaries to do further damage to African personality. Western missionaries did not leave much room for an African expression of Christianity. The theology of Western mission-founded churches in Africa was, for instance, not different from that of their parent churches in Europe and America. Many beliefs and practices of the African that did not sound comprehensible to the White missionaries were either disdained, suppressed or disallowed in African Christianity. The gifts of the Spirit were, for instance, distinguished into two (in line with Calvinistic beliefs) – permanent and temporary – the temporary ones (miracles, healing, prophetic utterances, etc.) being considered as having ceased with the death of the Apostles.[88] Scientific healing was more preferable to spiritual healing despite the fact that African concept of illness and healing was different from the Westerners'. Many Western missionaries suspected "that African medicine was coupled with superstition and fraud."[89] The existence and reality of demons and other evil forces were frowned upon. This was against the African view:

> ...the issue of witchcraft goes to the heart of the African psyche. African societies, like the biblical-Semitic world, have a religious and spiritual understanding of reality. We are surrounded by hosts of spirit beings – some good, some bad – which are considered able to influence the course of human lives. For that reason calamities are attributed to personal forces of evil. In such a setting it is an important role of religion to help free humanity from the tyranny of those forces of evil. It is useless to debate the reality of such spirit beings.[90]

The exorcism and healing inferences of Jesus Christ in the Bible were considered as suitable only for his age and time.[91] The veneration of ancestors by Africans was described as an abomination.

To many Africans, liturgy in the churches founded by Western missionaries became coterminous with lethargy. The liturgical languages – Latin, Portuguese, and English - were foreign to the worshippers. Western hymns, canticles, anthems, liturgical dances etc. were the norm in Western-mission founded churches. Very few Africans could comprehend the rhymes of hymns that were sung in churches. Pobee and Ositelu, therefore, ask, "What can an African villager make of hymns to the Trinity that use language like 'consubstantial, co-eternal, while unending ages run?"[92] The use of African musical instruments and dances were either not allowed or strictly controlled in the churches.

Many Africans, on being converted to Christianity, were persuaded to alter their allegiance to traditional rulers and societal norms. The Mission house,[93] usually the residence of the missionary, and other missionary townships inhabited by Christians became towns within towns with the missionary being perceived as the new authority.

In historical perspective, the effects of some of the policies of the Western mission-founded churches on African society was somewhat reminiscent of a similar situation – with a few exceptions – on the European society, described below, prior to the Evangelical Revival in Europe in the 18th century.[94]

> There were able preachers, but the characteristic sermon was the colorless essay on moral virtues. Outreaching work for the unchurched was but scanty. The condition of the lower classes was one of spiritual destitution. Popular amusements were coarse, illiteracy widespread, law savage in its enforcement, jails sinks of diseases and iniquity. Drunkenness was more prevalent than at any other period in English history. ..Furthermore, Great Britain stood on the eve of the industrial revolution that was to transform it in the last third of the eighteenth century from agriculture to manufacture.[95]

Western missionaries did not posit alternative strands to the beliefs and practices they undermined or banned. This created a big vacuum and left many African Christians with nothing to hold on to in times of crisis. Many Africans became disoriented socially, culturally, psychologically, philosophically and religiously. A serious identity crisis was the overall result.[96]

There was a breakdown of social order since the African convert did not know to what authority to pay allegiance – the church or the elders. Traditional rulers, accordingly, became suspicious of the motives of Western missionaries. This led the tense scenario of a grandnephew of an Ashanti King and Rev. Picot, a Methodist missionary who was seeking permission to have a missionary thrust in Kumasi, Ghana. The Ashanti royal told Rev. Picot, "…We will never embrace your religion, for it would make our people proud. It is your religion which has ruined the Fanti country, weakened their power and brought down the high on a level with the low man."[97]

Had the European missionaries allowed Africans to put Christianity in their own context, the Africans, with their knowledge of the nuances of their cultural elements, would have known what aspect of their culture that needed to be discontinued and what needed to be continued. Christianity would have become more meaningful to the Africans instead of being popularly tagged *White man's religion*. These cultural impositions and the intransigence of some of the Western missionaries and their African allies paved the way for the establishment of African Independent Churches. The dissection and integration of African culture by leaders of the Independent churches and its resultant acceptance by Africans amply prove that people take responsibility of the church when they can relate the church's beliefs and practices to their context, as we will observe in the life of Christ Holy Church International.

In conclusion of this section, attention needs to be drawn to the fact that not all AIC leaders were schismatics or loved to seek independence from western mission-founded churches just for the sake of leading a church. Some AIC leaders were not known to be members of any existing denomination prior to their claim of being called to preach the Gospel. In fact such leaders claimed they never intended to establish a denomination till certain circumstances compelled them to do so. An example of such leaders is Moses Orimolade Tunolase, who though an illiterate, began preaching in many Nigerian cities with no intention of establishing a denomination but ended up establishing Cherubim and Seraphim Society in 1925, one of the early AICs in Nigeria. Omoyajowo notes:

> It must be noted that, quite unlike most other African Independent Churches, the C & S came into existence by sheer accident. It was not a separatist sect, Nor was it directly the logical outcome of an organized series of evangelistic campaigns. Moses Orimolade was neither a general evangelist whose main concern was to win converts for Christ. To him, it

was not important to what denominations his converts chose to belong; what mattered to him was that they should become Christians.[98]

There were some other AIC leaders who after claiming that God had called them (either through a vision, prophecy or voice) to begin a ministry, left quietly, at times unnoticed or at times with the blessing of their leaders. Agnes Okoh belongs to this latter group of non-schismatic AIC leaders.

AIC Revivalism

The nature of the African Independent revival was drastic and radical, with so many similar traits to the Radical Reformation in Europe in the 16th century.[99] It covered three main areas: theology, liturgy, and evangelism. While maintaining the main strands of Christian theology in doctrines such as Christology, harmatiolology and eschatology, they made some radical theological addendums to what they received from Europe and America. As already noted, unlike the Western mission churches where women were not permitted to function as priests, most African Independent Churches found nothing wrong with feminine priesthood.

> The African independent churches ...offer them (i.e. women) another social group in which they are known and accepted as persons, in which they become full citizens of the Kingdom of God, in which they can take initiatives and responsibilities, and in which they can acquire a social position independently from their situation at home.[100]

Women were, thus, not only accepted as leaders, their gifts were distinguished from their gender. They were, therefore, given full recognition in the AICs. In some cases women were leaders.[101]

One other theological reinstatement by the AICs was on demonology. AICs hold an intrinsic belief in the reality of demons, witchcraft, and other malevolent spirits. Since they attribute every evil thing to the devil, they use the name of Jesus Christ and the promises in the Bible to extricate themselves from the fear and domination of the evil one. Pobee and Ositelu cite the following popular West African gospel song to support this view:

Satan, you don fall ground, O Macha macha you don fall for gutter eh, eh, you don fall for ditch, O kwatakwata	Satan you have already fallen you have fallen into the drain Hey! you have fallen completely into a ditch
Satan I hate your name Satan, you be trouble maker Jesus, he go face you now	Satan, I hate your name Satan, you are a trouble maker Jesus will face up to you now in a contest
With one blow, he settle that	With a blow, he will settle the whole issue
O man de tell am Na you dey cause am abortions na you dey cause	People are saying that you are the cause of the fight For you have been behind abortions caused by people
armed robbery na you dey cause	You have been behind armed robbery
I hate you, I don't like your name	I hate you, your very name is an abomination to me
Jesus don beat you two thousand years ago he don beat you again, O Macha macha	Jesus has already defeated you two thousand years ago He has already defeated you thoroughly
Satan, you don fall for ground Oh!	Satan, you have already fallen to the ground
You don fall for gutter Oh! You don fall for ditch Oh!	you have already fallen down a drain you have already fallen into a ditch.[102]

African Independent Churches not only use the name of Jesus to counteract the activities of Satan, as is shown in the song; they also use prayer and fasting. The importance of prayer was the reason some people called them "Aladura" Churches in Nigeria. *Aladura* is a Yoruba word that means "prayer"[103] In fact the emphasis on prayer is so strong that prayer has become an ecclesiastical title in most of the churches. Moses Orimolade Tunolase, for instance was given the title "*Baba Aladura*, a title that means "Praying Father"[104]

Heavy emphasis on the Holy Spirit has become a cardinal point in their teaching and practices. The Holy Spirit encompasses whatever they do.

Unlike the established missionary churches where one only hears of the Holy Spirit during preaching, teaching or singing, members of African Independent Churches do not only hear of the third person of the Blessed Trinity but experience Him in their lives and during worship. The African church leaders heal, give prophetic messages and see visions all in the name of the Holy Spirit.[105]

Seeing of visions, prophecies, the working of miracles and the use of many other pneumatic experiences are common aspects of AIC beliefs and practices. Healing[106] particularly has become synonymous with the mention of many AICs. Pobee and Ositelu, contrasting healing ministry in Western mission-founded churches to that of the AICs say:

> By contrast, the Western-initiated churches have ceded the healing ministry to doctors and hospitals and thus tended to overlook the depth of the healing of Jesus. In the historic churches moral and spiritual healing are provided for sacramentally; but miraculous cures are associated with shrines and saints…In Africa ministry will be judged deficient if it does not treat healing as a function of religion. Here the AICs have brought to the fore a tradition of the church which has been in danger of being lost."[107]

AICs do not only see Jesus Christ as their Savior and Lord, they acknowledge his authority over diseases of every type. Many people thus go to the AICs expecting a healing touch from Jesus, usually mediated through the leader of the congregation. Their claim of being healed serve as a stimulus of faith for both members of non-members.

Ecclesiology is another doctrine that has received attention by the African Independent Churches.

> The African We-feeling is a term that denotes the communal lifestyle of an African society – a society where no man is an island. The African We-feeling is entrenched in the spiritual churches to the extent that a whole congregation would fast for a member who is in trouble or in imminent danger… Members of spiritual churches feel a greater sense of belonging to a wider and more affectionate Christian family. People from poor and insensitive earthly families find spiritual churches a haven.[108]

Makhubu adds a South African experience to buttress AIC pastoral care which is akin to other AICs in other parts of Africa:

> With AICs it is not only the pastor who visits the sick. During the week, in the evenings, or on Sunday after service, all the church members present move to the bereaved or sick person's home for a short service and prayer, after which a collection is usually taken and given to the bereaved or sick person. Sometimes rent money or groceries are provided according to need. Women are asked to volunteer to help the sick person with household chores.[109]

Liturgical revival and innovations are considered one of the hallmarks of the AIC phenomena. While not abandoning some of the liturgical practices of the Western mission churches from which most of them seceded (such as the use of candles, incense, hymn singing, etc), leaders of most AICs encourage their members to use many African musical instruments and rhythms in their worship settings, apparently in accord with Psalm 150. Worship in most AICs is congregational, with everyone taking part. In most cases the pastor serves as an overseer while some members spontaneously get involved in ministries reserved for only ordained priests in many western mission-founded churches. Solomon Zvanaka describes a worship setting of the Zion Apostolic Church in Zimbabwe in this regard:

> A Zion service lasts for several hours or normally the entire afternoon in the case of Sundays. A theme for the occasion is selected, and several people are given a chance to preach. There are no written church calendars on which we base sermons. Instead, sermons are based on the inspiration of the Holy Spirit and on the discernment of the preacher. Normally, sermons are lively, punctuated by exclamations of 'ya-ya-ya halleluyah,' 'hamen,' and other cries of joy and approval...a preacher who talks on endlessly is controlled or disciplined by some women, who suddenly burst into song, dance, and movement, and thus bring liveliness of the worship service....As one preaches, the gathering from time to time responds to questions raised. The whole atmosphere is charged. It is time to celebrate...It is normal for the preaching to be interspersed with other spontaneous occurrences – like women breaking into rhythmic singing, dancing, and movement which assume an important place in the service...What activates both the singing and the dancing is the drum, the most essential musical instrument. All this is accompanied by ululating, clapping of hands, shaking of rattles, and blowing of the kudu horn.[110]

It is clear from the Zion Apostolic example that the hermeneutic is spontaneous because no one plans ahead of time. The hymnodic interruptions do not only serve as just hymns and songs but modes of supplemental exegesis. It is congregational because each member of the congregation is eligible to make a hermeneutical contribution to the sermon. Since the hermeneutic is all-inclusive and congregational, worshippers do not get bored or doze off during the sermon. There is physical evidence of active participation in the congregational hermeneutic.

The AICs have brought a new sense of missiology in African Christianity. They are known to have *mushroomed* in many corners of their countries of origin and into other countries. Odhiambo Okite describes some aspects of the new method of missions introduced by most AICs, particularly those in East Africa:

> The worship services of these new churches also present a challenge to the older churches. While some churches have the regular weekly hour of service on Sunday in a building, all of them are ready for a service any time, any place where a congregation can be gathered up.[111]

In many Kenyan cities, for instance, it is not uncommon to see some AICs parading joyfully with their flags on the streets before holding their services in the open – usually near a train station or a lorry park where many people wait to catch transportation to their various destinations. The open-air church services are not held for lack of an enclosed place of worship, in most cases. They are held for evangelistic purposes – so that passers by may have the opportunity to listen to the sermon and testimonies of the members and enjoy their vibrant worship services. Commissioning itinerant preachers has been another method of mission and evangelism among AICs.

With regard to the growth of the Cherubim and Seraphim Society in Nigeria, J. Omoyajowo states how a preaching band went to Sagamu and "preached at various centers in the town, and subsequently a branch was established..."[112]

Regarding the spread of AICs in Europe and North America, one needs to attempt to understand a paradox – how leaders and members of African Independent Churches, who are mostly poor, without seminary education and without missiological resources spread their faith abroad. An example of planting the Celestial Church of Christ (CCC) abroad serves as a bird's eye view of AICs' innovative missionizing or evangelism:

> The planting of CCC in Europe at the initial stage was essentially the handiwork of Nigerian students abroad or people in business and official assignments who had no intention of residing permanently abroad. When more than one Celestian found themselves in one city or community, the initiative came for them to meet and worship together. As their membership increases, the group becomes inter-ethnic and international in outlook.[113]

The resolve of some AIC members living abroad to either worship with another AIC or begin a prototype of an AIC in a foreign land is so strong that they prefer the discomfort of meeting in people's sitting rooms to joining Western congregations to worship in plush cathedrals. The desire may, at a face level, seem nationalistic or even racial but another paradigm of planting a Celestial Church of Christ congregation in Southeast London proves otherwise:

> The Harton Parish located in Deptford, Southeast London was the first branch founded in Britain in 1969. It was through the initiative of two Nigerians...both studying in Britain at the time. Upon arrival in London they came in contact with three other celestians who were also students. Thus, the idea of a prayer group was initiated where they could pray collectively for one another, discuss and share their problems and experiences, and in fact live a communal life where members are obliged to support each other...The nucleus group initially held their meetings in a sitting room, but as they grew larger in size, a church hall ...was rented every Sunday for the purpose of worship.[114]

The planting of the Celestial Church of Christ in Southeast London was not motivated by race, ethnicity or nationalism, but by the desire for intense spirituality and mutual We-feeling, two African ideals that may have different connotations in many Western churches. The AIC concept of mission is, therefore, patterned after the New Testament ecclesiology in many respects – emphasis on spirituality, and *oikonia*.

The main elements of the AIC revivalism – a closely-knit ecclesial community, lively and meaningful theology and liturgy, an empathetic style of pastoral care, respect for one's spiritual gifts rather than one's gender, intense prayer and fasting, healing and the demonstration of love among members – all culminate to their understanding of mission and growth. Christianity, to Africans, particularly the AICs, is no longer perceived as a "White man's religion." Christianity has become a non-Western religion, a religion for Africans.

The Role of Women in West African Independent Churches[115]

West Africa is a region where the prominence of AICs cannot be overemphasized. The ministries of William Wade Harris and Garrick Sokari Braide, two prophets who did not intend to establish churches in West Africa, set the tone for the increased emergence of many Independent Churches in the region.[116] Many of the Independent Churches are established Anglophone West African countries than their Francophone counterparts.

Women have played major roles in establishing some West African Independent Churches but scholars have either been reticent to report on their roles or not given them the prominence they deserve. For example, Christianah Abiodun Akinsowon jointly labored with Moses Orimolade Tunolase to establish the Cherubim and Seraphim Society in Nigeria. *"Her spiritual experience of June 1925 was the occasion for the founding of the C&S Society."*[117] Most scholars mention the name of the latter more often than that of the former. The itinerant evangelistic ministry of William Wade Harris in Ivory Coast and western Ghana has received wide publication but the same degree of prominence has not been given to Helen Valentine and Mary Pioka, two women who walked, barefooted, and ministered with Harris from 1913 to 1915, and jointly suffered persecution and imprisonment.[118] The pivotal role of Hannah Barnes in the establishment of the Muzama Disco Christo Church in Ghana is similarly submerged under that of Joseph Egyanka Appiah, the leader. With exception of Baeta who devoted three-and-half pages to Hannah Barnes in his history of MDCC, many scholars mention her name in passing.[119] Even though Elizabeth Isichei attributes the founding of the Twelve Apostles to Grace Tani,[120] most researchers claim that Grace and Kwesi John Nackabah jointly worked hard to organize the converts William Harris left behind in western Ghana into a church known as the Twelve Apostles Church in 1918. Nackabah is credited to be the leader. "While Grace Tani was the stirring figure in the Church who catered for the needs of members through divination, and healing – her role being essentially a charismatic role; somehow Nackabar seemed to have been recognized as the *de facto* leader."[121] In fact the Twelve Apostles Church in Ghana is also known as "Nackaba."

In eastern Nigeria where prophetess Agnes Okoh began her ministry, mention is made of prophetess Madam Nwokolo who established a prayer house in the 1960s but nothing more is known about her ministry.[122] Other Nigerian AIC women leaders who were contemporaries of Agnes Okoh but whose contributions are scarcely recognized are Lucy Harrison (affectionately called "Big Mamma Prayer"), who founded of the Church of Christ the Good Shepherd in 1946 and Theresa Effiong's Holy Chapel of Miracles, founded in 1947. Theresa Inyang founded The Church of God Lamentation of Jehovah, established in 1976.[123]

It is in regard to the aforementioned marginalization of the roles of women in African Independent Churches and the gradual definizmation of AIC leadership that the ministry and leadership qualities of Agnes Okoh in establishing the Christ Holy Church International in Nigeria will be given prominence in this book.

Summary

The profuse literary work on African Independent Churches spanning a period of over six decades – describing their genesis, nature, beliefs, practices, worship settings, persecution, and unprecedented growth in Christianity - clearly amplifies Jenkins' claim that the AICs "…collectively represent one of the most impressive stories in the whole history of Christianity."[124] Even though the beliefs and practices of some of the AICs still baffle observers, one needs to remember what they collectively stand for, as they attempt to justify their existence in their Manifesto.

> One main reason is because our leaders felt that the missionary zeal to save souls from eternal damnation with Christianity robed in foreign clothes did not take into account the fact that the Western God was spiritually inadequate and irrelevant to deal with the reality of many aspects of our lives. The result was a Christian faith and conviction which were only 'skin-deep' or superstitious, in spite of the successful spread of Christianity on the continent. There was and is still the question of how deep the Christian faith really is when so many of its affiliates still continue to visit the caretakers of the African traditional religions.[125]

African Independent Churches, as a result, perceive themselves as making Christianity more meaningful and relevant to Africans. On a continent where three major religions (Islam, Traditional Religions and Christianity) are in active competition for adherents, the AICs, by what they have stated in their Manifesto, seem to claim that they make Christianity very viable and responsive to the spiritual needs of Africans, to the extent that African Christians need not look to other alternative means of meeting their spiritual needs, thereby making more adherents to Christianity.

CHAPTER TWO

Nigeria: A Brief Introduction

Demographic Data

The Federal Republic of Nigeria is a country in west Africa with a geographical size of 923,768 square kilometers. It has been divided into 36 states and a Federal Capital Territory where Abuja, the capital city (the administrative center), and its enclosures are located. The accuracy of the total number of people living in Nigeria has been doubtful since it became the practice in the late 1950s that the results of census will be used as the criterion either to enlarge or decrease the number of seats in the House of Representatives.

The membership by regions in this house was allocated on the basis of a "*population quota.*" This was the number obtained by dividing the total population at the latest census by the number of constituencies. . . . It will thus be clear that the census now held a most important position in the political field.[126]

The disparity in census figures is still prevalent in Nigeria. The BBC country profile, quoting a 2003 United Nations source, puts the population of Nigeria at 124 million[127] whereas the *CIA World Factbook* of 2003 has 133,881,703 as the total population.[128] There is, however, one undeniable fact about the population of Nigeria: It is the most populous country in Africa.

The total number of religious adherents of the major religions in Nigeria is also debatable as the figures fluctuate from one source to another. As of 2003 the *CIA World Factbook* has the following data: Muslim 50 percent, Christian 40 percent, indigenous 10 percent.[129] Another source, during the same year has the following figures: Christian 52.61 percent, Muslim 41 percent, traditional ethnic 5.99 percent, non-religious/other 0.4 percent.[130] Since religion in Nigeria, like politics, is another hotbed in the lives of the people, statistical figures in that regard are generally problematic and, thus, highly controversial.

Politics and Governance
Colonial Era

Many different empires, kingdoms, and some city states were united to form the present day Nigeria.[131] Europeans began having contacts with people in the Benin kingdom, for instance, in the late fifteenth century, but it was not until 1860 that Great Britain had a stronghold in Lagos. At the Berlin Conference in 1885 where the then European powers distributed African countries among themselves, Britain claimed the Niger Basin and thereafter formed the Oil Rivers Protectorate, thus controlling trade in the Niger area. The British expanded their jurisdiction to other parts of Nigeria by treaties, diplomacy, and military force.

Although treaties were signed with rulers as far as north of Sokoto by 1885, actual British control was confined to the coastal area and the immediate vicinity of Lokoja until 1900. The Royal Niger Company had access to the territory from Lokoja extending along the Niger and Benue rivers above their confluence, but there was no effective control, even after punitive expeditions against Bida and Ilorin in 1897.[132]

Nigeria was finally colonized by Great Britain by 1903. The colonizer divided the country into three administrative regions—Northern, Western, and Eastern. The governor general, a Briton, resided in Lagos, then Federal Territory. The sovereignty of Britain was, however, consolidated through the political ingenuity of Frederick Lugard, then high commissioner of the Northern Region, who introduced the "Indirect Rule," a system of government which was entrusted into the hands of indigenes but controlled by the colonizers and their agents. In the north, for example, "the emirs [rulers] retained their caliphate titles but were responsible to the British district officers who had final authority."[133] The rules for each of the regions, under Indirect Rule, was unequal—an intentional policy to suit the different religious and political terrain of the respective regions. In 1914 the Northern and Southern protectorates were unified into one country—Nigeria. Afterwards, in 1916, Lugard formed the Nigerian Council, "a consultative body that brought together six traditional leaders . . . to represent all parts of the colony."[134]

As time went on, "the regional legislatures were enlarged and became sovereign bodies. Each region had a governor who presided over a cabinet; he was in no way subordinate to the governor general now placed at the head of the gederation."¹³⁵ A senate composed of select members from the regions and some other appointees was established in 1958. It is noteworthy, as Toyin Falola observes, that "Colonial Nigeria was nothing more than artificially constructed agglomeration of diverse and other loosely united groups. . . . One major problem with the federal system was that it exacerbated ethnic divisions."¹³⁶ Though united territorially, the unification of the various ethnic groups had been difficult, if not elusive. This has had a great influence on the ethnic composition of Christ Holy Church International.

Post Colonial Nigeria

The crave for political independence which swept through Africa south of the Sahara in the 1950s and the pressure for self-government by Nigerian politicians compelled Great Britain to organize an election in 1959. Prior to this election, Nigeria decided on a federal system of governance after independence. Political parties which contested in that election "revolved around ethnicity, since each one promoted itself as a representative of a major ethnic group."¹³⁷ With none of the political parties winning majority votes in the 1959 election, the Northern Peoples Congress and the National Council of Nigeria and Cameroon amalgamated to become the first post-independent government with Abubakar Tafawa Balewa as the prime minister and Nnamdi Azikiwe as the governor general. Nigeria became politically independent on 1 October 1960. Azikiwe later became the president of the federal government when Nigeria became a republic in 1963.

The first five years of post-independent Nigeria was a period of relative peace although there were some minor controversies over the authenticity of the 1963 census data. Niven affirms the peace of Nigeria with the following observation:

> Nigeria was the example to the world of what a well-balanced modern African democracy could be. The world outside watched this "giant in the sun" getting on with its business, quietly pursuing the paths of peaceful development, everything was African-controlled and inspired but associated with white men closely for the technical skills and know-how.¹³⁸

The "well-balanced modern African democracy" was short-lived and shattered by a series of events that led to a civil war.

The Era of Instability

The First Republic of Nigeria was characterized by political and constitutional crises, a disorganized society, corruption, and a plummeting economy. Some soldiers, mostly made up of Igbos, overthrew the constitutional government on 15 January 1966.

The *coup d'état* was violent. "Altogether on that dreadful night the prime minister, two regional premiers, the federal minister of finance, and all the army officers of the rank of colonel and above were killed, only one of them was an Ibo, and he was killed almost by chance."[139] The soldiers later instituted a military government with Major General Johnson Aguiyi-Ironsi, an Igbo, as the head of state. The low number of Igbos killed in the *coup d' état,* coupled with the great number of Igbos promoted in the Nigerian armed services and the numerous Igbo advisors appointed by the new administration fulfilled the suspicion of many Nigerians that the violent change of government was schemed by Igbos to serve their own interest. The simmering tension led to the massacre of many Igbos in the northern part of Nigeria, an action the Igbos did not take kindly. The Igbos retaliated and killed thousands of northerners living in Igboland.

After being in office for only six months, the first military government was toppled on 29 July 1966 by some army officers, most of whom were from the north. Many Igbo officers, including General Aguiyi-Ironsi, were killed. Lt. Col. (later General) Yakubu Gowon was installed as the new head of state.

The Biafra (Civil) War

Later disagreements over the structure of the army, the power of Federal Military Government as against that of Regional Governors, and the mode of governance of Nigeria (whether federal or regional) took precedence over a smooth administration of the country. Relationship between the East, led by Lt. Col. Chuckwuemeka Odumegwu Ojukwu, the military Governer of the East, an Igbo, and the rest of Nigeria, led by General Yakubu Gowon, the then head of the Federal Military Government, deteriorated to the extent that the Chiefs, Elders, and Representatives of Eastern Nigeria mandated Ojukwu to declare Eastern Nigeria a free and sovereign independent state with the name *The Republic of Biafra*—the mandate was carried out on 30 May 1967.[140] The declaration of a sovereign Biafra by Ojukwu compelled the Federal Military Government, after several attempts to resolve issues amicably, to preserve the unity of Nigeria. This led to a bloody civil war which was fought from July 1967 to 15 January 1970.

Col. Ojukwu's government started a policy of terrorism and intimidation in the minority areas fringing Iboland. The army looted the local treasuries and post offices and imprisoned leading civilians. This developed into murders of innocent people, mainly leaders of local opinion, into arson and pillage and seizure of possessions of many individuals.

This policy continued and intensified itself in the later stages, so long as these areas were in rebel hands. Thousands were murdered or were arrested in these areas, and hundreds of villages and hamlets terrorized, with considerable damage to private and official property.[141]

The civil war ended after Lt. Col. Effiong announced a surrender of Biafra on 12 January 1970.[142] One of the unrecorded effects of the civil war was the hatred and oblique perception of Igbos by non-Igbos, particularly those who were brutalized and traumatized by the Biafran army. How the civil war and its resultant unfavorable perception of the Igbos affected the growth of Christ Holy Church, because of her Igbo origins, will be discussed later in this book.

Post-Biafra Instability

The political history of Nigeria after the Biafran civil war has been a contentious issue among civilian politicians and the military. There have been seven military administrators as against two elected civilian governments from 1970 to the year 2000. General Murtala Mohammed overthrew the administration of General Yakubu Gowon in 1975, after the latter had reneged on his promise to return the country to civilian rule. Another attempt to overthrow the government of Murtala Mohammed was foiled in 1975, even though he was killed. General Olusegun Obasanjo was appointed to lead the government. Obasanjo later stepped down after he allowed an election to take place. A new civilian government under the leadership of Alhaji Shehu Shagari was inaugurated in 1979. After ruling for four years, Shagari's government was toppled in 1983 by the military, which named General Muhammadu Buhari as the new head of state. Two years later General Ibrahim Babangida ousted Buhari's government. He became the new head of state. After Babangida had annulled two general elections during his administration, he succumbed to intense civil pressure and resigned as a result. In 1993, he appointed Ernest Shonekan, a civilian, in his stead, but Shonekan's government was swept away after being in office for only four months in yet another *coup d'état* by General Sani Abacha, another soldier. Abacha died of heart failure in 1998. General Abdulsalam Abubakar succeeded Abacha. He supervised a transitional period and returned the country to elected civilian rule in 1999; the election was won by Olusegun Obasanjo, one of the past military rulers.

Corruption, nepotism, regionalism, allegations of rigged elections, human rights violations, mismanagement of the economy resulting in high cost of living, greed, unfair distribution of national wealth, despotism, and many other vices have been given as reasons for the constant change of governments in Nigeria. These activities caused chaos, killings, and displacement of many people, destruction of properties, armed robbery, and at times ethnic rivalry resulting in organized killings. Many Nigerians lived in fear under most of the military regimes. Falola's evaluation of the administrations of Babangida and Abacha, for instance, could be regarded as a summary of what happened in those chaotic years of military rule:

> No ruler in modern Nigerian history had acquired a more negative popular image. He [Babangida] earned this through a leadership style that thrived on duplicity, deceit, and dishonesty. Moreover, he was an autocrat and a cunning schemer skilled at minimizing opposition to his regime.
>
> By 1995 Abacha had shown himself as the country's most brutal leader to date. He jailed or killed his opponents, flagrantly violated human rights, and disregarded domestic and international opinion.[143]

The spate of political instability, the numerous military decrees, and the schemes of politicians, be they soldiers or civilians, to divide the ranks of religious leaders (to the advantage of the politicians) affected inter-religious relationship and the way Christian ministry was conducted in Nigeria as we will see in the life of Christ Holy Church International.

Ethnic Groups

Nigeria is a country that is said to have "more linguistic, cultural, and religious diversity than the whole of Europe put together: 250 language groups, several main culture areas, former Islamic states, and other communities with vigorous Christian traditions."[144] Johnstone and Mandryk record over 490 ethnic groups.[145] The main groups are Hausa/Fulani, Yoruba, and Igbo. Other groups are Kanuri, Tiv, Nupe, Ijaw, Ibibio, Efik, and many others considered minority tribes. The English language is, however, the *lingua franca* of Nigeria. More attention will be paid to the Igbos, since Christ Holy Church was founded among them.

The Origin of Igbos

The origin of Igbos, like many African people groups, is difficult to discover even though it is believed that the history of "their forebears goes back four thousand years or more."[146] Some scholars have attempted to strike some affinities between Igbos and the biblical Hebrews by identifying some similarities between Igbo and Hebraic cultures. Chief Solomon Amadiume posits thirty-one Igbo and Jewish cultural similarities and argues persuasively for Igbo-Jewish connections. He ends his comparison by saying, "Our elders say that whosoever sees an elephant should declare what he sees and not prevaricate, for such a situation does not admit of equivocation."[147] Basden confirms the Igbo-Jewish connections by affirming: "There are certain customs which rather point to Levitic influence at a more or less remote period. This is suggested in the underlying ideas concerning sacrifice and in the practice of circumcision. The language also bears several interesting parallels with the Hebrew idiom."[148] Speculations about the origin of the Igbo people may abound in many areas; scholars may debate the authenticity of such claims endlessly. Archaeological discoveries in Igbo-Ukwu in 1938 and two others in Nssuka and Ezira, however, indicate unambiguously that Igbo presence at their present habitation dates back to the Stone Age if not before.[149] Their geographical habitation in Nigeria has been described by Basden:

> From the coastline of the Bight of Benin, the Ibo country skirts the Ibibio, Aro-Chuku and Efik territories. After that its eastern boundary is formed by the Cross River. On the southern and western sides it stretches to the borders of the Ijaw Jekri, and Igabo and other tribes, and then spreads across the Niger to the confines of Benin. After passing 631° N. Lat., it narrows in once more, and extends in wedge-like formation until its northernmost limits reach the boundary between southern and northern Nigeria, where the Akpotos and Munshis are the nearest neighbours.[150]

The widespread nature of the Igbos and the distinctive features of some of them are not uncommon to some scholars of anthropology. Daryll Forde and G. I. Jones have, therefore, classified Igbos into five types which, for lack of appropriate description, they refer to as tribes, groups, and/or local communities. The groupings are: (1) the Northern or Onitsha Ibo which includes the towns of Onitsha, Nnewi, Awka, Ihiala, Aro-Ndizougu, Nsukka, Enugu, Enugu-Ukwu, and Okigwe. (2) Southern or Owerri Ibo has these towns: Orlu, Agbaja, Owerri, Umuahia, Aba and Bende. (3) Western Ibo. Some of the important towns are Ugwashi Uku, Kwale, Oguta, Aboh, Asaba, and Ahoada. Ndoni, the birthplace of prophetess Agnes Okoh is in part of Ibo land. (4) Eastern Ibo is also known as

Cross River. Afikpo and Arochuku are some important towns in eastern Ibo. (5) North Eastern Ibos have Abakaliki as an important town.[151]

The Unification of Igbos

The Igbos were formerly not a united people as they are today. Forde and Jones have stated:

> Before the advent of Europeans the Ibo had no common name and village groups were generally referred to by the name of a putative ancestral founder.... The Ibo are a single people in the sense that they speak a number of related dialects, occupy a continuous tract of territory, and have many features of social structure in common, but they were not formerly politically unified and there are marked dialectical and cultural differences among the various main groupings.[152]

Citing other sources, Forde and Jones trace the etymology of the word "Ibo" to a Sudanic word meaning *the people*. The word was contemptuously used by the Riverain Ibo to refer to those dwelling in the forest. The Igalas also used it in the same manner in reference to "slaves." It was later applied to the Ibibio due to their nearness to the river Kwa Ibo.[153] The early Europeans used the word "Ibo" to identify the people and language of the group of people presently called Igbos. Using the word Ibo to refer to a people and language does not automatically mean the people to whom the word is being referred have accepted it. This assertion raises the question as to why the Igbos have disregarded the contempt that went with the word and have now accepted it to describe themselves and their language. The translation of the Bible into a unified Igbo vernacular (as will be discussed later) by and large played a key role in defining the unity of Igbos.

The Religion and Worldview of the Igbos

The Igbos, like all other Africans, have their own cosmology that determines their actions and behavioral patterns. According to Chinoyelu Ugwu, Igbo cosmology is structured in two main realms, visible (natural) and invisible (supernatural). The natural level consists of empirical realities while the "supernatural realm is occupied by God, the deities, the disembodied and malignant spirits, and the ancestral spirits."[154]

Igbos have three names for the supreme being. The names, used interchangeably, are: *Chukwu*, (the great God or the high God), *Chineke*, (the Creator), and *Osebuluwa* (the sustainer of the universe).[155] Igbo names of the supreme being, therefore, indicate God's attributes. *Chukwu* is perceived as an all-good God who assigns everybody a personal *chi* (i.e., a creative destiny). "Next to *Chineke* is a pantheon of gods: *Anyanwu* (the sun god), *Igwe* (the sky god), *Amadi-Oha* (the god of thunder and lightning), and *Ala* (the earth goddess). There are other innumerable deities besides the aforementioned who are believed to have specialized in performing certain human activities, such as divination, herbal medicine, farming, adventure, and hunting. Igbos also believe in nature gods.[156] Principal of the shrines were the *Ubinukpabi* (the long juju) of Arochukwu, the *Agbala* of Awka, the *Igwe-ka-Ala* of Umunoha near Owerri, and the *Onyili Ora* near Agu-Ukwu, at Nri.[157]

Both Ugwu and Ilogu assert that Igbos do not have the concept of dualism[158] in their traditional belief systems. "The Igbo do not postulate an opposing being who is all evil and responsible for all evil. This is a thought foreign to the Igbo worldview."[159] To the Igbo, God has assigned some specific functions to the deities. The reality of evil is consequently attributed to a deity whom *Chineke* has endowed with the ability to effect the said evil. Such deities have the liberty to cause evil whenever they deem fit. The problem of evil[160] is, consequently, no problem to Igbos.

Other spiritual beings in the Igbo concept of the supernatural realm are the spirits of the ancestors, *Ndichie* or *Ndebunze,* who can be either malevolent or benevolent:

> Sickness and misfortune of every kind can be attributed to the influence of those offended among them. They can influence rainfall or bring good harvest; they can promote prosperity or cause adversity; they can also give protection and general well-being or cause disruption and calamity.[161]

Besides the ancestral spirits, Igbos also believe in spirits who are intrinsically evil, such as *Ajommuo, Akalogeli, Ogbonuke,* and *Ogbanje.* These spirits, according to Ugwu, "are incapable of good actions."[162] The belief in mystical powers is also prominent in Igbo society. The mystical powers "belong to the world of man. They are humanly-produced effects resulting from an exploitation of the inherent powers in nature. These forces include what different authors call *magic, sorcery* and *witchcraft.*"[163]

The Igbo use the word *Ogwu* for medicine, magic, sorcery, charm, talisman, etc., and *amusu* for witchcraft. The life and worship of the Igbo revolve around this cosmology.[164] The *Ogwu* is said to be an indispensable aspect of Igbo life. Igbos claim that it could be used positively to heal, protect, and improve the quality of life. It is said to be used also to cause every evil thing one can imagine. The medicine men are believed to have the power to make the *Ogwu* very effectual. They are believed to be able to manipulate the *Ogwu* for desired results, positively or negatively. "The concept of *Ogwu*," says Ugwu, "has a far reaching influence in the world-view of the Igbo. It affects their interpretation of reality."[165]

Unlike the *Ogwu* which can be used positively or negatively, Igbos believe that the *amusu* is used to do only evil things. "A witch (or a wizard) is believed to have an inherent psychic power that allows her (his) spirit to leave her (his) body while asleep to attack other people. . . Witches are believed to be capable of attacking their victims in various ways."[166] Igbo cosmology is one full of spiritual entities who have encircled human beings. Their lives are, as a result, intrinsically linked to the community and regulated by the *Omenani,* otherwise known as *Omenala.* The "*Omenala* here includes the different beliefs about the universe, the different taboos, regulations, prescriptions, and prohibitions as to what is proper in such a universe . . . for the harmony and equilibrium of the society."[167] Ilogu observes that:

> The relationship between man and the spiritual world is maintained through many channels. Obedience to the codes of behaviour and the customs *(Omenani)* approved by the ancestors, and enforced by the earth goddess through the priests and titled elders and heads of various extended families, is the most important channel. To the Ibo, therefore, the spiritual world is very real and intimate. Hence the belief in the existence of spirits in all aspects of nature and its various phenomena.[168]

From the aforesaid worldview and cosmology of Igbos, one can sense the need for one to be attuned to the spiritual beings so as to seek protection from misfortunes that could be effected by either the medicine men or other malevolent spiritual entities. Fear becomes a reality in such a supernatural worldview. This situation, and many others that space does not permit, was the socio-religious scene among the Igbos before the introduction of Christianity. We will see how this worldview posed a great challenge to the western missionaries, what they did to stem such belief, and how these very belief systems prompted Igbos to accept the ministries of African Independent Churches and that of the prayer homes. It must also be noted that these belief systems are still prevalent in Igboland.

CHAPTER THREE

Christianity in Southern Nigeria

Early Missionary Attempts

The enthronement of Joao II as King of Portugal in 1481 and his policy of using African chiefs as agents of bringing Christianity to their own people marked the beginning of a conscious attempt to introduce Christianity to some parts of the place now called Nigeria.[169] A Portuguese expedition to the Delta area in 1486 led them to contact the kingdom of Benin. In fulfillment of King Joao II's policy, a friendship with Ozolua, the Oba (King) of Benin, began through trading. Kings Manoel and Joao III of Portugal continued the advancement of Christianity but since the relationship was leadership-centered, the advancement depended on the interest of the reigning Oba. As a result, King Ozolua of Benin expressed interest in Christianity and allowed some Portuguese missionaries into his kingdom, permitting the missionaries to baptize some members of the royal family. The death of Ozolua, however, made Christianity less influential in the kingdom.[170]

The Portuguese pushed further into the Itsekiri (also known as Warri) kingdom and introduced Christianity through the ministries of Augustinian monks, Franciscans, and Italian Capuchins from 1574 to 1807. This initial attempt to introduce Christianity was not very successful. Sanneh attributes the following reasons, among others, to the failure of the early attempts: the identification of Christianity with European interest with the latter usually triumphing over the former, resistance by leaders of African traditional religions, the varying religious interests of the African rulers, high missionary mortality rate, and an inadequate number of missionaries.[171] There was a long period of Christian inactivity from that time until 1841.

The Evangelical Revival in Europe that led to the abolition of slave trade in Britain in 1807 heightened the need to engage in world missions. Thus Protestant Christians in Europe continued the task of evangelizing the world. Consequently, the period between 1841 and 1891 was seen as a period of more intensive missionary work in most parts of Nigeria as compared to that of the earlier one by the Portuguese Catholics. The Protestants decided to settle the freed slaves in Sierra Leone with the intention of using them as agents of evangelizing west Africa, particularly Nigeria.[172]

Some of the slaves were already Christians while others were not. The latter were given catechetical instructions while the former, with a desire to spread the Christian faith, began evangelizing the natives of the land and the newly recaptured slaves. They also taught in schools that had been established in Sierra Leone. The freed slaves in Sierra Leone became the pioneers of preaching the gospel to their own people and making some relevant studies of the culture and languages of the indigenes that made the proclamation of the Gospel very efficient.

In pursuit of halting the slave trade in Africa the British government developed a practice of positioning naval ships on the high seas to seize slave ships and set the recaptured slaves free by settling them in Sierra Leone. Thomas Buxton, a leading evangelical Christian and an anti-slavery campaigner was, however, not happy with the policy of recapturing slaves on the high seas. That policy, to him, was not an effective solution to end the slave trade. In his book *The African Slave Trade and Its Remedy*, Buxton argued that the efforts of Britain to stop the slave trade through diplomacy in Europe and naval patrols on the Atlantic had not visibly reduced the number of slaves taken out of Africa; that the only effective remedy was to attack the slave trade *at its source* of supply in Africa.[173] He was not advocating for a military adventure in Africa when he suggested that the slave trade should be attacked at its source in Africa. To Thomas Buxton, the trade in slaves would become less attractive when the African was educated in the Western manner, civilized, and empowered to be self-sufficient and productive. It is through such economic empowerment that Africans would acknowledge the value of humanity and act accordingly. The *modus operandi* of his concept of empowering Africans and supplanting the slave trade with a more viable trade and its expected results was articulated thus:

> We must elevate the minds of her people and call forth the resources of her soil....Let missionaries and schoolmasters, the plough and the spade, go together and agriculture

will flourish; the avenues to legitimate commerce will be opened; confidence between man and man will be inspired; whilst civilization will advance as the natural effect, and Christianity operate as the proximate cause, of this happy change.[174]

Buxton's idea of improving the economy of west and central African countries and thereby making the slave trade less attractive was laudable though it was developed under the false assumption of the prominence of western civilization. Later he introduced a slogan, "the Bible and the Plough," which was an indication that western civilization, Christianity, and a vibrant agro-economy were to be fused together to transform African nations.[175]

With the support of the British government and some evangelical Christians in Britain, mainly from the Anglican Church Missionary Society (CM S), Buxton's dream became a reality leading to the exploration of the Niger River with the purpose of unearthing the resources of the inner country and thereby empowering the natives with a decent and more viable economy. This was commonly called the Niger Expedition of 1841. Further expeditions along the Niger River were carried out in 1854 and 1857.

Six main missionary agencies were involved in missionizing Nigeria: the Anglican Church Missionary Society, the Wesleyan Methodist Missionary Society, the Foreign Mission Committee of the United Presbyterian Church of Scotland, the Foreign Mission Board of the Southern Baptist Convention of the United States, the Qua Iboe Mission, and the Catholic Society of African Missions of France. The missions operated mainly in the city states along the coastal areas, the interior of Yoruba land, and the Niger valley.

Western Missionary Initiative Among the Igbos

The Church Missionary Society

Major missionary work among the Igbos began during the Niger Expeditions dating as far back as 1857. The CMS and the Roman Catholics were initially the main mission agents who worked among the Igbos. The C.M.S used recaptive African Christians to spearhead evangelization of the Igbos. In the expedition of the Niger in 1857, John C. Taylor opened a mission centre at Onitsha while Crowther and Simon Jonas produced the first book in Igbo, the famous *Isoama-Ibo Primer*. Mission schools were opened by the CMS. Many Igbo leaders sent their children to the mission schools. The schools served as fertile grounds for the planting of churches. As a result, the CMS planted churches in almost all the Igbo hinterlands and in Port Harcourt on the coast.

Catholic Missionaries

The Catholic missionary work in Igbo land was pioneered by Father Joseph Lutz beginning in 1885. He sited his headquarters in Onitsha and went into the hinterland from there. The main points of mission were medical evangelism and social work. Many medical clinics were opened to treat diseases like fevers (malaria, jaundice of blackwater fever, sleeping sickness, cholera, typhus, yellow fever), dysentery, constipation, leprosy, sores and wounds, worm diseases etc.[176] Attention was also paid to the Christianization of slaves, social outcasts, and the helpless like twin babies, taboo children, lepers, and those accused of witchcraft. Vocational training institutions were established to train and integrate such people into the Igbo society. The Catholics opened schools and wrote some books. Father Aimé Ganot, a Catholic missionary, published an *Igbo Grammar* and *English-Igbo-French Dictionary* in 1899 and 1904 respectively.[177]

Evaluation of Western Missionary Initiative Among the Igbos

Initial challenges

Western missionary work among the Igbos was very difficult initially. Even though between 1830 to 1885 some traditional rulers rushed to invite the missionaries to establish churches in their areas of jurisdiction, the glee that usually went with the welcome ceremonies often turned sour when the rulers realized that missionary teaching undermined the culture of the land and the authority of the leaders.[178] Some of the most cherished cultural practices of the Igbos were disdained by the western missionaries. "The *Ozo* title, for instance, which was a sign of social status, was seen as a secret society. *Masquerading* which served as the traditional policing for maintaining law and order was considered something devilish; the traditional *marriage custom of paying dowry* to the family of the woman was seen as buying and selling of wives".[179] The western missionaries, with the active support of the British colonial government, opposed some practices like the killing of twins, ritual murder, and domestic slavery. The position of the missionaries and the government on these latter practices is seen as deserving by many scholars.[180]

Initial Successes: Education

In spite of the Igbo apathy and skepticism toward missionary activities, the tide changed in favor of the missionaries. The influence was so great that Christianity, in fact, became the most influential religion in Igbo land. By 1939 many churches have been planted; Christian schools and colleges were common. Many people had also been trained as teachers, clerks, preachers, nurses, and salesmen.[181]

Many other factors contributed to the growth and acceptance of Christianity among the Igbos apart from the evangelistic strategies of the various missionary agencies. Three of the factors will be highlighted, although not in their order of importance.

Initial Successes: Control of Epidemics

The first factor was rather circumstantial—the outbreak of epidemics. Ekechi mentions the following epidemics in Igbo land: the smallpox epidemics in 1873 and 1912 respectively, the spleen epidemic of 1903, and the influenza epidemic of 1918 -1919.[182] These epidemics were, for instance, said to have multiplied church membership at Onitsha. "For example, the smallpox of 1873, which caused great havoc at Onitsha, including the death of the king (King Idiari), reportedly triggered a dramatic 'rush to the church.'"[183] Catholic missionaries, in particular, were said to have doubled their memberships by actively treating and baptizing influenza patients. They, however, coerced some adult patients either to submit themselves to baptism or die and to be damned eternally in hell should they refuse baptism.[184]

Many Igbos flocked to the churches because the local diviner priests, who also served as medicine men, could not find any antidote to the epidemics. Instead, they "blamed the people…because they have forsaken the traditions of the land, broken the taboos and angered the spirit of the ancestors, by paying heed to the teachings of the missionaries."[185] With the provision of Western medical know-how, and the Igbo practice of abandoning gods who do not perform to the expectations of their adherents in favor of a more potent God,[186] it was not surprising that the people rushed to the churches.

Initial Successes: Contextualization

The second factor which endeared the missionaries (Catholic missionaries especially) to the hearts of Igbos was the contextualization of some of their local beliefs. Some Catholic missionaries adopted the Igbo concept of God (Chukwu) and consequently called themselves "Chukwu's messengers" (Ukochukwu). They called the Bible (Okwu Chukwu), God's word.[187] Some Western missionaries also accorded the Africans the dignity they deserved. Father Shanahan, for instance, used to say, "If you treat the African with respect and courtesy, you will find him a veritable treasure of goodness."[188]

Initial Successes: Provision of Relief Services

The provision of relief activities by churches during the Biafran war was the third factor. The Catholic Church, for instance, through *Caritas Internationalis*, supplied food, medicine, clothing, and other relief items to the wounded and displaced. The supply of the items was so profuse that some people thought the Catholic Church was in support of the Biafrans. The pope, however, refuted that impression at the Vatican in 1969.[189]

Writing on factors which promoted the growth of the church in Igboland, Ogbu Kalu, relying on his vast scholarly knowledge and reminiscence of the history of Christianity in Igboland, strongly believes that the color of the white man was a major factor to the growth of the church in Igboland. He argues "that favorable response to Christianity was often due to the presence of the white man. Mission bodies that used many white personnel as workers benefited."[190] Kalu supports his argument with five factors: fascination (i.e., the excitement of seeing a person with a different skin color), materialistic expectations (i.e., the use of gifts by the white missionaries to gain the favor and attention of their hosts), the perception of the white missionary as the forerunner of or a future emissary to the white colonial administrators, the need to adjust to new colonial patterns and administrative structures, and medical services. The paradoxical perception of the social status of the native missionary agents—the Sierra Leonean agents who were neither Igbos (though black) nor white people were pejoratively called "oyibo oji" (black Europeans)—was another strong point to substantiate the color advantage syndrome of the western missionaries.[191]

Initial Successes: Translation of the Bible

The contributions of western mission agencies towards the spiritual growth of Igbos would be incomplete if mention is not made of the translation of the Bible into the Igbo language. The resolve of western missionaries to vernacularize the Bible for African Christians was stated by T. J. Bowen in 1857:

> Our designs and hopes in regard to Africa are not simply to bring as many individuals as possible to the knowledge of Christ. We desire to establish the Gospel in the hearts and minds

and social life of the people, so that truth and righteousness may remain and flourish among them, without the instrumentality of foreign missionaries. This cannot be done without civilization. To establish the Gospel among any people, they must have Bibles and therefore must have the art to make them or the money to buy them. They must read the Bible and this implies instruction.[192]

The Bible, in the minds of the missionaries, was an important tool for effecting a viable Christian lifestyle and indigenous initiative, as stated by Bowen. All efforts were made, as a result, to reduce to writing the vernacular of the people among whom the missionaries ministered. The initial non-religious linguistic work of the missionaries served as stepping stones leading to the translation of the Bible into local languages, Igbo included. It was, thus, no wonder that the next linguistic work by CMS missionaries, after Samuel Crowther's *Isoama-Ibo Primer*, was the translation of the New Testament into Igbo in 1866[193] by Rev. John C. Taylor, who has been described as "a careful and methodical linguist."[194] Even though Anthony Nkwoka has stated that the entire Bible was "translated by Archdeacon Thomas J. Dennis between 1913 and 1917,"[195] that assertion is questionable since it tends to ignore the contributions of Igbo translators, particularly the contribution of Rev. T. David Anyaegbunam. Ben Fulford comments on Anyaegbunam's role in translation of the Bible:

> Dennis was of course highly involved, chairing his committee, and translating from the Greek and Hebrew himself in such a way. . . as to enable his co-translators, and Anyaegbunam in particular, to render each sentence into appropriate Igbo idiom, according to Union principles. Not only, then, were there several Igbo involved in the day-to-day translation of the Bible . . . but it was one of them, Anyaegbunam, who played the principal part in this process. . . . Three of the key Igbo translators of the Union Bible, Anyaegbunam and the Greens had lived through the transition to colonial period. . . . This [the Union Bible] was to a degree a genuinely indigenous Igbo project…framed by the vision of Dennis.[196]

The translation began in perhaps late 1906, but the dissimilarity of the various dialects in the Igbo language[197] was perhaps the reason it took nearly half a century to translate the entire Bible. Dennis, himself, was aware of the dialectical differences of the Igbos and the enormity of the task, but he pressed for the creation of "a cocktail of grammar and vocabulary that would be tolerable in terms of comprehensibility and local prejudice."[198]

The translation, which became known as the "Union Ibo" or "nobody's Ibo,"[199] caused a rift between Igbo Protestants and Catholics. While the Protestants acclaimed it as "a monumental translation,"[200] Catholics rejected it in 1929 and instead introduced a new orthography the same year. The reason for the rejection of the Union Igbo has been stated by Omenka: "When the Catholic authorities officially rejected it in 1929, they did so not so much for its inherent weaknesses as the fear that its growing popularity might adversely dilute the extraordinary concentration of native interest in Catholic schools, where English was given a place of prominence."[201] Thus the Union Igbo was not rejected because of lack of relevance to the literary work among the Igbos but because of denominational politics. The new orthography, which had its own imperfections, was reluctantly accepted by the Protestants.[202] Despite the variations of Igbo dialects, a problem "by no means resolved today,"[203] another translation of the whole Bible (Living Bible version) into the Igbo language was published in 1988.[204] Notwithstanding the rejection of the Union Igbo, Nkwoka claims that it is still being used by a cross section of Igbo Christians: "Nowadays all the new denominations from 'non-Christian,' 'messianic, revivalistic, and nativistic' Sabbath Churches to the most vibrant pentecostal churches, and in some cases even the Roman Catholics use the Archdeacon Dennis' Igbo Bible . . .had left an indelible mark on Igbo Christianity."[205]

In spite of the denominational politics surrounding the dialects of the Igbo language, especially as it relates to Bible translation, and also apart from the traditional role of the Bible in giving spiritual impetus and direction to users, the Bible has played a very meaningful role in unifying Igbos. Dennis began the unification process by inviting translation assistants from Asaba, Onitsha, Owerri in the Delta, Unwana, Arochuku, and elsewhere, thus fusing all the various dialects together.[206] The fact that all Igbos used the Union Bible without regard for their dialectical differences is evidence of the accomplishment of the unification process—something equivalent to the unification of the Yorubas through the translation of the Bible into the Yoruba language.[207]

The Emergence of African Independent Churches in Nigeria

Some Causes

The Struggle for Religious Independence

Nigeria has had her fair share of developments that led to the emergence of African Independent Churches (AIC). There were 4,200 AIC denominations with 20.3 million adherents in Nigeria in 2001.[208] This figure of AIC denominations represents about 32 percent of all AIC denominations in Africa.[209] Some of the mega-AICs in Nigeria are Christ Apostolic Church with 6,667 congregations and a potpourri of Cherubim and Seraphim Churches with 4,000 congregations in 2001.[210]

The fight for religious independence in Nigeria began as far back as the late 1800s when, with the withdrawal of American Baptists missionaries from Nigeria due to the American Civil War, some Africans and Afro-American Baptist members incorporated some African features in an attempt to make the church look more African. The American missionaries, on their return, disciplined the contextualization advocates, some of whom left to establish the Native Baptist Church in 1888. There was another spate of secessions from the Anglican community and the Methodist church in Nigeria. These led to the founding of United Native Church in 1891, The African Church (Bethel) in 1901, United African Methodist Church (Eleja) in 1917, and The Christ Army Church in 1918. Ayegboyin and Ishola consider these early AICs as precursors of AICs in Nigeria.[211] With the exception of the inclusion of some African cultural elements, such as polygamy in some of the above-named churches, their liturgies and belief systems were similar to the western mission-founded churches from which they seceded.

Desire to Find an Antidote to Epidemics

Many African Independent Churches were established in Nigeria after the period of the precursors. The causes, unlike that of those already discussed, were not always about the zeal for ecclesial independence but were also circumstantial. Sanneh gives four reasons that prompted the founding of AICs in Nigeria during this era: the worldwide influenza epidemic in 1918, the global economic slump of the 1920s, the bubonic plague in Lagos from 1924 to 1926, and a severe famine in 1932. He adds that the underlying factor of the urge to begin an African-initiated church was the immense role of the vernacular Bible.[212] These events made some Nigerian Christians look beyond the expectation of God to minister to them through word and sacrament. They needed a more pragmatic answer to their imminent danger in addition to being exhorted to have faith in God. The quest for answers and protection evolved into earnest prayer, fasting, and the use of blessed water for healing. Others went to the extent of having some glossolaliac experience. All these practices, considered as "unorthodox" by some western missionaries, caused the raising of some eyebrows and of course some concern in the missionary churches. The desire to stem these epidemics on the other hand and in some cases coupled with some precautionary measures taken by leaders of Western mission churches to preserve their churches' traditions, led to the founding of prayer groups which later metamorphosed into African Independent Churches.[213]

African Independent Churches Among the Igbos

The Braide Movement

The Garrick Braide movement, which gave birth to the Christ Army Church in 1916, was the first known schism from a western mission-founded church (CMS) in Eastern Nigeria, and, thus, reputed to be the first AIC in Igboland.[214] Circumstances leading to the founding of Christ Army Church were akin to those of other AICs. After the baptism of Braide, he devoted himself to personal spirituality till he heard a voice that commanded him to preach. He began preaching, asking people to depend solely on God, to abandon all trust in idols and other fetish paraphernalia, and to stop taking alcoholic beverages. The effect of his preaching and the miracles he performed gave him a large following. Braide, incidentally, fell foul of the authorities of the Anglican Church (after an initial affection) due to a said embellishment of his ministry and adulation of his personality by his followers.[215] He was also accused of claiming to be "Elijah II" and giving Bakana, his hometown, the name "Israel."[216] The CMS authorities perceived him as *enfant terrible* and consequently expelled him from the church. He was, afterwards, arrested by the colonial administration, prosecuted, and, as a result, convicted and jailed. He died shortly after serving his prison sentence in 1918.

Prayer Houses and Healing Homes

One other religious activity in Igboland that needs mention because of its connection with this work is that of prayer houses (Ulo Ekpere), also known as spiritual healing homes or compound churches.[217] They were quasi-ecclesial spiritual movements which were established to augment the spiritual needs of Christians in Igboland whose churches did not give any regard to the use of spiritual gifts. There were two kinds of prayer homes, the ones that claimed to be non-denominational and the ones that were operating as churches. Leaders of the former admonished their members to keep their memberships and pay their dues in the western mission-founded churches where they were members. For maximum and unhindered patronage, the prayer houses chose to meet on days and at times when members of the established churches could attend.

The most influential of the prayer and healing homes was that of the All Christian Praying Band of Prophetess Madam Nwokolo of Ufuma, also known as "Nwanyi Ufuma." Madam Nwokolo has been described as one "who in the early 40s started healing through prayer, fasting, and the use of holy oil."[218] Another Igbo prayer and healing home in the early 1940s was run by Prophetess Ozoemena, from Aboh Ndoni. Though not as influential as Nwokolo, Prophetess Ozoemena wielded immense influence on Agnes Oko, the founder of Christ Holy Church, as we shall see later.

Some Catholic seminary students, after studying four prayer houses in Igboland, outlined the following common characteristics: the purpose of healing both body and mind; the claim of leaders that they themselves were once sick but were healed; the practice of members to keep their memberships in western mission-founded churches; the desire to be reticent on what goes on among members; the emphasis of faith healing, fasting and prayer; the unquestionable acceptance of words, interpretations and the authority of leaders; the claim that all members are trained to see visions and prophesy; the claim of non-denominational status of the prayer homes; and the blessing of water, oil, and other elements as aids to healing.[219]

The Catholic seminarians obliquely evaluated the prayer houses, among others, as being led by false prophets, victims of self-deception who mislead others, people who are preoccupied with self, and promoters of faith who are not genuinely Christian (i.e., "faith which is only motivated and measured by cure)."[220] Though not doubting the possibility of miraculous cures through faith and prayers, the seminarians advised their readers "to be very cautious . . . before accepting stories of cures emanating from prayer houses."[221] Even the admonishing of leaders of non-denominational prayer houses to their followers to shun paganism, the use of charms, and to be loyal to their churches was described as "camouflage of orthodoxy . . . immediately one sees the actual doctrine and practice in some of these prayer houses."[222] They, consequently, cautioned their readers, especially Catholics, to be wary of patronizing the prayer houses so as not to lose fervor with the sacraments.[223] After expressing all these negatives, the seminarians, ironically, commended the prayer houses for rehabilitating mad people and awakening people to the necessity of prayer and fasting.[224]

In view of the popularity of the rayer houses among Christians of western mission-founded churches in Igboland,[225] the seminarians urged the Catholic church to be more pragmatic about the needs of her members; compose new hymns and prayers; introduce a more elaborate liturgy that would be relevant and meaningful to Igbos; bless sick children, houses, pregnant women, new fruits; and anoint the sick and establish prayer solidarities in every parish.[226]

The afore-said observations and recommendations can be rightly perceived as a normal academic discipline of seminary students and do not necessarily posit an official Catholic view of the prayer houses in Igboland. The reaction of the Catholic Church towards their members who patronized the prayer houses, however, tends to elucidate a point: Either the seminarians were reechoing the *vox populi* among Catholics or were influencing Catholics with their observations.

The archdiocese of Onitsha, according to G. C. Ikeobi, did not take any official stand on Catholics who patronized the prayer houses. Rather, priests were given the liberty to do what seemed right to them. Madam Nwokolo's prayer house, in particular, posed a great problem among Catholic priests, because of its non-denominational nature and popularity. While some priests did not see anything wrong with their members attending her meetings and other non-denominational prayer houses, others resonated the views of the five seminarians and thus saw the prayer houses as rival institutions. The former kept a blind eye to the patronage of prayer houses while the latter took some measures that made the patronage of prayer houses unpopular among Catholics. In some parishes those who openly participated in the activities of prayer houses were denied the sacraments and Christian burial. "Those who at some time come back from the prayer houses, and decided not to go there again, are made to kneel down before the congregation from the beginning of mass to the end for a given number of Sundays."[227] In fact until 1985, Ikeobi asserts:"The above, in a nutshell, has been and still is the way the Church in Onitsha Archdiocese deals with her members who, in spite of repeated warnings, continue to frequent these prayer houses."[228] The hatred of the prayer houses was not peculiar to Catholics. Ikeobi observes that the prayer houses were ridiculed by members of the established churches.[229]

Conclusion

An effort has been made to trace briefly the historical, political, sociological, geographical, and religious situation of Nigeria—with special focus on Igbos as a people; their cosmology, worldview, and the resultant beliefs; and the seeding and growth of Christianity in Igboland. The emergence of African Independent Churches and their variant prayer houses or healing homes in Igboland and their ramifications on the Igbo society and western mission-founded churches have become an indispensable and veritable phenomenon in Igbo Christianity. It also enforces the fact that people tend to seek spiritual relief somewhere when their spiritual needs are either ignored, suppressed, or met in a manner that does not fall in line with their respective worldviews. In a nutshell, the history and growth of African Independent Churches in Igboland amplify the belief that people do their best to propagate the gospel (without expecting any foreign aid) when it becomes meaningful and relevant to their respective contexts. The purpose of recounting these socio-political and ecclesiastical events is to enable readers to understand the context of the life, ministry, and challenges of both Agnes Okoh and the history of the Christ Holy Church International—the locus of our study.

PART TWO

Leaders and Growth

CHAPTER FOUR

Christ Holy Church International: Early Beginnings

Agnes Okoh

Her Early Life

Agnes Amanye Okoh was born in May 1905 to Onumba Emordi, a farmer, and Ntonefu, a trader. Emordi, her father, was a native of Ndoni, a town in the Ogba/Egbema/Ndoni local government area in Rivers State, Nigeria. The town is divided into three villages and twelve quarters. Onumba Emordi was from Umu-Agbidi quarters in Ogbe-Ukwu village. Ntonefu, her mother, was from Umikem quarters at Onitsha, also in Igboland, in eastern Nigeria. Emordi and Ntonefu got married at a time when child mortality rate in Nigeria was very high. As a result they gave birth to thirteen children but had to bury twelve of them. Agnes was the only survivor. The parents of Agnes were not Christians, but she worshipped periodically with a nearby Roman Catholic congregation.

Agnes was not educated in any of the numerous mission schools in Igboland. The reason may be ostensibly attributed to her gender and the Igbo perception of the roles of women in society. Comparing the privileges and responsibilities of Igbo males to their female peers in 1921, Basden observes:

> The women and girls are not so free, though they enjoy themselves well enough in their own way. Almost as soon as they can walk, girls take a share in the household duties. They begin by carrying water, collecting firewood, rubbing floors, assisting in the preparation of food, and then they are initiated into the technicalities of trade. . . . Unless a girl can read before she is twenty it is safe to assume that she will never learn at all.

This will serve to illustrate the uniformly low level of intellectual attainment with which Ibo women are satisfied.[230]

In fact, Ilogu notes that the education of Igbo women was taken seriously from 1939 to 1964,[231] a period when Agnes was approaching her mid-life.

At the death of her parents she left Ndoni to live with some relatives at Asaba, a town close to her mother's hometown, Onitsha. She was a petty trader, buying and selling textile, until 1924 when she was married to James Okoh, a Ghanaian immigrant sailor in Nigeria. James Okoh was a Ga from the Kwakwaranya We (clan) in Accra, Ghana. After the marriage, she became legally known as Agnes Okoh. James and Agnes Okoh gave birth to a daughter, Anyele, on 5 May 1925 and a son, Marius Anyetei, 5 April 1927.

Her Religious Experience and Call

James Okoh died in the early 1930s. Agnes did not remarry. While Agnes, now a single parent, was recuperating from the grief of losing her husband, Anyele, her only daughter, died on 1 April 1938, at the age of 13 while at a middle school at Asaba, in Delta State. Agnes struggled hard to overcome her grief and the challenges of single parenthood. She developed a migraine and began seeking healing from one mission hospital after another. When it became evident that her migraine defied the potency of western medicine, she visited some native doctors, known among the Igbos as *dibia*. The native doctors also failed to provide any relief. She became restless, consequently. Not many African Independent Churches and their variant prayer houses or healing homes were in Igboland at that time. Some of the few operating in eastern Nigeria were the Cherubim and Seraphim Church, the Christ Apostolic Church, and Madam Nwokolo's prayer house of Ufuma.[232]

After falling sick and being in a state of despondency for over four years, she met a friend in 1942 who led her to the prayer house of prophetess Ozoemena, popularly known as Ma Ozoemena, at Enugu. Agnes spent fourteen days with prophetess Ozoemena who incidentally was also from Ndoni; she was totally healed through prayer, in the name of Jesus. She, subsequently, committed herself to faith healing and studied under Ma Ozoemena who became her pastor and spiritual mentor. According to Rev. Enoch Okonkwo, the first general evangelist of Christ Holy Church (now retired):

> Odozi-Obodo[233] [i.e., Agnes Okoh] was very close to her [Ozoemena] and they worked together. Odozi-Obodo used to

receive counseling, advice, and tutelage from Ozoemena on how to be self-conscious of God's calling. Odozi-Obodo was advised by Ozoemena to be careful, always prepare herself ready because God wants to use her for great work. They worked together.[234]

Agnes later recognized that she had the gift of prophecy since all her prophetic utterances were said to have been fulfilled exactly. Prophetess Ozoemena was said to be so overwhelmed with the accuracy of Agnes' prophecies that she in turn prophesied to Agnes that God intended to use her in the future to spread the gospel. The prophetess, however, cautioned Agnes not to rush into ministry; she asked her to wait until God's appointed time.

In April 1943, while returning from a market at Enugu, Agnes Okoh claimed to have heard a voice saying, "Matthew 10," repeatedly. She turned around each time she heard the voice in an attempt to see the speaker but did not see anyone. She quickly ran to the home of a friend and asked her, "What is Matthew 10?" The friend, who was semi-literate, told her that "Matthew 10" is part of the Gospel of Matthew in the New Testament. They sought the help of a young man who read the entire chapter of Matthew 10 to them in Igbo language from the Union Igbo translation of the Bible. The two women then rushed to the prayer house of Prophetess Ozoemena. After hearing the religious experience of Agnes, Ma Ozoemena reminded her of the earlier prophecy of God's intention to use her. She reiterated the divine warning that Agnes should not rush into the ministry; she should wait for God's timing. Meanwhile Agnes continued in her textile business at Enugu market. She became so resourceful that she was able to finance her son's education and looked after him till he got a job.

Her Itinerant Evangelistic Ministry

Prophetess Agnes Okoh had a stint in proclaiming the gospel in 1946 before becoming a full-time itinerant evangelist: "One night," said the prophetess, "while I was at Enugu, our Lord called me and asked me to go to Afikpo (in the present Abia State in Nigeria) and that I should use only ten shillings (one *niara*) for the journey. On the following morning, I obeyed his word and went."[235] She returned to Enugu and waited for a further divine directive as advised by Prophetess Ozoemena.

In 1947, Prophetess Ozoemena told Odozi-Obodo [i.e., Agnes Okoh] that they had to relocate to Onitsha as God had instructed. They left Enugu for Onitsha and lived at Ilo-Oroja. On 15 December 1947, Prophetess Ozoemena called holy prophetess Odozi-Obodo to go and find a place to conduct her own prayers; they will no longer be together according to God's directive."[236]

She commissioned her to begin an itinerant evangelistic ministry right away. In accordance with some of the injunctions in Matthew 10, backed by a said revelation from God, Agnes immediately discontinued her textile business. She sold all her merchandise and distributed the proceeds to the poor and needy. She left Ma Ozoemena's prayer house and began fasting and praying, imploring God to empower and direct her in the ministry that had been entrusted to her. She claimed to have been assured of God's presence in a dream in which she was asked to use John 10:10, "The thief comes only to steal, and kill, and destroy; I came that they might have life, and might have it abundantly,"[237] as the thematic message of her ministry. She then bought a handbell and began preaching from one place to another.

Agnes began her itinerant ministry in late 1947 at Onitsha, a town known for its commercial activities in eastern Nigeria. Faith in God was her major emphasis. Matthew 10 was her favorite Bible passage. Her motto was, however, John 10:10. She went to many places in Igboland wearing a white garment[238] with a white head scarf. She held a Bible in her left hand and a handbell in her right hand. Her medium of communication was the Igbo language. She, however, spoke Pidgin English[239] when ministering to non-Igbo speakers.

At Onitsha, usually at market places, she announced her presence by ringing the handbell, singing a Gospel song and then preaching. She would challenge her audience, saying: "Why are you having sleepless nights? Why don't you have meaning in life? What does life mean to you? Jesus is inviting you to come so that you might have life and have it more abundantly. There is new life in Jesus. Jesus wants to exchange your meaningless life with a brand new one. The joy that you are supposed to have in life has been stolen by the devil. If you come to him, he will give you the meaning of life and make your life new."[240] She was said to have usually ended her preaching by praying for her audience.

The thrust of her message centered on repentance, righteousness, and holiness. As people were coming to her with their problems she realized that she had the gifts of healing and seeing visions in addition to prophesying. Her healing and prophetic prowess attracted many people to her. Those who were healed began spreading the news about the new prophetess. Her popularity, therefore, became as widespread as a bush fire. Many people began inviting her to their towns and villages.

She honored people's invitations to minister in their villages and towns in the south eastern and Niger Delta areas of Nigeria.[241] At other times, however, she was said to have been prompted by the Holy Spirit, through dreams, visions, or intuition to go to certain places and preach the gospel.[242] Depending on the accessibility of the area, she traveled either by public transport—buses and trains—or on foot. At the villages, she sought permission from the elders, as traditional protocol demands, before beginning preaching. She would then stay at the village for months praying and healing people until she would claim that God had directed her to move to another place.

Her Centralized Evangelistic Ministry

Finally, she settled at Onitsha and coordinated the affairs of her prayer centers from there, albeit continuing her evangelistic ministries in Igboland. Among her early converts were ten men and two women who helped her to proclaim the gospel from one place to another. The twelve were Hezekiah D. Mbaegbu, Pa J. A. Ifeajuna, Benedict Aroghalu Mbamalu, Paul Ifeduba, Pa Onyejekwe, Winifred Nweje Ifeajuna, Cecilia Obi, Michael Obi, Brother Job, Patrick Egabor, Enoch N. Okonkwo, and David O. U. Nwaizuzu.

Agnes Okoh used an uncompleted building at Onitsha as her headquarters. After an itinerary ministration she would retire to that building and be praying for people. "Many people who had known her while she was with Ozoemena and those who heard of her fame as God uses her marvelously were going to receive prayers."[243]

Though her ministry had some of the features of prayer houses of her time, it was different in some respects. Unlike most of the prayer houses that were conducted in a centralized location where people had to travel so as to receive prayers from the head prophet or prophetess, Agnes' ministry was planted in many towns and villages in Igboland. She was not the central figure in the ministry whom every one wanted to visit so as to be prayed for. Rather she trained her own pastors and commissioned them to take care of the spiritual needs of the people. The ministry was therefore not centered on her personality or her gifts only. The ministry, at this point, was considered non-denominational.

Her Refugee Status and Ministry

At the outbreak of the civil war in Nigeria in 1966 she closed down all the prayer centers that were in the towns and villages where soldiers were doing battle. The center at Onitsha was also closed. Prophetess Okoh and most of the members sought refuge at Arondizougu, also in

Igboland, where there was relative peace. Though a refugee, she continued to pray, comfort, counsel, preach, and heal the other refugees and people living in and around Arondizougu. Her services were not limited to the civilian population; her followers claim that some soldiers went to her for prayers. She became very popular and opened more prayer centers at the environs of Arondizougu. She stayed at Arondizougu untill the war came to an end.

What impressed people and convinced them of God's presence with her was her ability to quote the Bible from memory even though she was illiterate. According to Rev. Enoch Okonkwo, "She was eloquent like the prophets of old, though she was an illiterate, but God wrote the Bible in her brain. There is no portion of the Holy Bible she did not know."[244] She was, as a result, said to have held her audience spellbound by showing profuse knowledge of the Bible by either quoting from memory or asking some people to read several texts from the Bible in support of the subject matter. Before quoting from the Bible or asking someone to read a text, she would ask, "*Obu na ife na ekwu adiro na akwukwo nso?*" meaning, "What I am saying, is it not in the Bible?"[245] Many people found it extremely difficult to believe that the prophetess could neither read nor write any language.

Her Persecution

Some people viewed prophetess Agnes Okoh's evangelistic ministry with some cynicism. Those who were amazed at the effectiveness of her healing gifts but found it hard to believe that God would use a woman in such magnitude began attributing the source of her powers to Mami Water, "a name applied by Africans to a class of female and male water divinities or spirits that have accreted elements from several European, New World, and Indian cultural traditions."[246] The blessing of water as an element of healing by the prophetess was seen by many as a legitimate proof of the Mami Water syndrome. Some people, as a result, made fun of the church, calling it "Mami Water Church." Some also speculated that she had a shrine at Ndoni, her home town. Whenever her attention was drawn to what the cynics were saying about her, the prophetess would either say, "*Adigh m anu okwu ekwensu*" which literally means, "I do not hear the voice of the devil," or "*Chukwu me kwalu fa ebele*" ("May God have mercy on them").[247]

Rev. Enoch Okonkwo recollects how someone wanted to kill the prophetess at Onitsha in 1954. The assailant knocked at her door at night. When the prophetess asked about the identity of the one knocking on the door the person mentioned his name, but the prophetess claimed that a voice warned her not to open the door. The intruder's persistence compelled the prophetess to call some of her assistants (including Rev. Okonkwo) from her window and asked them to check the identity of the one knocking at the door. The man was found to be holding a machete, so he was overpowered and handed over to the police.[248] Members of the church were taunted for attending a church founded by a woman, perhaps due to the aforementioned poor image of women in the Igbo society. It was even alleged that some members of western mission-founded churches and some charismatic churches made fun of Christ Holy Church members for dancing, clapping hands, and shouting "Hallelujahs!" during worship times. They were, as a result, popularly ridiculed as "Hallelujah Church." Some people who donated lands for the church were alleged to have been persuaded by some Catholic leaders to take back their lands.

The Emergence of the title "Odozi Obodo"

The prime concern of Prophetess Agnes Okoh was to get land to build a worship center for her new believers in Christ. The purpose was to stabilize them in the faith. Some of the beneficiaries of her healing and prophetic gifts gave land free of charge to begin the ministry.[249] At some places where the believers were not wealthy enough to donate land, elders of the communities donated *ajaw-awfia*, (i.e., bad bush) or *ajo oshia* (i.e., evil forest)[250] to the leadership of the prayer ministry. Some of the towns where evil forests were donated, according to Rev. Samuel Ejiofor, a former head of the church, were Abba, Umuoza, Ogbunike, and Achalla.[251]

In those days, according to Basden who published his book about the Igbos in 1921, when Agnes was a teenager, free-born men who died of natural causes were buried in the foregrounds of their homes. Married women who died of natural causes were, however, buried at their husband's village, except when a wealthy son of the deceased arranged that the mother be buried at her hometown. Such arrangements were usually preceded by some negotiations with the relatives of the deceased's husband and the payment of fees by the son.

> The Ibo will endure everything demanded of him in this life; will put up with hardships, the misbehaviour of his children, indeed anything, in order to insure that his burial will be properly performed. His whole future welfare depends upon this, and hence it takes, at all times, a most prominent place in a man's calculations.[252]

Igbos believed that an improper burial was a disgrace to the departed person, an act that could result in the punishment of the living. Igbos, therefore, performed second burial rites to ensure that things were done properly. Basden states some of the eschatological beliefs of Igbos:

> When men have run their course in this world they return to their master—the supreme being—and live with him in the spirit world. In their spiritual state they are endowed with never-ending life, and, until the ceremony of second burial has been observed, they continue to haunt this world, wandering at will in the houses, compounds and farms, invisible, yet ever present, and taking a distinct yet unremitting interest in the affairs of the individual and the community with which they associated in life. After the rites of the second burial have been completed the "spirits" depart to their appointed place and rest in peace until their reincarnation, i.e., as long as they behave themselves.[253]

The importance of the second burial is demonstrated by the steps some Igbos took to ensure its reality. This is seen in the fact that poor relatives had to "sell old people, especially a woman decrepit and sick . . . and the money obtained by the sale was devoted to the expenses of the second burial, this being considered much more important than her latter end on earth or the disposal of her actual remains."[254]

In spite of the importance Igbos attached to burials, not all Igbos were given proper and decent burials. At death, slaves were hurriedly buried. Some people in the Igbo society were not even buried. Such people—lepers, those who die of communicable diseases such as small pox, women who die at childbirth, lunatics, those who commit suicide, those murdered, and those who died accidentally through drowning or burns—were simply thrown into the bad bush. Those who were considered as social misfits were also cast into the evil forests. This practice is corroborated by Chinua Achebe in his novel *Things Fall Apart,* a novel about tensions between western missionaries and some beliefs and practices of Igbos:

> Unoka was an ill-fated man. He had a bad *chi* or personal god, and evil fortune followed him to the grave, or rather to his death, for he had no grave. He died of the swelling which was an abomination to the earth goddess. When a man was afflicted with swelling in the stomach and the limbs he was not allowed to die in the house. He was carried to the evil

forest and left to die. There was a story of a very stubborn man who staggered back to his house and had to be carried again to the forest and tied to a tree. . . . He died and rotted above the earth and was not given the first or the second burial.[255]

It was customary at that time to kill some people, believing that they would accompany deceased chiefs and kings in the other world. It was a popular belief that such victims would serve the departed chiefs and kings. "The corpses of all these victims were not buried; they had to be cast away in the *ajaw awfia* (bush dedicated to receive corpses of outcasts) where the remains of human sacrifices were deposited."[256] Those who were thrown into the evil forest were believed to have been later killed by the evil forces that inhabit the forest.

The act of throwing corpses into evil forests was antithetical to a very prominent Igbo belief about the supernatural. The fear that the living would be haunted by the ghosts of the dead for not performing the rites of a second burial was very prevalent in some Igbo communities. Some Igbos bore the brunt of the irony of burial discrimination as against the fear of being haunted by the ghosts of those who were not given proper burials, particularly those who were not buried at all. The evil forests, as the name implied, was dreaded because it was deemed to be the resting place of spirits who felt disgraced and humiliated by the living. The spirits of those thrown in the forest were believed to have been filled with vengeance. It was, therefore, believed that they used every opportunity to punish the living. It was a general belief that people who dared to enter the evil forests or were thrown into it alive either had scratches all over their bodies, developed swollen bodies, or never returned.[257]

Agnes Okoh and her followers were not the first people to be offered an evil forest. Giving evil forests to religious leaders seems to have been an old practice among some Igbo elders. The elders, in their bid to get rid of religious leaders, pretended to be generous while in actual fact acted treacherously. Chinua Achebe concurs with the claim by members of Christ Holy Church on this issue by giving an account of a similar "donation" to some western missionaries who asked for land to build a place of worship:

> Every clan and village has its "evil forest." In it were buried all those who died of the really evil diseases, like leprosy and smallpox. It was also the dumping ground for the potent

fetishes of great medicine men when they died. An "evil forest" was, therefore, alive with sinister forces and powers of darkness. It was such a forest that the rulers of Mbanta gave to the missionaries. They did not really want them in their clan, and so they made them that offer which nobody in his right senses would accept. . . . They want a piece of land to build their shrine. . . . Let us give them a portion of the Evil Forest. They boast about victory over death. Let us give them a real battlefield in which to show their victory. . . . They offered them as much of the Evil Forest as they cared to take. And to their greatest amazement the missionaries thanked them and burst into song.[258]

The claim by members of Christ Holy Church that some evil forests were "donated" to Agnes Okoh, their leader, can therefore not be doubted. The gift at its face value seemed generous, yet it was "a gift" that tended to test the genuineness of her claim of serving a powerful God whose power knows no boundaries. The "gift," similar to the Trojan horse, was also a grand trap to cause the death of the prophetess and her followers and thus curtail her ministry on earth. The gifts could also be perceived as a contest between two deities—the gods of the villagers and the God of the prophetess.

The prophetess, being an Igbo and knowing the beliefs about the *ajo oshia* among the Igbos, accepted the offer, prayed at the entrance of the forests, encouraged her followers that the God they were serving is mightier than the evil forces in the forests and then entered. She and her followers then built some huts and made the forests their habitation. Many villagers instantly became members of her church on hearing and seeing that the prophetess and her followers entered and lived in the evil forests without any mishaps. Within a few months the prophetess invited all those who were not afraid to live in the forests, either to build some houses in the forests or to use some portions of the land to farm. These bold and generous acts of the holy prophetess increased the economic power of many villagers in view of the fertility of the forests, and thus made the poor rich in no time.

In recognition of her ability to overcome evil forces, healing people of all kinds of sickness, and turning dreaded forests into a more useful venture for her followers and other inhabitants of some villages, many observers of her ministry began calling her *Odozi Obodo*[259] which literally means "town repairer" or "nation builder." The title *Odozi Obodo* has been translated by Peter DomNwachukwu as "one who shapes society and keeps it morally pure."[260] It is a title which nearly obliterated the name of prophetess Agnes Okoh, because those who knew her and the effects of her ministry were said to have had no doubt that the name was a befitting honor for her. She was known by and large as Odozi Obodo. Christ Holy Church International has been popularly known and called "Odozi Obodo" or "Odozi Obodo's church." Until 2000 all billboards of the church had Odozi Obodo written in parenthesis after the name of the church. Due to the multicultural policy of the church, the name Odozi Obodo has been substituted with "Nation Builders" on the church's bill boards.

The ministry did not have an official name prior to 1950. It was loosely called Odozi Obodo's prayer ministry. In 1950, after receiving some administrative help from some leaders of Christ Apostolic Church, the prayer ministry was officially named Christ Apostolic Church (Odozi Obodo). That name was later changed to Christ Holy Church of Nigeria in 1975.[261]

Some personal qualities marked Prophetess Agnes Okoh as a prophetess called by God. The qualities were leadership, healing, prophecy, philanthropy, and faith. These qualities endeared her to the hearts of those who came close to her. The qualities will be discussed one after the other.

Her Leadership Qualities
Societal Background of Her Leadership

The traditional role of women in Igbo society is a subservient one like many other African societies. H. Onyema Anyanwu underscores this fact in the everyday perception of Igbo women: "In traditional society women are really portrayed quite consistently as appendages of men. They are looked upon as possessions of men, as goods which may be sold, disposed of, given away, traded or just ordered about by men, as things which might better be seen and not heard."[262] This practice is followed strictly when it comes to occupying leadership positions.

Throughout the traditional society it is the norm to find men occupying the positions of authority and command. Men are the rulers, the generals, the judges, the priests, and the landlords; not because of their proven ability to undertake such roles or because of any inability among women, but rather simply because such roles are unquestionably and automatically reserved for them. Men are specifically designated to fill those roles.[263]

Although Anyanwu praises missionaries for their tireless efforts at restoring feminine dignity in Igbo society by integrating them in church organization and educating them,[264] the religious roles of Igbo women, before the missionaries arrived in Igboland, were paradoxically highly respected, as stated by Dom Nwachukwu:

> Igbo women are active participants in the religion. They lead in every aspect of worship except *igo oji* (blessing and breaking of the *kolanut*) and *igo ofo* (using the *ofo* stick ritually and ceremoniously).... There are many cultural norms which delimit women's societal life, but in the arena of religion, Igbo women enjoy enormous freedom. They serve as priestesses, diviners, messengers, and worshippers. The most important deity in Igboland, *Ala* (earth goddess), is female. Her chief minister is always a woman.... This is the substance of Igbo religious life before the advent of Christianity.[265]

In spite of these significant religious roles, Anyanwu claims that the societal marginalization of Igbo women still persists. "The presentation of women in the society is consistently condescending, patronizing, derogatory, and in many places downright insulting . . . this traditional conception of women has not been completely eradicated despite the efforts of the missionaries."[266] The prophetess, Agnes Okoh, began her ministry and continued ministering in Igboland in such a chauvinistic society and under the circumstances described above.

Her Motherly Role in Leadership

Her inability to read and write any language was an additional societal setback, yet she did not allow such limitations to impede her leadership role in the prayer ministry that eventually became a church. Instead, she used the very thing that has been disdained by Igbo society—womanhood—to display optimum leadership. Prophetess Agnes Okoh has been popularly known among Christ Holy Church members and admirers as "Mama," a designation that connotes dignity, honor, and the acknowledgement of some characteristics to which masculinity does not have alternative equivalence. In an answer to a question, "Why do you call Prophetess Okoh 'Mama'? Is it because of her old age?" Rev. Samuel Ejiofor replied, "I worked with her for sixteen years. She regarded everyone as her child. She never discriminated."[267] To the Very Rev. Daniel Chukwuenyem Dike, "Mama was a disciplinarian who did not tolerate any form of nonsense or anything that was contrary to her call. She believed in truth twenty-four hours. If you do not have truth you will never be part of Mama."[268] To Rev. Emmanuel Alamanjo,

> Odozi Obodo fed everybody with spiritual and material food. From the time the church was founded till 1976 when

she retired, she single-handedly fed all workers of the church, even during the war when there was a shortage of food. She used the gifts she received from people to feed people who came to her and all the workers."[269]

Her Use of Appellations at Training Others

While training her pastors, Prophetess Agnes Okoh was said to have taken recognition of the special qualities of her trainees and, consequently, gave them appellations (motivational names), which resonated those distinctive qualities.[270] Rev. Enoch Okonkwo is, for instance, called *Agu* (Lion), an appellation depicting his fearlessness at healing diseases that had hitherto defied every type of healing. For his ability to crush spiritual problems into pieces, Rev. Daniel O. U. Nwaizuzu is called *Enyi* (Elephant). Rev. Gabriel O. Chiemeka's ability to command and subdue stubborn evil spirits to come out of people, in the name of Jesus, earned him the appellation, *Ochiaga* ("commander"). She used the appellations to call them, build their faith, encourage and challenge them, and to motivate them into action. Her trainees were, consequently, said to have accomplished many feats they thought they could not do, all things being equal. She used to call the entire membership of the church "*Umu Chineke!*" ("children of God!"). She used these appellations to counsel them to live lives befitting the appellations.

Her Use of Repetition at Training Others

Prophetess Agnes Okoh was a leader who was able to use the pedagogy of repetition to influence her followers with what she liked and disliked. She used this method to pass on her leadership policies and personal faith in God to her followers any time she was with them. Some of her most famous sayings which many of her followers remember are: "*Ka anyi nu onu Dinwenayi.*" ("Let us listen to the voice of the Lord's voice,")[271] "*Rapu ife nine n'aka Dinwenanyi.*" ("Leave everything in the hands of the Lord,") "*Ne ekpe ekeple*" ("Be prayerful,") "*Kwusia ike na Jisus Kraist.*" ("Stay firm in Jesus Christ,") "*Eme kwana ife ga emegide okwu akwukwo nso nifi na Jisus Kraist n'aba ozo.*" ("Do not go contrary to what the Bible says because Jesus is coming soon,") "Temptations only stop when River Niger dries up."[272] "I do not listen to the voice of the devil." "If I fear God there is no one else to fear." "Fear comes into your life whenever you deviate from God." "Trust in Jesus." "Go and stand on the Word of God." These sayings of hers have been imprinted indelibly on the minds of those who worked with and heard her.

Faith and Humility as Leadership Qualities

Her faith in God was said to be unflinching. She did not only communicate her faith in God to her followers, she demonstrated it even to the disbelief of her followers at times.[273] Rev. Okonkwo testifies about Agnes Okoh's faith in God:

> Odozi Obodo will never consider anything that will change the word of God. She will rather prefer death. As long as it is written in the Bible, she will neither divert to the right or left. This gives rise to the popular sayings within the church "I do not hear the voice of Satan." She always stood firm and nothing shook her faith in the word of God. This made her very unique. She would forfeit anything she had, to ensure progress of the work of God. She would suffer anything possible to advance the work of God. She would prefer to starve than allow God's work to fail. I witnessed all these qualities in her, having lived with her for six years at Ndoni.[274]

The humility and contentment of Prophetess Agnes Okoh were some of the hallmarks of her leadership. Although it was through her that the prayer ministry came into being and later grew into a church, members of Christ Holy Church International claim that Prophetess Agnes Okoh was aware of the biblical injunction on female leadership in the church.[275] Therefore, she never considered herself as a pastor and leader of the church. She was content with her prophetic ministry in the church and thus referred to herself as "prophetess of God." According to Rev. David Nwaizuzu, one of her early followers, "she did not see herself as one who will be in charge of the affairs of the church. She never coveted the position of a leader. When men began joining the church she gave them leadership positions. Mama never baptized, she never gave a communion, and she never ordained anyone."[276]

As a result, very early in her ministry, in early 1948, she appointed Pastor Hezekiah D. Mbaegbu leader of the prayer ministry. She claimed that God asked her to make that appointment. Mbaegbu was the leader of the ministry until he was suspended in 1956 after a misdemeanor. So resolute was her avowed policy of allowing men to lead the ministry that she did not take advantage of the vacancy in leadership position during Mbaegbu's suspension, albeit she perceived it as a setback. In his stead, the prophetess appointed Rev. Enoch Okonkwo and Rev. David O. U. Nwaizuzu in 1956 as co-leaders. She claimed, again, that these appointments were made upon divine instructions.[277]

Agnes Okoh's decision not to lead the church or assume the role of pastor, apart from her interpretation of the headship of man, may have been motivated by either the male chauvinistic nature of the Igbo society or the influence of her Catholic background,[278] though she could have taken advantage of the favorable Igbo perception of the religious roles of women to lead the church. She was under no obligation not to lead the church. With the exception of her sole prerogative of appointing leaders of the church, a function she usually claimed was revealed to her by God through prophecies or visions, she did not use her position as the founder to usurp the functions of the male leaders, running the church from the backstage. Instead, she instituted a democratic administrative body called "The Elders Committee," thus, dismantling any self-ego of indispensability. At Onitsha, the headquarters of the church, she used to sit at the side of the altar, during church services, while the leaders sat behind the altar, a place of leadership influence and honor. She served as a mother to the leaders and other pastors, using her spiritual and motherly dispositions to observe, encourage, counsel, and train them. She was, nevertheless, a disciplinarian who held people accountable to their commitments.

Accountability and Total Dependence on God as Leadership Qualities

According to Rev. Christian Chukwuemeka Obiefuna, "If she knew that you are responsible for this table and something on the table was needed she would insist that the one responsible would bring it. She held people responsible for their tasks. She was careful that things were done in order."[279] Rev. Daniel C. Dike recalls that the prophetess used her maturity in life to control their youthful exuberance. "Whenever anything went wrong Mama would ask us to wait on God's time. She calmed us any time we wanted to take some hurried actions. She used to advise us never to fight for God, since God is himself a warrior who does battle in his own time."[280]

Prophetess Agnes Okoh's sensibilities to the promptings of the Holy Spirit were overwhelming. "She did not do things except God directed her. Even when you suggest something to her she would say, 'Let's hear from God.' Only when God gave her an answer would she move, and when she moved she would not look back."[281] Such faith and obedience to the promptings of the Holy Spirit were seen as unrealistic by some members, particularly the educated ones, and consequently caused some tensions between them and the prophetess. Three examples will be given in this regard. When in 1956 Prophetess Agnes Okoh appointed

Rev. Enoch Okonkwo and Rev. David O. Nwaizuzu joint leaders of the church, Catechist Ekueme, who was more educated than the appointees, challenged the appointment on the basis of his education. He claimed to be more qualified than Okonkwo. The prophetess, while not denying that fact, insisted that the appointment was divinely revealed.

The second disagreement between the prophetess and Ekueme was with regard to preparing a preaching timetable. While Prophetess Okoh was used to waiting on the Lord's directives before going to a place to preach, Ekueme wanted her to establish a timetable and adhere to it. The prophetess, again, did not compromise.

Finance was the last point of tension between Ekueme and Prophetess Agnes Okoh. The prophetess claimed, at the early stages of her ministry, that God asked her neither to collect money from anyone nor allow her leaders to collect money in exchange for their services for a certain unspecified period. She was even said to have rejected moneys given to her by Marius, her only son who was gainfully employed during this period with the public works department of the colonial administration.

Rev. Enoch Okonkwo makes a reference to this policy when asked to reflect on the nature of the ministry at their time: "Money played less important role at our time"[282] [sic]. This policy plunged the leaders into great financial stress and abject poverty. The prophetess resisted a proposal by Ekueme, who asked her to review that policy in view of the financial difficulties in which they found themselves. She told Ekueme that God's directives are non-negotiable. She, however, assured him that God had promised her that if she and her workers were able to obey that prophecy, a time would come when leaders and workers of the church would lack nothing. These disagreements provoked Ekueme and a few members to leave the church in 1956.[283] This is reported to be the only time some people left in protest of church policies since the beginning of the ministry in 1947. Leaders of the Ihitenansa Superintendency, however, claim that Ekueme did not establish any church, so most of the members who followed him became disappointed and, thus, returned to the prophetess' prayer ministry. They, therefore, do not consider it a secession.

Her Ability to Inspire Communal Lifestyle

Through her selfless and humble leadership, the life of the early members of the church was said to be communal, caring, and affectionate, akin to that of the early church in Jerusalem. Mud houses were built for widows whose husbands died intestate. According to Chidi Mbadiwe,

Fasting in proxy for barren women was the norm in the early 50s. The barren women had no knowledge that some members were fasting and asking God to make them fertile. When God answered their prayers members brought all kinds of gifts—food, clothing, money—to the new mother and child before the dedication of the child in the third month after birth."[284]

Free manual labor was provided by some members for other members who were either too poor to hire laborers or too weak and sick to work on their farms. Those who benefited most from the free manual labor were women. Wealthy members who owned houses were said to have reserved one room in their houses, as a tithe, for some of the workers of the church. The members provided the basic needs of other church workers who were housed on church premises. "The members," according to Rev. John Ekweoba,"gave their clothing to poor and hungry church workers. Even church workers who had more than one pair of trousers gave the other to those who had none…We used to walk for ten or fifteen miles to preach the gospel."[285]

Members of the church were neither compelled nor persuaded to meet the needs of others. The pedagogy of giving was based on the example of the prophetess. "She was a prophetess who taught with examples, always setting an example with her own self. When Odozi Obodo tells you to give and promises you that what you have given will be given back to you, she will first give so you can see it."[286] The generosity of the members, therefore, emanated from the exemplary lifestyle of the holy prophetess.

Very Rev. Clement Obiokoye claims that another regular feature of the early life of the church was the revelation of some people's secret deeds and thoughts during their meetings. What some members did in secret was revealed through prophetic utterances when they met at worship services—the presence or absence of the object of the revelations were not important.[287] It was a general practice of members to follow up on absentee members to find out what had prevented them from being present.[288] Miraculous healings became commonplace in the church, as will be discussed later. Members of the church were, as a result, awed with the activities of the Holy Spirit and did things with circumspection.

Reflecting on the lifestyles of the church members in the mid-50s, Rev. Enoch Okonkwo says: "Our church in our time was built on Almighty God through his Son Jesus Christ and the Holy Spirit as the totality of our abiding faith and deeds."[289] Prophetess Agnes Okoh combined her natural motherly instincts with humility, the fear of God, and the desire to obey God no matter the circumstances to lead the church. "Mama was generous and approachable. I can liken her meekness to the biblical Moses, because we never saw her quarreling with anyone."[290] She had the desire to raise up men and women who would do the work of God without necessarily looking up to her. Her leadership influence over them was consequently immense. Her leadership was couched in the cultural milieu of the Igbo context. As a result, she was able to adapt aspects of the culture that do not contradict the teachings of Christianity while rejecting the ones that are contrary to plain biblical teaching.

Her Healing Ministry

Initial Practice of Faith Healing

Prophetess Agnes Okoh's ministry was filled with numerous healing miracles. Her own experience of being healed of a migraine in 1942 gave her a first-hand knowledge of God as a healer. Commissioned to preach a life-in-Christ message (John 10:10), she considered healing as an integral part of the life-in-Christ package and, therefore, did not hesitate to pray for all those who were sick in body and soul.

The church initially practiced a strict form of faith healing, one that does not permit members to make other choices when sick. "Nobody was allowed to take any form of medicine in the early stages of Christ Holy Church, from the 50s to the early 70s. Those who sneaked to take any form of medicine were exposed by the Holy Spirit. It was an abomination for a member of this church to take medicine when sick."[291] The church set aside healing homes for those who were seriously ill and handicapped. Rev. Alamanjo, who was himself healed in the church, gives a description of the importance of healing in the early years of the church:

> In those days every station had three buildings—the worship center, teacher's quarters, and the healing home. Mad people were in chains; there were blind people, lepers, those enduring serious satanic attacks, who came to live in the church. Those with serious cases lived in the healing homes. They came with their mats, pots, stoves, and kettles. The mad people stayed for about three days to three weeks, depending on the severity of their lunacy. No sickness was incurable; sickness was never a terror to anybody because members knew that once the name of the Lord was invoked, the sickness will rUn away. Every member was as strong in prayer as a gospel minister.[292]

Prophetess Agnes Okoh was said to have healed many people of all kinds of diseases. "She raised dead people and healed those who were mad, lame, and blind. I am an eye witness to all these miracles. That is why her people believed her claims, and I personally decided to follow her."[293]

Using Water from Streams to Heal

The apex of her healing ministry was in 1963 when she claimed that God had revealed a stream to her (in a dream) to use to heal.[294] She described the site of the stream to some of her pastors and asked them to go and locate the stream. After many failed attempts, the stream (Nkissi stream) was spotted in the northwestern part of Onitsha.[295] The Nkissi stream looked dirty, but as she and her workers began to weed around the stream, clear spring water gushed out, something they considered as a confirmation of the revelation. The prophetess sent her workers to announce to the populace of Onitsha to assemble at the stream with all their infirmities. The workers initially traveled to all the nearby towns and villages using megaphones to announce the dates and times the prophetess of God would go to the stream and bless it for healing.

For six months in 1963 the prophetess went to the stream on every other Tuesday morning at 9:00 a.m. At the stream, the prophetess, dressed as simply as any elderly Igbo woman would dress, led her workers to sing songs of praises and gave a sermonnette which was usually about the purpose of the earthly ministry of Jesus Christ and the need to put one's faith in him. She would then bless the stream, drink from it herself, and ask her pastors to take a drink before ushering those who had assembled to take a drink in order to receive healing. Those who came with some containers would then be allowed to fill them with the water after everyone had drunk from the stream. The water in the containers was given to sick friends and relatives who could not make a trip to the stream. It was even reported that some sick people were forcibly taken from their hospital beds and transported to the streamside.

There were numerous claims of healing after using the consecrated water. News about the stream of healing spread to many parts of Nigeria so the numbers of the crowds swelled to such an extent that, after a while, owners of the land bordering the banks of the river, thinking that the prophetess was enriching herself by using the water to heal, began putting some impediments in the way of the prophetess and those who went there for healing. The prophetess, consequently, stopped using the stream to heal.

A similar revelation was made to the prophetess in 1973. This time the Olo Ogwashi stream at Ogwashi-Ukwu at Aniocha South Local Government Area in Delta State was used. The procedure and the results were similar to those of the Nkissi stream, but an eyewitness account by Rev. Christian Obiefuna, who was one of the ministers who spotted the stream after the prophetess had sent some pastors to look for it, is worth noting:

> She used to go to the stream at 10:00 a.m. every Monday to pray and ask some of her pastors to read a portion of the Bible. She then asked the reader to explain the scripture that had been read. Then the leader of the pastoral team announces, "Now it is time for the holy prophetess to bless the water." Mama would bless the water and drink it first. She then asked her leaders to drink. After that she would tell the people, "Go and take your own and drink." As people drank the water they began to shout for joy and give testimonies of instant healing. Then they filled their containers with water. It usually ended by 2:00 p.m.[296]

The only difference between the ministries at the Nkissi and the Olo Ogwashi streams was the length of period in which the two streams were used. While the former was used for a half year the latter was used only five times.

Apart from using water from the two streams, the prophetess also blessed oil for healing. She also asked members who were sick to bring water from their homes to be blessed for healing. The prophetess, it must be noted, did not make water and oil medicines to be taken when one was ill.

Some Testimonies of Agnes Okoh's Healing Prowess

She used diverse means of healing. "What surprised me about Mama," says Rev. John Obiakor, "was that she healed diseases that had defied medicine just by simple prayer. For example, in 1964 when she visited the congregation at Awkuzu, at Oyi Local Government Authority, three female mental patients were at the healing home. She did not even say a prayer; she only took a long look at them and commanded that they be released from their chains because they had been healed."[297] In February 1976, a lame man was brought to the Prophetess during a worship service at Onitsha to be healed. "Mama did not pray; she only looked at the man and commanded him, saying: 'Get up in the name of Jesus and glorify the Lord with the other worshippers.' The man immediately got up and joined the singing."[298] When she prayed for the sick her prayer was usually described as "simple." She was not used to praying for long hours. According to Rev. Enoch Okonkwo, who was himself healed by the prophetess in 1952, "A simple prayer from Mama settles the sickness that had defied every type of medication. . . . What was surprising about her healing ministry was that she did not charge money. She did not ask people to bring anything from the house; she only prayed for people just as they came."[299] Another dimension of the healing gift of the prophetess was midwifery.

On Friday, 2 February 1951, during a prayer meeting the Lord revealed that all pregnant women among the congregation should go to the prophetess whenever they are in labor for delivery. Consequently, women in labor went . . . and were delivered safely. A lot of women were delivered through this way and most of the babies born are fullgrown men and women.[300]

The prophetess trained many women in midwifery, also known in west Africa as traditional birth attendants. One of the roles of wives of pastors in the church is to perform the duties of a midwife. Suffice it to say that the prophetess added a wider dimension to her ministerial functions—a dimension which was very relevant to female leaders and members.

Her Prophetic Ministry

Her Concept of Prophecy

Prophetess Agnes Okoh is widely remembered for the exact fulfillment of her predictive prophecies and other prophecies warning people of impending omens if they did not stop their sinful practices. She was also known to have exposed the secret deeds and thoughts of some people, thoughts that were inimical to the fellowship in the church and humanity. "When she told you that something would happen tomorrow, you dare not challenge her because her prophecies were fulfilled exactly."[301] Her prophetic utterances were not preceded with any bodily gestures or ecstatic noises. She prophesied while having a conversation with people.[302] She considered prophecy not as guess work but as a word from God. She was, therefore, always prepared to prophesy no matter the perception some people would accord the prophecy.

The Efficacy of Her Prophecies

Three specific prophecies of Prophetess Agnes Okoh have endeared her to the hearts of many. Such people do not doubt her claim of being a prophetess of God. The first of the prophecies was about the outbreak of the civil war in Nigeria.

>In 1965 she prophesied that…Nigeria will be in turmoil, that Nigeria will lose so many souls and spill so much blood. It sounded like a joke then. She said that there will be hunger. That corn which is being sold at fifteen for three kobo will be sold at one for sixty kobo. Everyone was saying how could that happen, when there was relative peace in Nigeria.[303] [sic].

The fulfillment of this prophecy was the Nigerian civil war that raged on from 1966 to 1970.

The second prophecy, which baffled many people, was also with regard to when the civil war will end.

>Two and half years after the war started, in October, 1969 during the annual harvest at Ojoto, I was present. The late Rt. Rev. M. A. Okoh was the officiating minister at that harvest, and he announced, that the holy Prophetess Odozi Obodo through revelation has said that the war will end after December 1969. People were asking who will win the war. He replied that the Almighty God did not reveal who will win, but that the war must surely end after December 1969. I went to Rt. Rev. Okoh and asked him, what are we to do. He said that, we should announce it without fear. . . . So I was one of those who went about telling people that the war will soon end.[304]

This prophecy was pronounced during the heat of the civil war. "During that time Enugu, Okigwe, Aba, and many other towns were war zones so people were confused and doubted the prophecy."[305] The prophetess uttered this prophecy, when she and most members of the church were refugees on the Biafran side. The announcement of the prophecy, the command to her members to broadcast the prophecy, and the uncertainty about the winner or loser of the war caused a great stir in Igboland, particularly among the Biafran soldiers. The Biafran soldiers considered the prophecy as false rumor. They tried to suppress the spread of the prophecy by intimidating and persecuting some leaders and members of the church. Evangelist Cyril Ofoedu narrates his ordeal at the hands of some policemen for spreading the prophecy about the end of the war:

>On 25 December 1969 as I was preparing to have a Christmas dish of rice and corned beef stew I heard a knock at my door. I was arrested by two policemen immediately as I opened

the door. They took me to a police station at Ezinifite-Nnewi where there were sixteen other pastors of Christ Holy Church. I was told that I had been arrested for reiterating Odozi Obodo's prophecy that the Biafran war will come to an end immediately after December 1969. I was taken to a dungeon and interrogated. When I admitted that I heard the prophecy of the holy prophetess, I was tortured and slapped several times. I was detained in a cell till 12 January 1970. While there, I heard that the wife of the district police officer pleaded with her husband to tell his men not to torture me anymore because she saw me in a dream rejoicing with some people that the war had come to an end. Other members of Christ Holy Church were also arrested and brought to the cell. On 12 January 1970 General Effiong broadcast an unconditional surrender of Biafra and the cessation of the civil war. I was carried shoulder-high at the prison.[306]

The announcement of Biafran surrender by Lt. Col. Effiong on 12 January 1970 marked the fulfillment of this prophecy. As a result, many people flocked to register their names in the church. The prophetic ministry of Agnes Okoh was extended to other prominent people of Igboland. Deaconess Victoria Njoku, who was the house helper of the prophetess, reveals:

During the Nigerian civil war, the Biafran war leaders, Odumegwu Ojukwu, Okoko Ndem, and others came to Arondizuogu to ask Mama about the state of the war, whether Biafra will win or not. Mama told them that "the uncircumcised will rule them." She told Ojukwu to find a way of escape, for there was a plan to catch him. So after four days Ojukwu left for exile, and not too long after that the war ended.[307]

The third prophecy was about mission in foreign lands. In the late 1950s, following the successful mission work by some Nigerian AICs in other west African countries, some leaders of the church began pressuring Prophetess Agnes Okoh to send some of the evangelists of the church to establish some congregations in Cameroon and other neigboring countries. The prophetess did not bow to pressure from her leaders. Typical of her, she counseled her followers to wait for God's own time. In 1963 she prophesied about an evangelistic timetable which she said will be brought about in God's own time. A musician in the church immediately composed the prophecy into a song:

Early Beginnings • 93

> Ayi ga'bu kwasi ndi ama—ndi ama Chukwu
> Nime Nigeria, Nime Ghana, rue ebe nine nke
> Ayi ga'bu kwasi ndi ama—ndi ama Chukwu Africa
> Rue Jerusalem, rue Samaria, rue ebe nine uwa soturu

The translation of the song in English is:

> We shall be witnesses—witnesses of God
> In Nigeria, in Ghana, up to all parts of Africa
> To Jerusalem, to Samaria, unto the end of the earth.

Members of the church began singing that song anytime they met to worship or anytime the issue of international evangelism was raised till 1999, when the church, for the first time in their evangelist campaigns, bought land in Ghana and registered the name of the church. The first congregation in Ghana was established in July 2000. The partial fulfillment of this prophecy had evoked some confidence in the prophetic prowess of Prophetess Agnes Okoh.

On the authenticity of the prophecy, Rev. Pastor Emmanuel Aniago argues that Nigeria is bordered on the west by Benin, in the north by Niger, northeast by Chad, and east by Cameroon. Unlike Nigeria, whose *lingua franca* is English, all these countries speak French as *lingua franca*. The only exception is Cameroon, which has both English and French as national languages. Even though the national medium of communication in Ghana is the English language, Cameroon is ironically closer to the Igbos than Ghana. Benin and Togo separate Nigeria from Ghana so one would have expected that the leadership of the church would find evangelism in Cameroon more expedient than Ghana, but, true to the prophecy, the first congregation of Christ Holy Church beyond the boundaries of Nigeria was established in Ghana—not by design but through some coincidental circumstances that are hard to explain, all things being equal.[308]

It is in view of the healing miracles and the exact fulfillment of Prophetess Agnes Okoh's prophecies that Rev. Enoch Okonkwo asserts that God used her like, and even more than, the prophets of old.[309]

Her Philanthropic Activities

The most common testimony about prophetess Agnes Okoh by those who knew her is "Odozi Obodo loved everybody." Apart from meeting the spiritual needs of people, she tried as much as possible to meet their physical needs—food, clothing, cash, etc. Her love and kindness, according to her followers, was not limited to members of her church. She used to tell her members that they should not dislike those who were not members of her church. She entertained all, irrespective of religious and denominational affiliation.

The people of Ndoni, her hometown, fondly remember her for her philanthropic work. She allowed the leaders of the town to use a house which was built for her by the church as the guest house of the town. She offered rooms and hospitality to government officials and magistrates who were on duty at Ndoni. According to the Most Rev. Daniel Okoh:

> Mama was the first person that provided pure water for the people of Ndoni, and a public tap was available free of charge. She gave both financial and moral support to both the primary and secondary schools....When the secondary school was established in 1977, the prophetess offered her bungalow in order to accommodate the principal and some national corp members.[310]

The Most Rev. Daniel Okoh further asserts:

> There was a time when the remoteness and terrain of the town did not encourage teachers to take up teaching positions. The payment of salaries of those who took up teaching positions at Ndoni was delayed unduly by the Nigerian government. It was a big problem. At one point Mama helped to pay the salaries of the teachers."[311]

The prophetess built a nursery and primary school (which was later named in her honor—Odozi Obodo Memorial Nursery and Primary School) in her hometown in 1994, one year before her death. Tuition was free. She also paid the salaries of the teachers. The fee-free policy of the school, enabled the poor to give their children education, at least to the primary level. In recognition of her support to educational advancement at Ndoni, the prophetess was, accordingly, honored by the Rivers State with a certificate of recognition during the launching of the Women's Education Campaign on 8 July 1987. The Ndoni Pioneers Social Club accorded her another honor on 19 September 1987 for the same reason.

In 1984 Prophetess Agnes Okoh single-handedly built an eight-room maternity home for Ndoni and the surrounding villages. Services at the maternity home are free for both members and non-members of the church. The midwife and four other workers were all paid by the prophetess. "People come here to give birth free of charge. The only items we require them to buy are detergents to wash their things and kerosene to light their lanterns. At the end if they have anything to give they give."[312]

According to His Royal Highness, Chief Gabriel Okeyia, the awo (chief) and Okpala-Ukwu (the eldest person) of Ndoni, "She helped many poor people. When there were no roads at Ndoni, she gathered people to construct roads and streets. It has been said that 'a prophet has no honour in his hometown,' but she was an exception. Everybody liked her."[313]

The prophetess also spent money freely in the church. "It is most exciting to understand that the church [building] at Ndoni was entirely built, furnished, and electrified [wired] by the general prophetess, Odozi Obodo, alone and finally donated same to the [Christ] Holy Church of Nigeria."[314] During the church's three-day convention at Ndoni, 13—16 February 1976, she "provided seven fat cows, numerous goats and chickens, numerous bags of rice, beans, and garri, grosses of yams, drums of oil, bags of salt, baskets of fish, cartons and crates of several assorted drinks, and indeed a lot of other items of foodstuffs with which she had entertained nearly one million guests for three days during and after the convention."[315]

Her Retirement and Home-calling

For many years the prophetess never visited Ndoni, her hometown. When asked to give reasons for not going to her hometown regularly she replied that God had told her that her hometown would be the last place of her ministry, so when the time came God would ask her to go back and settle.

Prior to her retirement there was a belief that Ndoni could never be developed. This belief was deepened by the claim that those who attempted to build any standard house with corrugated roofing sheets died mysteriously. The evil forces in the town were believed to have considered such people wealthy but not worthy to enjoy their wealth, so they died under mysterious circumstances. Those who used dried grass to roof their buildings, a sign of poverty, lived to see the completion of their houses and enjoyed the fruits of their labor. Many indigenes of Ndoni who were wealthy, consequently, refused to go to their town, let alone build and settle.

The return of the prophetess to Ndoni in February 1976, after many years of absence, was, therefore, phenomenal. When she began building her bungalow many people warned her not to roof it with iron sheets, lest she die, but she derided that belief even though there were said to be numerous proofs to substantiate it. She told the inhabitants that the God she serves is mightier than any other god. She, therefore, encouraged her town folks who were stuck in other people's cities for fear of being killed by evil forces to come home and build. Her continued existence, coupled with her perfect physical health after building the edifice at Ndoni, authenticated her claim of serving an omnipotent God. She consequently used members of her church who knew Ndoni indigenes in diaspora to intensify her "come-home-and-build" campaign. Many citizens, as a result, returned and gave the town a new identity. That was not all; her presence attracted many people to the town:

> While the holy prophetess lived on earth, members of Christ Holy Church and people from all walks of life, including governors, presidents, government and business chieftains and more importantly the downtrodden usually throng Ndoni to pay homage and seek God's blessings and grace in their lives, through the prayer of the holy prophetess.[316]

It is in recognition of these contributions that prompted the chief of Ndoni to say: "Her presence at Ndoni brought many changes to the town. We will always remember Odozi Obodo."[317] Ijeoma Nwachukwu, who had lived in the town for more than half a century, was more ebullient on this issue:

> Before God called Odozi Obodo, people of Ndoni knew God, but they did not know that God is a living God. It was through Odozi Obodo that people of Ndoni came to realize that there is a living God. Whatever this town is today and however it is known in Nigeria or internationally is what Odozi Obodo made it to be. Ndoni was an unknown town in Rivers State or across the Niger River. It was Odozi Obodo who made the name of Ndoni popular among Nigerians. That is why she is called Odozi Obodo—a town repairer.[318]

Prophetess Agnes Okoh finally retired from active ministry and settled at Ndoni in 1985, at the age of 80. Leaders of the church financed the making of her statue in front of her house with the inscription beneath it, *Ugwo Olu zulu oke,* meaning "complete reward." The significance of the inscription is based on one of the popular sayings of the prophetess. She used to say that God does not owe anybody and that when it is time for God to reward someone they are rewarded in full. On her retirement a poultry farm was built for her so that she would be free from boredom. A member bought some local cattle and put them in a pen close to the prophetess' residence. Feeding the cattle also kept her busy. She did all this in addition to having time for her guests who visited her for various reasons, chiefly among them were those who went to her to be counseled. She was called home at 9:00 a.m. on Friday, 10 March 1995, at the age of 90. Leaders of the church are building a cathedral that can seat 3000 worshippers in her honor at Ndoni.

Conclusion

Prophetess Agnes Okoh lived through many tumultuous times in the history of the world and Nigeria. She lived through the First and Second World Wars. She witnessed many landmarks in Nigerian history as well. Such landmarks were colonial rule, the unification of Nigeria, political independence, the civil war, the numerous military regimes, and the second civilian administration. All these events evoked fear, apprehension, uncertainties, short-lived hope, famine, and human trepidation. With the exception of the First World War, which occurred when she was in her early teens, she was counselor, trainer of trainers, prophetess, intercessor, healer, encourager, teacher, leader, and a mother to many people in these pivotal periods in Nigerian history.

She was seen as an embodiment of hope, comfort, discipline, assurance, integrity, and Christ-likeness to many people. Through the use of her diverse gifts and talents many people claim that their lives were turned around—from nonentities to spiritual celebrities, from insanity to human dignity. She was able to portray the paradoxical attributes of God, holiness and love. As a result, God was perceived as immanent, one who is keenly interested in the physical and spiritual well-being of humanity as against a whipping deity who is to be feared and approached with extreme caution. Through her ministries and her selfless philanthropic activities many people were said to experience the love and mercy of God in practical terms. The practicability of the teachings of Jesus Christ is no longer perceived as impossibilities by many of her followers. She was said to have touched the lives of many with the love and power of God in Jesus Christ. The Very Rev. Clement Okoye asserts: "The history of Christianity in Africa without mentioning Mama's contribution is a grand misnomer and a great injustice to the recognition of the role of women in African Christianity. Mama's exemplary lifestyle, her faith in God, and her leadership qualities are her most enduring legacies to African Christianity."[319]

CHAPTER FIVE

Development of Leadership in Christ Holy Church International

Introduction

The church, being a divine institution of human beings, cannot be left without a leader. With the resolve of Agnes Okoh not to lead the church, this chapter discusses how she approached the question of leadership from the beginning of the prayer ministry to the present state of being a full-fledged church of God.

Hezekiah D. Mbaegbu

Hezekiah D. Mbaegbu joined the prayer ministry in 1948 from an Apostolic Church, though not from Christ Apostolic Church. Prophetess Agnes Okoh appointed him to lead the prayer ministry in the same year that he joined the ministry and designated him "Catechist." Unlike the prophetess, Catechist Mbaegbu was educated. He was credited with the writing of the first order of service for the ministry. He might have had some knowledge in Christian ministry and doctrine since one of his main activities in the prayer ministry was teaching. He taught the members about Christian doctrine and other related issues until he was suspended for four months in 1956 after he admitted to the truism of a prophetic utterance that he had murmured and told lies about a fellow member of the prayer ministry. He was recalled from suspension after showing signs of repentance. He, however, lost his leadership position in the Church.[320] Catechist Mbaegbu is credited with instilling the discipline of Bible study in the prayer ministry. He used his education to steer the prayer ministry towards theological education until Marius Okoh was called to lead the ministry. He is fondly remembered for using the experiences of his own faith journey to guide and encourage younger pastors.

Enoch Okonkwo

Enoch Okonkwo was born in 1922 to Alonta and Mary Okonkwo, peasant farmers at Enugu-Ukwu in Njikoka Local Government Area of Anambra State. Though his parents were adherents of a traditional religion, he was converted into Anglicanism in 1935 when he became a house boy of a man who was an Anglican. Because of poverty he dropped out of school when in Standard One (ninth grade).

He suffered from tuberculosis for many years without cure, despite the fact that he had visited many western hospitals. At a certain point his father invited a native doctor to live in their home so as to effect an uninterrupted healing. Even though the native doctor initially boasted that if he were not able to heal Okonkwo no human being could cure the disease, he later advised him to seek prayers from somewhere else when it became apparent that Okonkwo's condition was deteriorating. In 1952 someone directed him to Prophetess Okoh who healed him after praying and blessing water for him to drink and to bathe. The inability of the native doctor to heal him in contrast to the divine healing he received at the prayer ministry increased his belief in faith healing. He consequently became a member of the prayer ministry of Prophetess Agnes Okoh.

In 1956, the prophetess, after praying for Enoch Okonkwo and David O. U. Nwaizuzu at a church service, told them that God had elevated them to the ministry. They were appointed "as catechists without formal training nor orientation. The Holy Spirit was the orientation teacher."[321]

Enoch Okonkwo was the first person to be promoted field evangelist in 1958. He was commissioned to plant churches. He was ordained in 1961. During the civil war he took the risk of supervising some churches; he "was trekking to Arondizougu on a weekly basis across the war fronts to supply the needs of the general prophetess [Agnes Okoh] and the church."[322] After the war he led a team of evangelists to plant many churches in Bendel State. He was promoted to the rank of a superintendent in 1972. He was appointed the chairman of the board of superintendents in 1980 till his retirement in 1982.[323]

Rev. Enoch Okonkwo's gift of healing overwhelmed many observers. He is noted to have healed many people who were sick of various diseases. According to Rev. Pastor Emmanuel Aniago:

> During his [Okonkwo] active days he was marvelously used by God. After preaching he would pause and tell his audience, "It is now time for your problems to be solved. Everything depends on you. If you are blind and want to see, why don't you open your eyes and see? If you are a cripple, why don't you make an attempt to stand? Stand up!" People would begin to shout in excitement.[324]

Even after being retired from active ministry he used his gift of healing to heal many. He is said to have healed two lunatics who are now pastors of the church. One of his many healings that made him very popular was the healing of two lame sisters. He recounts the healing:

> It happened that I went to pray for some people at Abagana and saw a young lady, and she was lame. I persuaded her helper to bring her to me and after three days, she started walking. The lady hailed from Umunya, and her immediate elder sister was also lame. She went to her village to inform her sister of the salvation of Christ. Her sister was brought, and she was healed and started walking.[325]

Rev. Okonkwo, affectionately called *Agu* (Lion), was an itinerant evangelist who visited many congregations and led many outdoor revivals. Many of his healing miracles happened at such outdoor evangelistic revival meetings.

Rev. Okonkwo, the octogenarian, attributes his healing prowess to his faith in the Lord. He claims that he has never taken any form of medicine (when sick) for over half a century, since he became a member of Christ Holy Church in 1952. "The promises of Jesus in the Bible," according to Rev. Okonkwo, "are not just sayings to make people feel happy; they have some potency in them."[326] On his major contributions to church, Rev. Okonkwo believes that he instilled in most pastors of the church faith in Jesus Christ. He remembers telling them that Peter the apostle was an ordinary person like any other person, yet when he placed his trust in Jesus he saw extraordinary results. He claims that the prophetess prophesied that God would increase the finances of the church through his ministries. This prophecy, to him, has been fulfilled in view of the vast number of people who joined the church through his outdoor revivals which were characterized by many healing miracles. Many people in the church have memories of his unflinching faith in the omnipotence of the Triune God, particularly as regards healing. His love for spreading the gospel (with many miracles following) is said to be one of his greatest contributions to the church. Though not highly educated, he relished recording what God has done so that posterity will not lose faith in God.

David Ozioma U. Nwaizuzu

David Ozioma U. Nwaizuzu is the son of Isaac Nwakwo Nwaizuzu, an Anglican catechist, and Eunice. He was born in 1930. He started elementary school at the age of eleven and graduated with a middle school leaving certificate (equivalent to high school diploma). He was employed by a transportation firm and rose to the level of a manager but he later resigned to establish his own business.[327]

He was poisoned by some friends and, thus, visited many hospitals without any success till he visited a brother at Onitsha in 1954, where he was told that a woman could heal him. He went to see Prophetess Agnes Okoh who told him that if he had faith in God he would be healed. He was healed in two weeks. He left the Anglican Church and became a member of Agnes Okoh's prayer ministry. He was appointed a catechist in 1956 and later a field evangelist before being ordained in 1961. During the civil war, he secured a shelter for the prophetess and some members of the church at Arondizougu, his hometown. After the war he was promoted to superintendent and later the first auditor-general of Christ Holy Church. He retired in 1982.

> He is noted to be an extraordinary church planter who planted over twenty congregations within the period he was elevated to a catechist until his retirement. Rev. Emmanuel Aniagor describes Nwaizuzu's revival services:

Rev. Nwaizuzu is a quiet man but full of faith in Jesus Christ. He used songs mostly to minister. He would sing songs about the working power of Jesus ChrisT, moving here and there, and then you would hear people screaming and proclaiming their healing and deliverance. That is why he is called *Enyi*, the elephant."[328] He considers the establishments of the church in Lagos and Benin City as some of his greatest contributions to the spread of the church since those stations were established outside Igboland.

Marius Anyetei Okoh

Marius A. Okoh was born on 15 April 1927. He was the only surviving child of James and Agnes Okoh. He is considered as one of the few privileged boys at Ndoni to have access to western education. His mother was a Catholic; Marius was baptized in the church and later grew up to become a mass server in the Roman Catholic Church at Ndoni. He was employed with the public works department in 1947, the same year that his mother began the prayer ministry. He was sponsored by his employers to further his education at Yaba Higher College in Yaba, Lagos. He graduated with a diploma in civil engineering. With graduation he became one of the top personnel of the public water department in Nigeria.

He married Pauline who gave birth to seven boys, but only one survived. Marius witnessed the sickness and healing of his mother, but he was at first skeptical of his mother's claim that God had called her. The resoluteness of his mother finally convinced him that she was not deceiving herself.

The Call to Ministry of Marius Okoh

His mother once told him that God would call him sometime into a full-time ministry, but he derided that prophecy, particularly at the time when he was contemplating furthering his education abroad. Nevertheless, he took a correspondence course with *The Voice of Prophecy Bible Correspondence School,* then located at Ibadan in western Nigeria, and was awarded a diploma in 1952. He was awarded a certificate of advanced Bible lessons by the same school in 1953.

On 11 June 1956, the call to serve as a fulltime minister came through the Prophetess in a revelation, and some committee members were sent to inform him about the new development. The messengers went with a lorry that was virtually empty, planning to bring Marius and his wife, Pauline, back home to answer the call of God. When the ministers arrived [at] Umuahia from Onitsha and gave the message to Marius and Pauline, he took his wife and their property and came down immediately to Onitsha. He resigned officially from the public works department on 20 June 1956.[329]

Marius was appointed secretary to the board of elders of the church. While serving as secretary to the board of elders, he became a friend of the Rev. Dale Collins and Rev. Cook, American evangelists working in Igboland at that time. The American evangelists gave him some lessons on the importance of evangelism and later ordained him.

In 1958, he was appointed the general superintendent[330] of the church. His appointment marked the beginning of three cardinal characteristics of Christ Holy Church: administration, evangelism, and education and training.

The Administration of the Church Under Marius Okoh's Leadership

Marius Okoh, a hefty six-feet-plus person, made great use of his education and work experience at the public works department to lay down some administrative structures in the church. Prior to his appointment as the head of the church the only functionable groups were the board of elders and the choirs. He began forming auxiliary groups in the church, such as women's groups. He also formed various committees to run some aspects of the church's business. He expanded the order of service which was first written by Catechist Hezekiel Mbaegbu. Marius wrote an order of service for each day of the week. He also wrote an order of service for other events in the church, such as, weddings, baptisms, Lord's Supper, ordinations, death and burial, laying of foundation stones, and other important events in life. In some cases he wrote the order of service in the Igbo language. He ensured that every property of the church was duly registered.

He led the board of elders to write a workable constitution for the church—defining the organizational structure, stating the roles and functions of committees and officials, setting the criteria for selecting officers, stating the procedures of doing things properly, spelling out disciplinary measures and what might cause one to be disciplined, and laying down measures aimed at ensuring financial propriety in the church. He licensed all the itinerant pastors and workers of the church and stated a *modus vivendi* expected of all pastors and workers of the church.

The Rt. Rev. Marius Okoh designed a simple accounting principle of recording the income and expenditure of all the congregations. He encouraged the recording of attendance of men, women, and children at church services. He also encouraged all the pastors to keep exact records of all miracles in their respective stations. One thing he did which endeared him to the hearts of many was registering a new name for the church. In consultation with the central executive council, the name of the church was changed from Christ Apostolic Church (Odozi Obodo) to Christ Holy Church in Nigeria. He registered the new name in January 1975.

What many ministers remember about Marius' personal administrative emphases are his hard work and insistence on punctuality. "He worked from morning to night in order to ensure that what he wanted was done. There were times that he would not go to bed until what he wanted done was done just as he wanted it to be done."[331] He was perceived by many as a taskmaster, but he considered those who perceived him as such to be lazy people. Marius' love for punctuality is told by Daniel Okoh, his son:

> After Marius left school, he learned about an employment opportunity in Public Works Department through one of his uncles and prayerfully prepared for the interview. On the day of the interview, young athletic Marius left home early and ran all the way to the venue of the test due to the fact that he had no money for transportation. But as he was running in order to arrive early enough, he did not realise that the interviewer saw him as he drove past him. So at the venue he was identified as somebody who had the zeal to work and was offered a job on the spot. It could be said, therefore, that his love for punctuality, for which members and workers of Christ Holy Church later knew him, helped him to secure the job.[332]

Rev. David Nwaizuzu concurs on Marius' punctuality: "He was very strict and did not play with punctuality. He was always around 15 minutes earlier than the appointed time. He instilled that in his trainees."[333] His sense of urgency, as a pastor and administrator, is depicted in his favorite scripture verse, Revelation 22:12: "Behold, I am coming quickly, and my reward is with Me, to render to every man according to what he has done."

The Spread of the Church Under Marius Okoh's Leadership.

The leadership of Marius Okoh and his love for evangelism were inseparable.

> By November 1957, American evangelists Rev. Dale Collins and Rev. Cook joined Marius Okoh and the other ministers of the church to organise one of the greatest evangelistic campaigns east of the Niger River. The revival meetings which were held in open fields recorded many miracles—the blind received their sight, the lame walked, and people testified of freedom from the power of charms and darkness. . . . Apart from the Americans, African evangelists like Apostle J. A. Babalola, Prophet D. O. Babajide, and Pastor J. A. Madaiyese assisted Marius Okoh in spreading the gospel.[334]

The success of the first outdoor evangelistic revival set the tone for a series of indoor and outdoor revivals in the church. "He selected some young men and trained them to carry out the task of evangelizing the communities in Igboland. These include Enoch Okonkwo, David O. U. Nwaizuzu, H. D. Mbaegbu, Godwin Obikwelu, W. O. Orafu, W. N. Asoh and Christopher Okereke."[335] In order to proclaim the Gospel without any hindrance, Marius Okoh "bought a Volkswagen bus from Collins at the cost of seventy-five pounds (£75.00) to help propagate the gospel. This bus, which was bought single-handedly by Marius, became the first gospel van of this ministry."[336] The purchase of the van allowed Marius and his team of pastors to proclaim the gospel in many new places. Daniel Okoh sheds some light on the spread and results of the evangelistic campaigns:

> Major villages in the east that benefitted from those early campaigns include Nnewi, Arondizougu, Agulu, Ogidi, Ajalli, Otoucha, Awka, Aba, Amaigbo, and Nkwere. In all these campaigns, many miracles were recorded, and multitudes abandoned their shrines and evil ways for Christ. Many witch doctors that heard the gospel and saw the miracles openly burned their idols and turned to Jesus Christ. Praise God! People, who were healed of all sorts of diseases and those who accepted the gospel of Christ as was preached by Marius Okoh and his team went home and happily donated pieces of land to the church for the purpose of establishing the church for the benefit of their communities. The church responded quickly to this kind gesture by sending evangelists to these new and fertile areas.[337]

Officials of Christ Holy Church International refer to the Rt. Rev. Marius Okoh as the "foremost African evangelist." When asked by *Glad News* to give reasons for that description, Enoch Okonkwo said:

> "He did a lot of great works. He trained us. We started as full-time workers before him, but he trained us. God gave him a lot of spiritual gifts which enabled him to distinctively evangelise, counsel, pastor, teach, and perform miracles in the name of our Lord Jesus."[338]

At the time the Rt. Rev. Marius Okoh was called to eternity, "Christ Holy Church had gone beyond eastern Nigeria to spread to Northern and Western parts of the country like wildfire. . . . The church had over 300 branches [congregations] in the four cardinal points of Nigeria."[339] The significance of the spread of the church under the leadership of the Rt. Rev. Marius Okoh is significant when one realizes that there were less than ten congregations before he was called to lead the church. His emphasis on outdoor evangelistic campaigns, his ability to identify with people from other ethnic backgrounds as a result of his public service outside of Igboland, and his education broke the dominance of Igbos in the church. The church attracted Yorubas, Hausas, Efiks, Tivs, Urhobos, Ishans, Kalabaris, Itsikeres, Ojos, Ibibios, Igaras, and some Ghanaian immigrants in Nigeria.

Pastoral Training During the Leadership of Marius Okoh

When Okonkwo and Nwaizuzu were asked to identify Marius Okoh's major contribution to the church, they unanimously and unhesitantly exclaimed simultaneously, "Training of workers!"[340] Prior to his leadership the church adopted the Elijah/Elisha type of training, i.e., the mentoring of a person on a one-on-one basis. He changed that system to a formal type of training. Training of the catechists of the church became a priority after the success of the evangelistic campaigns. The pressure that the ministry received from the communities to open stations prompted Rev. Marius Okoh to start a more formal training of catechists in 1963.[341] He set up the Christ Holy Church Catechists Training School (now known as the Marius Okoh Memorial Seminary—MOMS) at Onitsha in 1963. The purpose of the school was to teach the catechists about evangelism, the Bible, and pastoral ministry. According to Rev. Nicholas Udemba, the general secretary and assistant general superintendent of the church, Marius sensed that some of the pastors had their own gifts that needed to be developed. Another thing that caused him to set up the school was the need for uniformity of training.[342]

The initial curriculum included an introduction to the Bible (book by book); some basic doctrines of Christianity; the history, nature and purpose of Christ Holy Church; the church's philosophy of ministry, preaching, and administering of the sacraments. Studying at the school was mandatory for all catechists. Thus everyone, including the leaders who preceded him, went through the educational process of the school. Tuition was free. He was initially the sole teacher, in addition to his numerous other functions. Students at the school were intentionally trained to expect and endure hardships. As a result, the students were denied the comfort of sleeping on mattresses. They were made to sleep on mats spread on hard floors so that they would learn to undergo hardships should they encounter one in their pastoral stations. Depending solely on God for one's sustenance was greatly emphasized. Respect for authority without regard to age and personality was another cardinal principle at the school. Students were also taught to be humble and care for one another.

The results of the training have been phenomenal in the life of the church. "The school which was sown like a seed in 1963 had trained more than 5000 ministers of God, both male and female who have transformed many citizens of this country through the Word."[343] The Rt. Rev. Marius Okoh is fondly remembered for the training he imparted to the pastors of the church. "He came in with his education and modified many things. He trained many people and ordained them."[344] To Very Rev. Innocent Afunwa, "Rt. Rev. Okoh . . . made Christ Holy Church to be what it is today. We learned many things from him."[345]

Publications During Marius Okoh's Leadership

Rt. Rev. Marius Okoh did not limit the education and training program to only the pastors and staff of the church. He appointed a board of publications and charged it with publishing a church magazine. A quarterly magazine, called *Good Tidings*, was published as a result. The purpose of the magazine is stated in the third issue:

> Surely, God has never outlived any generation or century without manifesting his miraculous power to them through his holy prophets and chosen servants. Our age not exceptional; hence the floating series of the *Healing* and *Miraculous* magazines from various parts of the world to prove God the same yesterday, today, and forever. Good Tidings is one of its kind. It is far from politics, fiction, exaggeration, and denominational malignity. Therefore every page of Good Tidings contains plain truth, divine inspiration, healing testimony, and inspired sermon and commentary. It has been designed to satisfy the curious thirst for the immediate Christian literature the country now needs.[346]

Contents of the *Good Tidings* included poems by some members, teaching material on some topics selected by Marius Okoh, healing testimonies, news, and events. *Good Tidings* was, thus, a tool for educating the *corpus* of Christ Holy Church on the beliefs and practices of the church. The testimonies and news sections were aimed at building the faith of the members both in the church and in the Lord Jesus Christ. Some members with literary flair were given the opportunity to demonstrate their skills by writing. His love for education led him to sponsor the education of some poor members of the church.

The Healing Ministry of Marius Okoh

Marius Okoh was not only an administrator, evangelist, and teacher; he was also a gifted healer. He was said to have healed many people, but one miracle that has stuck to the memory of many is the raising back to life of Elder Benedict Aroghalu Mbamalu, one of the early members of the Church who at the time he died was a very wealthy member of the church. In 1961, while leading a harvest service at Onitsha, the Rt. Rev. Okoh was told the news of the death of the elder, but he did not tell anyone. He was also not in a hurry to go and console the bereaved family. He took his time to conclude the harvest ceremony before he told his team of pastors about the sad news. He and his team proceeded to the deceased's house at Isiokwe, a suburb of Onitsha. He got there in the evening, several hours after the man had breathed his last breath. He sent away all the women who were weeping in the room where the corpse was laid. He began praying. After a long prayer, whitish mucus came forcefully from the dead man's nostrils, and he opened his eyes wondering why he was in that state. It is said that Benedict later lived to a ripe old age of 110 years before he died again.[347]

Post-Biafran War Activities of Marius Okoh

His leadership acumen was noticed when the civil war ended. The ending of the civil war brought many challenges to the leadership of the church. As the leader he was faced with the challenge of settling many members who lost properties. Those who lost their limbs needed to be comforted. The entire administration had to be reorganized because many of the stations in the war zones were closed down. Many members were, consequently, displaced from their homelands and farms. Marius Okoh stood above the challenges by challenging those who were less affected by the war to help those who were affected the most. His emphasis was on being one another's keeper. Members, thus, used their own resources to support those who lost properties during the war.

The Popularity and Death of Marius Okoh

The quality of his leadership style earned him the appellation *Igwe*, a title reserved for traditional leaders of Igbo communities or towns. It literally means "sky," but in Igbo communities it stands for "authority." He was said to be impartial and a good listener, a man who listened to and respected people's views no matter the status of the person in the society. His affection and popularity among the clergy and laity of the church can be gleaned from the way he was welcomed to Enugu when he went there to dedicate the church building:

> As the great crowd were anxiously waiting for the arrival of the general superintendent at the appointed time on Sunday 1 August 1976, there was explosion of jubilation as the Mercedes car of the general superintendent, the Rt. Rev. M. A.

Okoh glared from a distance. Until he arrived, there was an unceasing cheers of Igwe! Igwe!! Igwe!!![348]

The Rt. Rev. Marius Okoh had a motor accident in August 1979 while traveling from Asaba to his office at Onitsha. He suffered an injury to his spinal chord that affected the way he walked for the rest of his life, but the accident did not slow him down. He continued doing his pastoral duties until he died in his sleep on 2 March 1980, at the age of 53.

Many people guess that his death might have been caused by complications from the motor accident and his tight schedule that left no room for rest, but others think otherwise. They think that it was time he left the world. The belief of the latter is based on Marius' action and pronouncements at the general meeting he held with all his pastors at Onitsha in December 1979. At that meeting he was said to have told the gathering that he had finished his work, and so he wanted to go and rest. Some leaders of the church, reading between the lines, asked him to withdraw that statement, but he refused, justifying his position that when a person's work comes to an end the person must necessarily go and rest. Before closing the meeting Marius Okoh promoted the pastors *en masse* and told them that the mass promotion is in appreciation for their support of his leadership.[349] The most unprecedented thing about the mass promotion was the promotion of Samuel Ejiofor from a pastor to assistant general evangelist. To the surprise of the meeting Marius Okoh promoted Ejiofor again to the position of assistant superintendent. That meeting was the last time he met his pastors and workers.

The Central Executive Council, which is the highest decision-making body of the church, in consultation with the general prophetess, and in recognition of his immense contribution to the church, posthumously proclaimed him "Co-founder" of the Church. An epitaph at his burial ground at Ndoni reads:

> Here lies the body of the Rt. Rev. Marius Okoh, a foremost African evangelist, the first general superintendent and a co-founder of Christ Holy Church who slept in the Lord on Sunday, March the 2nd, 1980. Rest in perfect peace.

After the death of Marius Okoh, Rev. Enoch Okonkwo temporarily led the church from 1980 to 1982.

Samuel Ejiofor

The next leader of the church was Samuel Ejiofor. His leadership appointment was by prophecy. Ejiofor became the leader of the church at the age of 36. He was, at that time, the youngest person in the history of the church to become the leader. He was, therefore, affectionately called *Eze Nwata,* literally meaning "a king in his youth" or "young king." He became a member of the church through the influence of his parents. He married Nwodichi when he was 20 years old; they have five children. Rev. Samuel Ejiofor led the church from 1982 to 1988. He continued the evangelistic campaigns and planted many congregations in Igboland. During his active ministry, he was said to be a dynamic preacher with a combination of in-depth hermeneutical skills and practical application so that many people who heard him preach found it irresistible to come to Jesus Christ. In this regard, Rev. E. N. Iloabuchi says: "When you hear Ejiofor preach and you do not repent, your chances of repenting next time will be very slim, if not impossible."[350]

He introduced a new dimension into the church's evangelism by rewarding pastors who opened more congregations with promotions. He wanted to begin opening some congregations beyond the Nigerian borders, but the prophetess asked him to wait until God inspired him. Samuel Ejiofor was retired at the age of 42 after many members prophetically spoke that it was time he retired. When asked why he agreed to retire at a young age and at a time when he was healthy and robust, he replied that it was God who promoted him to be the leader of the church, so he saw no reason to disobey the will of God when it came to his retirement. He is still a member doing jobs assigned to him periodically by the leadership and some pastors of the church. He is considered to be an example of selflessness and humility in the church.

Gabriel Onuorah Chiemeka

Gabriel Onuorah Chiemeka was a member of a Catholic Church in Nigeria before he joined Christ Holy Church International in 1964 as a result of healing he received from the church. In 1988, through a prophetic utterance, he was appointed the leader of the church when he was already a senior superintendent. He continued managing the affairs of the church until many people began prophesying that, for the church to grow faster than at the pace it was growing, he should step down to allow Daniel Okoh to lead the church. These prophecies were unprecedented in the history of the church because Daniel Okoh was then a student at Port Harcourt University, not even a pastor of the church. He obeyed the prophecies and stepped down in 1993 when Daniel Okoh was then a junior pastor. He is, however, still serving the church as general evangelist and assistant general Superintendent. In addition to being the head of the Nnewi

Superintendency, he manages the Ndoni office of the church, the office formerly occupied by the holy prophetess during her retirement days.

When asked by *Glad News* why he stepped down from the topmost position to a subservient one in the church, the assistant general superintendent said:

> Christ Holy Church is a spiritual church with its own God guided set-up. Every role performed by anyone is more or less with the authority of a caretaker. The owner of our ministry is Christ Jesus who by the measure of holiness we endeavour to imbibe sends his Holy Spirit to direct our steps, decisions, and occupations. . . . It was the divine will of God that Most Rev. Daniel Okoh will assume the office of general superintendent. . . . There was no question of moving from number one to number two. Even now, Christ is still and will remain number one. . . . It is the Lord's doing, and there is no conflict whatsoever.[351]

Apart from the fact that he obeyed the voice of Jesus Christ, Rev. Chiemeka considers his present position, general evangelist and assistant general superintendent, as more honorable than the previous one. "These are higher positions and promotions from the Lord God than the previous position of senior superintendent."[352] To him, being positioned at Ndoni seems equivalent to occupying the seat and performing the duties of the holy prophetess, roles he considers a privilege. It must be noted, however, that these positions and functions were not prerequisites for stepping down from being the incumbent. He stepped down before the board of superintendents elevated him to these positions. His leadership and selflessness are seen by many as an embodiment of humility and the desire for a united church.

Daniel Chukwudumebi Okoh

The Birth of Daniel Okoh

Daniel Chukwudumebi Okoh was born on 12 November 1963. He is the last and the only surviving child (out of seven) of the Rt. Rev. Marius and Pauline Okoh, both deceased. When Daniel was growing up he knew that he would one day be a minister of God, but he did not know when that would happen. This knowledge was based on what his parents and grandmother told him.

Felix, the sixth child of Marius and Pauline Okoh, was said to be a handsome and brilliant boy, but he died in 1960 at a young age just like five other siblings who preceded him to eternity. His death was unbearable to the Okoh family. As they were grieving, a certain woman confessed that she used some charms to kill Felix. Some people became infuriated and decided to march to the woman's house to mete instant justice to her, but Prophetess Agnes Okoh dissuaded them from their intended action. She prophesied in 1962 that God would vindicate the Okoh family by giving them a boy who would grow up to do the Lord's work. As a sign of fulfillment, the parents were told that one of the hands of the boy to be born would have a fairer complexion than the other. "I was told that when I was born one of my hands was fairer but I cannot remember whether it was the left or right."[353] Daniel Okoh claims that there were other prophecies in the church regarding his mission on earth when he was growing up.

The Call to Ministry of Daniel Okoh

The parents of Daniel did not rush him into the pastoral ministry; they rather gave him good education; he graduated with a bachelor of science degree in political science from the University of Port Harcourt, Nigeria, in 1988. At age 27 he married Fidelia. They have a son and a daughter.

Daniel's response to his call to the ministry was slow and with some reluctance, since he wanted to further his education after earning a University degree.

> When I was growing up I heard many divine messages confirming the earlier one before I was born, but I did not know that it would be fulfilled so soon, because in those days it was the norm that only elderly people were called and ordained as pastors. In view of this perception, when I was called I was a bit hesitant, because I thought that the time has not yet come for me to be a pastor.[354]

He, nevertheless, enrolled at the Catechists Training School of the church in 1989 and went through the process of becoming a pastor without being accorded any preferential treatment before beING ordained by Gabriel Chiemeka in March 1991.

The Elevation of Daniel Okoh to Leadership Positions

On 25 January 1993, at the age of twenty-nine, he was elevated to the position of general superintendent, the highest position in the church. He was, as a result, officially designated, "His Grace, The Most Reverend." The Most Rev. Daniel Okoh was still skeptical whether the timing of his elevation to the leadership of the church was right or not, so he inwardly asked for a sign from God.

> I prayed to God and requested that he give me the kind of spirit he gave to King Hezekiah in the Old Testament, because I am impressed by the restoration work King Hezekiah did. I asked my followers, therefore, not to resist any change or throw away the basics of our beliefs and practices because the power of Christ is the same."[355]

The sign did come during an outdoor evangelistic crusade (revival) in 1996, a year after his elevation.

> In 1996 during the Owerri Crusade at the Grasshoppers stadium there were many miracles. On the second day of the crusade a certain blind man was healed. On that night it rained heavily, but the crusade went on, nevertheless. At the close of the crusade the blind man was returning to his home on a chartered vehicle. He was still blind. Before he boarded the vehicle his aide suggested that he put some blessed water on his eyes. The man did that and began feeling some scales dropping from his eyes. After some two minutes the man started shouting, "I can see! I can see!!" His exclamations drew many people to the scene because they were still within the vicinity of the stadium.[356]

The healing of the blind man and the other miracles during the crusade were perceived as a confirmation of his call to lead the church. The miracles occurred "at a time when many Nigerians thought miracles were no longer a present reality, so the miracles that happened during the 1996 crusade proved to the world that the power of the Lord has not changed. The miracles confirmed that God has given me the spirit of King Hezekiah."[357] Daniel Okoh further elaborated on the other significance of the 1996 evangelistic crusade:

> The crusade led to a change of impression that Christ Holy Church is only for illiterates and Igbo tribes, as many saw the caliber and tribes of some of the members of the church. Many members of the church who are university graduates later came to declare their willingness and readiness to serve the church in their own area of specialization."[358]

The Most Rev. Daniel Okoh has continued the evangelistic campaigns of the Church.

The Spread of the Church Under Daniel Okoh's Leadership

The church now has nearly eight hundred congregations with over one million members in Nigeria. One significant contribution of Daniel

Okoh is his role in the establishment of the church in Ghana. He convinced the central executive council of the church to raise money to buy land and build a three-story house on the plot before leading a contingent of pastors, singers, and other members to begin a three-day outdoor evangelistic campaign in Accra, Ghana, in late July 2000—one of the commendable achievements in his leadership. By the end of 2002, the church had four congregations in Ghana with an average membership of 500.

Unlike his predecessors who concentrated on solidifying the church in Nigeria and, therefore, never traveled outside the country, Daniel Okoh has attended many international ecumenical programs and has been a host to many international Christian leaders. "These have helped boost the image of the church as an International church. To the members, what is happening is a fulfillment of a prophecy of Odozi Obodo. Christ Holy Church is no longer seen as a local, backyard church."[359] When the church was established in Ghana the name (Christ Holy Church of Nigeria) became a misnomer, so in May 2001 the central executive council gave the church a new name, Christ Holy Church International.

In addition to his internationalization program, the Most Rev. Daniel Okoh has devised a program of integrating multiculturalism. He saw the need for such a program after he attended an international network conference organized by the Multi-Cultural Ministry Network which was sponsored by the World Council of Churches in Australia in 1999 and Thailand in 2002. The Multi-Cultural Ministry Network is a network of churches that are interested and are involved in multiculturalism. "Getting involved in this ministry opened my eyes to see that we are all people of one God with basic commonalities."[360] His emphasis on multiethnic ministries has brought in ethnic groups like Ewes, Gas, Akans (in Ghana), Ijaws, Idomas, Etsakos, and Igbiras.

Prior to the leadership of the Most Rev. Daniel Okoh, the church did not have a written Mission Statement. A synopsis of the beliefs of the church written on baptismal certificates was all that was previously documented. In his desire to create a uniformity of purpose he sought assistance from the Good News Theological College and Seminary, Accra, Ghana, to formulate a mission statement for the church and expand the synopsis of their beliefs into a creedal document entitled, "Statement of Faith of Christ Holy Church International."[361] It is perhaps the most elaborate Statement of Faith any African Independent Church has ever written. Both the Mission Statement and the Statement of Faith were written on the 2003 wall almanac of the church. The purpose was to ensure that everyone read and understood what the Church stands and hopes for.

Under his leadership, the use of computers has been introduced in the church. He has also introduced a better retirement scheme for fulltime workers and pastors.[362] Some of the leaders who were retired before his leadership have been settled comfortably.[363] He has also formed a central finance committee, education committee, youth council, almanac committee, central disciplinary committee, central building committee, music festival committee, and Sunday school manual writers committee.

Theological Education and Training Under Daniel Okoh's Leadership

Education and training of the clergy and laity has been improved under the Most Rev. Daniel Okoh's leadership. The curriculum of the Catechist Training School has been upgraded and expanded. The standard has also been raised to a seminary and renamed in memory of Marius, Marius Okoh Memorial Seminary. With the guidance of the faculty of Good News Theological College and Seminary, fifteen persons were selected to undergo a seminar in the dynamics of writing Sunday school materials for adults in 1998. Another group of persons was trained to teach adult Sunday schools. The church now publishes 3,000 copies of Sunday school study materials bi-annually. Members of Christ Holy Church International spend the first hour of their Sunday worship studing the Bible corporately based on what has been written in their material. This is a practice that can be found among very few African Independent Churches. Rev. Pastor Emmanuel Alamanjo, chairman of the Sunday school manual writers committee, speaks about the continued training and preparation of the manual writers:

> We are always guided by the Holy Spirit. The manuals are not written carnally but under the inspiration of the Holy Spirit. He directs us on what to write. We give different texts to every member of the committee to write and then we edit. We run periodic seminars for Sunday School manual writers at the national headquarters and at district and superintendency levels. Manual writers improve themselves with fasting, prayers, and constant Bible studies. Joshua 1:8 has been their watchword. There has been a big improvement in the quality of the contents of the study manuals as a result.[634]

As to the impact of the Sunday school Bible studies, Alamanjo claims:

> Many have testified that the manual has changed their perception about Christ Holy Church, a truly evangelical church. It has endeared the hearts of so many people who were otherwise speaking evil of the church. It has greatly enhanced the

image of the church. Sunday school teachers do write to the committee expressing their difficulties and joy. Our members read it and regard it as daily food. It has, as a result, increased the Bible knowledge of the members.[365]

The importance of teaching the Bible in the church is seen in the fact that the leader of the church himself selected the manual writers and the Sunday school teachers and was part of the first training sessions offered by the Good News Theological College and Seminary. He encouraged both the manual writers and Sunday school teachers to augment their teaching tools with Bible dictionaries and concordances.

The education and training policy of the Most Rev. Daniel Okoh has been geared to the women of the church and other contemporary issues like HIV/AIDS. Since 1998 annual conventions for the women have brought a new wave of respect for womanhood. The church has taken up the challenge of educating the youth on how to stop the spread of HIV/AIDS.[366]

What many people love most about Daniel's leadership is his ability to keep the traditions of the church while introducing new ideas. The most admirable thing about the leadership style of Daniel Okoh, according to Emmanuel Asadu, is his affability:

> The Most Rev. Daniel Okoh is an example of humility. You can see him talking freely and sharing jokes with ordinary members. Some general superintendents in Nigeria are usually escorted by macho body guards so it is not even possible for you to approach your head pastor; you have to sign some forms and observe some protocols before you can see your minister. Most Rev. goes to the people. He does not even wait for the people to come to him.[367]

Rev. Samuel Ejiofor summarizes the contribution of the Most Rev. Daniel Okoh as follows:

> The church was a Nigerian church, but today it is an international church. The history of the church is now about to be written; we now have organized committees that take care of certain aspects of the church. Our workers were formerly confined, but now they are encouraged to attend conferences and seminars. He has introduced organized Sunday schools, women's seminars, computerization of records, and in-service training for workers. He has also upgraded the semi-

nary. The image of the church has brightened with the reception of overseas guests. His wisdom, intelligence, humility, understanding, and simple lifestyle are his personal traits that have enhanced his leadership.[368]

Conclusion

The development of leadership has been done gradually and with a lot of commitment. The prophetess designated some members as catechists and mentored them, giving them the freedom to make decisions and be responsible for their decisions. The coming of Marius Okoh and Samuel Ejiofor marked some intellectualism in the leadership of the church. However, intellectualism was not raised above spirituality. The church depended on the role of the Holy Spirit in leadership development. The appointment and duration of offices were dictated by the Holy Spirit.

The elevation of Daniel Chukwudumedu Okoh to the position of general superintendent and the able support he is receiving from his predecessors who are much older than he are seen as the apex of the blending of spirituality and intellectualism. The church is now making great use of these two qualities. Leaders of Christ Holy Church International, though without any higher seminary education, have made great contributions to the church's growth and direction. With fortitude and equanimity they braved the rigors of the Biafran civil war, disregarding their refugee status, to continue building the church. They have, thus, demonstrated that the will to succeed is tied to total dependence on God.

CHAPTER SIX

Christ Holy Church International: Nature and Growth

The Nature of Christ Holy Church International

Christ Holy Church International is a fulfillment of the Church Missionary Society's desire in the nineteenth century of creating an African church which would be self-governing, self-supporting and self-propagating.[369] This chapter describes the way the church developed its selfhood in the areas of support, administration, and growth—aspects that are totally African initiated, without any Western assistance. The growth of the church will also be examined quantitatively and qualitatively.

Composition and Membership

The ethnicity of members of the church in Nigeria is dominantly (80 percent) Igbo. The leadership is also heavily Igbo-dominated. Pastors of the Church, however, disagree to a suggestion that the church is an Igbo church. Below is Rev. Eusebius Iloabuchi's argument:

> We have congregations in Ghana but there are no Igbos in Ghana. The Catholic Church was at first made up of Italians, but it was not considered an Italian church. The Anglican Church too was begun with many English people. Every church must begin from a particular tribe and then spread to others. We have stations in Calabar and the Rivers State; they do not speak Igbo.[370]

To become a member one is expected to have heard the gospel of Jesus Christ, believed in the vicarious death of Jesus Christ, openly confessed him as Lord and Savior, and expressed a preparedness to abide by the mission statement, rules and regulations, and faith in the church's statement of faith. The open confession is made when one willingly goes to a pastor and declares his/her intention to become a member. The person's name will be recorded in the membership book, and then a prayer will be said. Those who fail to go forward and declare their intentions of becoming members are considered as "regular visitors" irrespective of their commitment to the church. Unlike popular assertions that women outnumber men in African Independent Churches, the female/male ratio is almost equal in most congregations.

Membership avenues to the church are usually through healing, parental influence, big-time evangelistic revivals, teaching, and preaching. Members of the church facilitate the work of increasing the membership by inviting non-members to the functions of the church or for prayers. In a few instances there are other spectacular conversion experiences apart from the traditional ways of becoming a member. An example is that of Elisha Anyalebechi:

> Victoria Anyalebechi's children died shortly after birth. She went from one place to another to find the solution to her plight but she did not get any tangible answer until in 1960 her mother, Mrs. Agnes Uba, led her to Christ Holy Church at Ama Okpara in Nkwerre Local Government Area for the church's prayers. There was a revelation that God would bless her with many children, but for that to happen her husband, Elisha Anyalebechi, also had to go to the Church to receive prayers. Elisha, who was then living in Rivers State, angrily tore up three letters inviting him to come down for the prayers. At a point, when his wife went to him to invite him personally, he retorted to his wife, "Why will not God call me to Maria Assumpta Cathedral at Owerri or to some other big church instead of inviting me to that hut called Christ Holy Church."
>
> One Friday, Elisha, full of anger, bought a small plastic container and filled it with petrol. He traveled to Ama Okpara with the intention of setting the worship center ablaze. On that day, unknown to Elisha, the congregation was praying and fasting, and had, therefore, gathered at the worship center. Elisha met the people worshipping. His mother-in-law, Mrs. Uba, saw him from afar and began rejoicing that her son-in-law was at last coming to the church for prayers. She told the pastor so, when Elisha reached the worship center, the pastor invited him to come forward for prayers. Elisha stood for a moment and reluctantly went forward. After the prayers, a woman pointed to him saying that God had revealed to her that Elisha had planned something diabolical against the church;

so he had to confess before he would be blessed. Elisha did confess and pulled the container filled with petrol and a box of matches he had bought for his deed. The whole congregation, though surprised, asked God to forgive him. Afterwards, he and his wife gave birth to many children, one of which is Evangelist Anthony Anyalebechi.[371]

Three groups of people are usually attracted to the church—pagans, members of other churches, and those who were born into the church. On the second week of December all the members congregate at Onitsha, the headquarters, for an annual convention. The two-day convention is usually a time to take stock, share testimonies to build up faith, and praise the Lord for God's goodness. Leaders of the church take the opportunity to brainstorm and strategize for the following year. The annual convention is also a time for prayer and the promotion of pastors.

Pastoral Calling and Ministry

In December 2002, the church had a full-time pastoral staff of 1,471. The pastors are mostly middle school leavers (equivalent to high school graduates) with a few graduates and post-secondary school leavers. Most were, however, traders before responding to their pastoral calls. A great number of the pastors were formerly members of western mission-founded churches (particularly Catholic and Anglican). The pastoral staff of Christ Holy Church International is mostly composed of men who are aged 30 to 59.

The Role of Women

The church does not ordain women as a matter of policy. The ordination of women is considered unbiblical. The title "pastor" is used broadly for all those who do the work of shepherding. Among the pastors, therefore, are those who are ordained, those yet to be ordained, and women performing the duties of their male counterparts but not technically designated as pastors. They are called "channels." Women, nevertheless, play important roles in the church. Out of the pastoral staff, 623 were women performing some ministerial functions such as visitation, intercession, counseling, leading church services, and preaching. They are, however, not allowed to baptize, ordain, officiate at the Lord's Supper, bury the dead, bless children, or bless water. The highest position for female members used to be general prophetess but with the death of Prophetess Agnes Okoh, who held that position, the highest position now for the female is deaconess general. Other positions women can occupy are Christian mothers, treasurers, and financial secretaries. Both genders can be appointed elders, church wardens, youth leaders, and choirmasters.

Certainty of Pastoral Call

Certainty of call to the pastoral ministry is very important to leaders of the church. Many ministers claim that God communicated his desire to call them to full-time ministry through dreams and visions. When some pastors were asked (in a questionnaire) how they became certain that God had called them into the ministry, 85 percent of them listed dreams and visions. In such instances dreams and visions are not considered gifts, they are considered a one-time means of divine communication to certain people regarding their vocations. A typical example is that of Rev. Nicholas Udemba, general secretary of the church:

I was sick with hepatitis in 1971. After going to many hospitals I was finally hospitalized at London Hospital, Apapa, Lagos metropolis, where three doctors told me that I would not live because I had so many wounds in the liver so I should go home and wait for death. I was then a building draughtsman with Julius Berger in Lagos. While waiting for my people to carry me home, I had a dream on my hospital bed. I saw myself in a very deep and large pit. A beggar came to me and asked for alms. I dipped my hands into my pocket and found four pennies. I gave the beggar two pennies and kept the rest. Immediately the man changed and became sparkling white. This man told me, "This is not your place; follow me." While following the man we came to a big gate with wild guard dogs as big as cows. When the dogs saw us coming they lay on the floor like lambs. The gate opened by itself, and we passed through. When we got outside of the gate I saw many doctors and native doctors standing by the side of the road. Each of them was asking me to come to them for healing, but I said, "I will not come; I have been told to go." I continued moving, moving, moving, until I woke up from my dream.

The following day some family members came to the hospital and took me to my hometown. When I got home I saw many people crying because they knew I would die soon. I could not eat, drink, talk, breathe well, or stand on my feet. In fact I was dying. My elder sister, who was a member of Christ Holy Church, hired a vehicle and took me to Onitsha to receive prayers from Mama Odozi Obodo. When we reached Onitsha I was carried to the holy prophetess. She began to pray and said, "*Na fa Jisos*" ("In the name of Jesus"). Immediately she stopped and asked someone to call Deaconesses

Ifeajuna, Obi, and Nwabuzor. When the deaconesses came she told them that she had called them to be her witnesses because "God says that this man will serve me; he will be my minister. He should be taken to Isiokwe, in Onitsha, for him to make a vow before the altar that he will serve God. If he makes the vow, he will be healed within three days." When they took me to Isiokwe, I tried to say the vow but had some difficulty. I remember saying "If God heals me I will work for God." They took me back to the general prophetess. I was healed exactly on the third day. I was so strong that on the fourth day I joined the church at a gospel crusade at Onitsha. My healing took place in the first week of February, 1971.[372]

Rev. Udemba perceives his dream as very significant in his life due to events that led him to the presence of Prophetess Agnes Okoh and the prophecy leading to his healing. To him what the beggar-turned-angel told him, "This is not your place, follow me," is enough evidence of his call to the pastoral ministry. All these events, to him, confirm his call to the pastoral ministry. In spite of the belief in dreams, it is the policy of the church to give training to all those who claim that they have been called into the ministry. They are trained and observed before being ordained. Almost all the pastors are bilingual, speaking their local languages and English.

How the Church Takes Care of Pastors

The church believes in full-time pastoral ministry. The pastoral ministry is considered as the most dignified work on earth, so they ensure that the needs of pastors are met so as to maintain their pastoral dignity.[358] Senior Evangelist Michael Martey Mensah has this to say regarding the church's policies on meeting the needs of pastors:

Provisions and regulations have been laid for every station to care for their workers and ministers—paying of stipends, some allowances, providing food, kerosene, and other basic amenities. It is a policy in this church to provide free accommodation to her pastors; it may be a small place at first until a satisfactory place to stay is rented for him. If, for instance, certain circumstances compel one to rent a house outside the church premises, the church pays the rent. In all cases, the church pays all utility bills as well. Wherever a minister goes on official duties, money is provided from the station's coffers for the minister's transport fare or petrol. The members have been trained in that way; they already know what they are to do. They make sure that their ministers are well-dressed. If the pastors are not neatly dressed, they will not be proud enough to point at them and say, "This is our pastor." Stations make sure that they provide cars for pastors and motorcycles for evangelists and those below the rank of evangelists. If a station is not resourceful enough to buy a vehicle for her pastor, churches in the district to which the station belong come together to buy the means of transport. The means of transport are given as irrevocable gifts to the person in whose name it was bought. [373]

Members of a congregation also pay all expenses pertaining to the wedding of their pastor. Some congregations in the rural areas (countryside) buy land and farm on it for their pastors. Other important ministry tools such as cellular phones are bought for most of the pastors ministering in the cities and metropolis.

Administration: Personnel and Finance

Administrative structure

The church is administratively divided, in descending order, into superintendencies, districts, parishes, and stations. The superintendencies are equal to dioceses in the Episcopal tradition. A superintendent minister is, thus, equivalent to a bishop. The head of the church who has oversight over all the pastors, is designated general superintendent. He is assisted by the general evangelist who is presently himself as superintendent minister. A central executive council made up of the general superintendent, general evangelist, assistant general superintendent, financial secretary, general treasurer, superintendent ministers, and the general deaconess is the highest ruling body of the church. There are some functioning committees that are equally important for other aspects of the administration. The committees are central disciplinary, central building, education, music festival, and almanac.

Self-financing

The financial sources of the church are weekly offerings, tithing, freewill pledges (in case of fund raising), donation of properties, and proceeds of bazaars. Each year congregations organize a harvest (bazaars) as a means of raising funds to meet the budget of the congregation. It is usually held on a Sunday. On that day, after the usual morning service, members bring various items—foodstuff, farming implements, dairy and poultry products, clothing, stationery, building materials, etc.—to the place of worship. The items are brought with extreme joy amidst non-stop jubilant singing and rhythmic dancing; a long line of people come holding (waving) or carrying their items to the feet of an elder or pastor standing before the congregation. The items are sold (bazaar sales) in a non-egoistic atmosphere characterized with joy and hand clapping. The proceeds are put in the congregation's fund.

Each station is required to open an account with a commercial Bank where the church's money is expected to be deposited. There is, however, a central account in which funds are set aside for special purposes; for example, funds for evangelism and the care of widows, are deposited. The financial transactions of each station are mediated through a financial committee. The first Tuesday of every month is financial accountability day. It is a day when substations render accounts (income and expenditure) of the previous month to their district pastors. The district pastors, in turn, render accounts to their area superintendents, while the area superintendents also give account of their financial stewardship to the general superintendent. The local financial committee members have to endorse the financial statement as being a true reflection of the income and expenditure of the station before the statement is presented to the higher authority. It is not a practice in the church to render accounts regularly and openly to all the members of the congregation. members of the financial committee, however, tell any inquirer the financial position of the congregation.[374]

Worship and Liturgy

Members of Christ Holy Church worship God twice daily seven days a week. They worship at dawn (with the exception of Sundays when they worship in the morning) and in the evening from Monday through Sunday. The members are committed to the twice daily worship services. When Catherine Asor was asked to state some of the uniqueness of the church in Nigeria, she proudly said: "We are the only church in Nigeria that worships twice daily for seven days."[375]

Dawn and Evening Services

The dawn services are similar to individual morning devotions in some Christian traditions. The only difference is its congregational nature. Members who patronize the dawn service sing praises to God and give thanks for "guidance, protection, and deliverance from worldly perditions."[376] A prayer asking God to forgive their sins is said by the leader. They are exhorted by the pastor to demonstrate their Christlikeness in their daily activities. The congregation then spends time in prayer—

committing their body, soul, spirit, school children, all pastors and missionaries, the poor and needy to prayer. They also ask God that they may come back in the evening full of joy to thank him. The pastor sends the members off with a benediction. This is how members of Christ Holy Church International begin their day.

In the evenings they reassemble to thank God and ask for forgiveness of sins. They pray for divine protection and deliverance throughout the night. Again a benediction is uttered by the leader before members leave for their various homes.[377]

On Fridays members worship from dawn till midday, praying and fasting. They reassemble in the evening to continue worshipping. With the exception of Friday morning offerings which are used to meet the needs of the poor and needy, the church does not take advantage of the dawn and evening services to enrich herself. The only other day that offerings are taken is on Sundays—morning and evening.

The Nature of Worship

As many other African Independent Churches, the worship services of Christ Holy Church International are lively and long with the singing of western hymns and local gospel choruses accompanied by both western and African musical instruments. Vigorous and ear-splitting hand-clapping, instinctive choreographic movements to traditional rhythms, and loud shouting of "alleluias" are the main characteristics of Christ Holy Church International worship. According to the order of service used by the church, members shout "alleluias" ten times at various sections of the service.

Music plays a great role in their worship services. The singing of songs is led either by the gospel band or the choir. Christ Holy Church has many good choirs which have won ecumenical singing competitions. When Linda Guy, an associate seminar leader of Abiding Life Ministries International, New Zealand Office, spoke at a Christ Holy Church Women's conference in 2000 and later worshipped with them, she could not hide her impressions:

> The music and dancing in Christ Holy Church is amazing. I wish I could just jump up and join in; and occasionally I attempt to. But I just love sitting and watching . . . watching your enthusiasm, your joy and happiness at being together with God's people, your talent and natural abilities to dance so beautifully and energetically.[378]

In all worship services they leave time for members to give testimonies and thanksgiving about what God has done for them. Members are also encouraged to come before the congregation to tell them of puzzling dreams they have had the previous nights, a vision they have seen, and a prophetic utterance they want to make.

Women are required to cover their heads when worshipping. Worshippers at Christ Holy Church services are grouped according to their gender. When asked to give reason behind this policy the consensus was that it has no cultural connotation. Other popular reasons: (1) to avert seduction; nothing seduces a man more than sitting close to a woman; (2) to avert distraction during worship service since, they claim, not all men and women can maintain self-control; (3) husbands who are not members would not be happy seeing their wives sitting beside other men; it could cause a breakdown in some marital homes.

Every worship center has two kinds of places set aside for pastors to sit—one is outer; the other is inner. They call these places "altars." The perimeters of the altars are not covered with any cloth; they are plain. They are reserved for pastors only. The inner ones are for the ordained pastors, while the one in front of the inner ones is for those who are yet to be ordained, though serving in various pastoral categories such as evangelists, catechists, etc. The inner ones are inscribed "Holy, Holy, Holy." The worshippers sit on long pews or benches.

A sixteenth-century type of high-rising Victorian pulpit with steps leading to the platform of the pulpit and lecterns are the two main types of pulpits used in many congregations. The Victorian-type pulpits are usually placed on either the far end right or left side of the worship center, while the lecterns are usually placed in the middle. Preachers are free to decide which of the pulpits to use. The lecterns are most often used. Every worship service regularly ends with the congregation singing the following song:

Praise God from whom all blessings flow;
Praise him, all creatures here below;
Praise him above, ye heavenly host;
Praise Father, Son, and Holy Ghost.

They sing this song of praise (either in English or Igbo) to affirm their faith in the Triune God.

Uniqueness and Ecumenicity.

Uniqueness

Despite the numerous similarities between Christ Holy Church International and other African Independent Churches, members of the church see some major differences and do not hesitate to mention them so as to state their uniqueness. "We do not wear special garments. We do not have dietary restrictions. We do not burn incense and candles. We do not charge money for healings and prayers. We do not have holy grounds. We do not remove shoes before entering our places of worship. We do not use palm fronds to bless water."[379] These assertions, as well as others like spirit possession, ecstatic gestures, and belief in angels that are very common with most African Independent Churches, are not the beliefs and practices of Christ Holy Church International. The Church is, therefore, different from some other African Independent Churches in many ways.

Ecumenical Activities

Christ Holy Church International does not isolate herself from the activities of other African Independent Churches in spite of her uniqueness. The church is a member of the Organization of African Instituted Churches (OAIC), Nigeria Chapter, which is an affiliate body of the Christian Association of Nigeria (CAN), an ecumenical body of all Christians in Nigeria.[380] Other congregations of the church join some ecumenical activities such as choral festivals and open air evangelistic campaigns.

Major Factors of Growth

Trend of Growth

The church had grown from 12 members in 1947 to 300 congregations in 1980 when Marius Okoh was called to eternity. This indicates the phenomenal spread of the church. On average the Church plants 14 congregations annually. Dr. Michael Wells, director of Abiding Life Ministry International at Littleton, Colorado, U.S., an evangelistic and counseling institution, expressed his wonder at the growth of the church when he visited Nigeria in February 2000:

> Come to think of it, who would have believed that somewhere in the world there was a woman that was used so marvelously by God to start a church in 1947 that has expanded to over 700 solid branches. This is basically the story of Christ Holy Church, and it is possible for the church to spread all over the world.[381]

Church Growth Policies

Christ Holy Church International has some daring policies of church growth that have slowed down the rate of the growth, no matter the rate of expansion. We will discuss such policies in detail.

Self-housing

The church has a policy of self-housing. Many churches in West Africa worship in public classrooms, cinema halls, and other rented facilities. Christ Holy Church International, however, has a policy of worshipping only in its own properties. As a result the church does not begin a congregation at any place until land has either been bought or donated and a place of worship built. The worship center is usually built with the pastor's residence attached to it. Rev. John Obiakor traces the historical background of the policy to the leadership of Marius Okoh.

> When the church was begun a hut was usually raised for worship purposes, but the ministers were living in rented homes. One day Marius visited a minister to settle a misunderstanding between the minister and his landlady, but the landlady was not happy about the arbitration. So she poured dirty water on Marius for no apparent reason. Marius then gave a directive to the whole church that henceforth no minister should live in rented houses.[382]

Some elders at the Nsukka congregation told of many incidents where property owners ejected members of the church. "The members scattered," they said, "and we had to start all over again. So to make sure that such incidents do not happen again, when we start, we start on our own land."[383] Speaking further of the policy, the Most Rev. Daniel Okoh says that past experiences of the church amply demonstrate that worshipping in rented facilities is like thrusting the future of the church into the hands of the property owners, since property owners who do not have any regard for written agreements evict pastors and members from their leased properties at their own whims and desires.

Self-financing

Another related policy of the church that needs mention is the resolve not to borrow money from anyone. According to Rev. Christian Obiefuna, the treasurer of the church, "Christ Holy Church does not borrow money from any person or institution—not even the banks. We do not owe anyone anything."[384] Members of the church are expected to finance every project or venture undertaken by the church through free-will offerings.

These policies make the spread of the church a costly venture due to the high price of buying land and building materials in Nigeria, the long and meandering processes one has to endure, and the poverty of most of the members. When asked to name one major challenge facing the Lagos Superintendency, Chidi Mbadiwe, an elder of the superintendency, has this to say: "Lagos is like Nineveh; there are some good things but there are also many things that can distract the attention of people from being committed to God.... We have bought many lands but we lack money to develop them."[385] The planting of a congregation by Christ Holy Church International, thus, means a lot more than just gathering people to worship God through Word and Sacrament. These policies, inhibitive as they are, do not stop leaders of the church from planting one congregation after another.

Factors of Growth

To understand the growth pattern, we will have to discuss the factors of growth in the context of Africa and Nigeria. Many factors contribute to the growth of Christ Holy Church International. Three main factors, however, will be discussed. They are evangelism, miracles and healing, and teaching of the Word of God. We will not discuss these attractions in any order of preference or priority.

Outdoor Evangelistic Campaigns

Even though the church began evangelistic crusades[386] (revivals) in the 1950s, they intensified such revivals from 1963 onward. The prominence of evangelism in the church can be deduced from the content of the mission statement. The mission statement is stated thus:

> The mission of Christ Holy Church is to worship the Triune God in holiness and to teach and spread the Good News of our Lord Jesus Christ across borders, race and cultures urgently, powerfully, faithfully, wisely, and fearlessly till Jesus Christ comes again.[387]

The Mission Statement can be said to be the evangelistic statement of the Church. In fact, drawing a line between evangelism and the Mission Statement is impossible. This is indicated in the Most Rev. Daniel Okoh's launching of the Mission Statement. He urged the members to be evangelistic-minded so as to face the challenges of the new millennium: "To face these challenges and overcome, we the members of Christ Holy Church should always see this Mission Statement as our guide in evangelism."[388]

The Mission Statement clearly indicates that evangelism in Christ Holy Church International encompasses the teaching of the Word of God as well. Members of the church do not perceive any dichotomy between teaching and evangelizing. They evangelize as they teach and teach as they evangelize. Their objects of evangelism, therefore, are not only those who have not heard the Good News but also those who have already heard and responded to it. Having a deeper knowledge of the Word of God, to them, enhances one's desire and willingness to share the Good News with others without any fear of being intimidated. Their evangelistic campaigns are, as a result, done both indoors and outdoors. The indoor compaigns are meant for their members while the outdoor campaigns have non-Christians in mind.

The *locus classicus* of their evangelistic campaigns, as the mission statement shows, is the Good News of our Lord Jesus Christ. Since Prophetess Agnes Okoh did not build the ministry around her personality, taking a low-key role in leadership and administration, members neither project her personality nor her gifts as a means of attracting people to the church. When over two hundred members of the church were asked to state two things that attracted them to join the church, none of them mentioned the name and numerous gifts of Prophetess Agnes Okoh. The proclamation of the Good News is what matters most to members of the church. When the Rt. Rev. Gabriel Chiemeka was asked by *Glad News* how he would describe Christ Holy Church to non-members, he did not mention the name of the prophetess or how God used her, although they are important contributions to the growth and popularity of the church, he stressed their adherence to the Word of God:

> To the best of my knowledge, Christ Holy Church believes totally in the New Testament and the Old Testament as confirmed by Christ. This Church believes totally in the word of God; in the Bible. . . . We do not divert to the left or right because of difficulties or problems. Rather we always stand to see that the words of God are observed fully to its letter.[389]

The evangelistic aspect of the Mission Statement leaves no room for a myopic evangelization. It looks beyond the numerous borders, races, and cultures of Nigeria and elsewhere. This influences the preparation of its ministers and workers on how to proclaim the Gospel. "Christ Holy Church is an African-instituted church that abides by the word of God and we also use idioms to express our Christianity."[390] This statement by Rt. Rev. Gabriel Chiemeka indicates that the church does mission to suit the understanding of the objects of evangelization—no matter the cultural differences—without necessarily compromising the purity of the gospel.

The adverbial descriptions of the proclamation of the Good News in the Mission Statement—urgently, powerfully, faithfully, wisely, and fearlessly— are indications of the extent to which they are prepared to go in order to proclaim the gospel effectively to their hearers. This shows their willingness to wait and depend on the Holy Spirit to equip and direct them to minister meaningfully to peoples and cultures beyond their knowledge. It is also an indication of their preparedness to make use of educational opportunities available to them.

The urgency of their evangelistic campaigns is embedded in the mention of the Second Coming of Jesus Christ in the Mission Statement. Even though there are numerous references in the Bible about the certainty of the return of Jesus Christ, the exact date, day, and time of the coming are hidden from humanity. The indefiniteness and imminence of the time of Jesus' return behoove Christians to do things urgently.[391] The dedication and commitment of Christ Holy Church members to evangelism can be explained by their belief in eschatological events. With such belief they know that the soon-coming Christ will not only appreciate their efforts, he will reward them as well.

As a result of their faith in the second coming of the Lord Jesus Christ, the reward they stand to gain, and the need to evangelize, members of the church contribute money to finance their evangelization campaigns and building of places of worship. Leaders of the church raise funds on the last Sunday of every month for the purpose of evangelism and related issues like purchasing land, musical instruments, and gospel vans. There is also periodic fund raising to meet some special needs like buying a particular plot of land. When the church needed money to buy plots of land in Ghana, for example, the Central Executive Council made an appeal that states *inter alia*:

> First in the series of support, we urgently solicit the acquisition of plots of land. Brothers and sisters, due to the high cost of land and buildings all over the world, the cost has been broken down in bits to enable everyone to participate fully. Cities: N20,000 per sq. metre, Urban: N5,000 per sq. metre, Rural Area: N8,000 per sq. metre. Kindly choose from the above schedule how many square meters of land you would like to give to the Lord at this crucial hour and receive your blessings.[392]

The proceeds of both the regular and periodic fund raising are saved in a separate bank account so that monies for evangelism can be used when the need arises.

Records at the headquarters of the church show that major outdoor evangelistic crusades are coordinated by the Central Executive Committee on an average of three every year. Other superintendencies organize their own outdoor campaigns on a smaller scale as and when, they claim, the Holy Spirit directs.

The outdoor evangelistic campaigns by leaders and members of Christ Holy Church are usually preceded by prayer, fasting, and waiting on the Holy Spirit by all the members living in and around the community where the crusade (campaign) will be held. Their willingness to wait on the Lord is so obvious that even their guests can see it. Dr. Michael Wells, who claims to have traveled to more than 50 countries, comments:

> I have seen churches all over the world, some built on evangelism, others on Christian principles and values to suit their worship. But, Christ Holy Church is the church I have found that is built on Christ's humility, waiting on Christ and listening to his voice, so thoroughly built on abiding in Christ.[393]

While waiting on the Lord, the location of the place to be evangelized is usually determined by either a prophetic utterance, an invitation from someone to the church to begin a ministry, a donation of land, and or money, or some circumstances lending themselves to divine direction. Whatever the indication might be, members commit the campaign to intense prayer for assurance from God while preparing for the campaign.

Another important aspect of the campaign is the printing of posters stating dates, venues, number of speakers, and a theme. A typical example is:

CRUSADE! CRUSADE!! CRUSADE!!!
CHRIST HOLY CHURCH OF NIGERIA
Date: 9—11 March 1999
Time: 5 pm each day
Venue: Old Parade Ground, Area 10, Garki, Abuja
Theme: Moment of Restoration
Seven Speakers
Come; let Jesus restore your life, health, wealth, peace, joy.
Come and be blessed.

The posters are plastered all over the towns and cities for the sake of publicity. Gospel vans are used to go to neighboring villages and vicinities inviting people to the crusade grounds.

Themes for the campaign differ from one place to another; at times they are repeated. Some of the popular themes are: "Total Healing for the Nation," "My People Are Born to Live," "Power Explosion," "Moment of

Restoration," "Amazing Grace." The most common of the themes is "My People Are Born to Live." Even though *Chinoyelu* Ugwu has stated that "the basic motivation of the Igbo to religious practice is 'life' (Ndu) which is of supreme value to the Igbo,"[394] one cannot base the importance of life to the Igbo only on the fact that one is an Igbo. This perhaps explains the significance of Agnes Okoh's life-in-Christ thematic preaching based on John 10:10, a theme that has been prominent in the church's evangelist campaigns. By preaching abundant-life-in-Christ messages during their evangelist campaigns, Christ Holy Church International gives their audience the opportunity to know the causes of their struggles in life and the preparedness of Jesus Christ to rectify their situations. The church, thus, gives a wider meaning and implication to the Igbo concept of life.

In most cases those who are invited are the ones suffering from all kinds of diseases, those looking for jobs, infertile couples, those who find life meaningless, and others who find themselves in some circumstances they deem as having no natural explanation. People, therefore, attend the evangelistic campaigns expecting their problems to be solved. The attention of those gathered at the evangelistic meetings is usually focused on the ability of Jesus to save and deliver people from the enslavement of the devil and diseases. For instance, the invitation on the posters of the outdoor crusade held at Ijebu Ode, on 18-21 February 2001 states: "Come to the Cross and receive Healing, Complete Life, Peace of Mind, Fruit of the Womb, Prosperity, Joy, Employment. Jesus is Lord." Asked whether the church is a prosperous church in view of the references to prosperity on the evangelistic posters, Emmanuel Asadu, the technician/audio engineer of the Nation Builders Band, which is the national gospel band of the church, replies:

> Prosperity, from the perspective of Christ Holy Church, starts from the spiritual aspect of the individual's closeness to his maker and his commitment to serve God even if his resources are very little. Outward prosperity is considered a secondary matter. Members of Christ Holy Church do not attach much importance to material prosperity. I have seen a minister of Christ Holy Church giving his car as a gift to another minister to use as his own.[395]

Prosperity on the evangelistic banners, according to Asadu, is a call to establish a life-lasting commitment with Jesus Christ first, and then serving him no matter the circumstances.

Activities on the crusade grounds begin usually at 5:00 p.m. and end at 9:00 p.m. The gospel band leads the gathering to sing some common gospel choruses backed with western and African musical instruments. Powerful microphones are usually used to carry the Christ-centered messages far and wide, such that even those who for some reason do not go to the crusade grounds hear the messages in their homes.

The wide posting of the invitation to the crusade, the long duration of the evangelistic campaigns, the smart dressing of the gospel singers, the invigorating music at the crusade, the force with which the Christ-centered messages of the preachers penetrate some people's homes, and some people's claims of being healed are all forms of showcasing the church, thus making people aware of the existence of the church and what God can do for them through the church. Prospective members are given the opportunity to review a broad spectrum of aspects of the church so that they can base their decisions to become members on facts, not hearsay. Senior Catechist Eugene Okere Ogbonna testifies about how he became a member of Christ Holy Church:

> In a dream in 1984 I saw some people building a worship center on an empty parcel of land in my hometown. Later I saw a picture of Jesus hanging on one of the walls of the worship center so I went to stand before the picture and said, "Jesus, so it is here you are, and I am looking for you while I am suffering in life. Jesus, if you are here then I will worship you." Two months later some people came clearing the same parcel of land for a church building. After building the church there was a crusade. On the day of the crusade, the preacher's message was about how some people are suffering in the world trying to find meaning in life. The examples the preacher gave were very similar to what I had been going through for the past four years. The man preached as if he were living with me. In the end he said, "It is only God who can help people to find meaning in life." The message touched my heart so I went forward to accept Christ. My life has changed for the better since that time.[396]

Many members of Christ Holy Church International have testimonies similar to Catechist Ogbonna's experience. In fact when some members were asked to state how they became members of the church, most of them said they were invited to evangelist crusades. The church attracts people from other churches without necessarily inviting them personally. Such was the experience of Emmanuel Asadu, who was a member of a pentecostal church which, according to him, paid lip service to evangelism:

> Evangelism in this church is a supreme task. This is one of the things that attracted me to this church, because evangelism is my heartbeat. The church makes financial contributions to evangelism. The church is a prophetic ministry so we approach evangelism in that respect.[397]

The outdoor evangelistic campaigns often yield fantastic results that are beyond the expectations of the organizers.

Indoor Revivals

Members of Christ Holy Church International are the focus of indoor evangelist revivals. Such revivals are done by individual congregations. Some congregations do it routinely, once monthly, while others do it as the need arises. The indoor revivals usually last for either three days, a whole week (Monday—Saturday), or in some cases a fortnight. Each meeting usually begins at 6:30 p.m. and ends at 9:00 p.m. The long period affords the pastors time to exhort and teach the members about the need to tell the gospel, the dynamics of telling it, and, how to live it among people in a Christlike manner. Leaders of the church take every opportunity to remind the members of the need to tell the gospel. When writing on the mission statement, the Most Rev. Daniel Okoh, for instance, reminded members of this need:

> Every member of this church is called to spread the good news and so you must see yourself as an evangelist wherever you may be at any point in time—at home, in the office, in your market stalls, during your business or social gatherings, in vehicles, trains, and airplanes. We have to witness to the ignorant about the name that is light, the name that heals all kinds of diseases, the name that gives life, the name that opens up doors of prosperity, and the name that brings freedom from sin and gives absolute peace. This name, Jesus Christ, is the name above all names.[398]

One of the greatest legacies that Agnes Okoh left to members of Christ Holy Church International is the imprinting of her religious experience on their hearts. Her mandate to read Matthew 10, a passage about how Jesus sent his disciples to proclaim the Gospel, has been the bedrock of Christ Holy Church. As has been already noted, all the leaders of the church have emphasized the importance of evangelism in both word and deed. The contrast between the destruction of life by the devil and the abundant life one can find in Jesus Christ has become the clarion call of the evangelistic campaigns of Christ Holy Church. The church, therefore, has grown from strength to strength.

Healing and Miracles: Background Information

Healing is a ministry that attracts people to the church more than any of the other ministries. Out of two hundred members interviewed, forty-five percent became members after being healed. Forty percent of the pastors interviewed were also healed before becoming members. Before we can understand the phenomenon of healing in the church, we need to take notice of the Igbo, and to a larger extent the West African concept of sickness, causes of sickness, and processes of healing.

Writing on the concept of health and sickness in the Igbo worldview, *Chinoyelu* Ugwu observes:

> Health for the Igbo could be used restrictively to denote the physical state or condition of the body and mind. . . . But in a more encompassing sense, health is not restricted to the state of the body; it extends to a person's general condition in his world of relations. Health or well-being involves the ability of the individual to relate harmoniously to both his physical and metaphysical worlds.[399]

The cosmology of the Igobs, to a larger extent, influences their concept of health, causes of sickness, and the healing process. They, like many Africans, live in a world of realities; they, thus, expect to be ill sometimes in their lives. Sickness is nothing new to them. What matters most are the direct causes of sickness, how treatable the sickness is, and the circumstances leading to the sickness and, in fact, any misfortune that overwhelms their comprehension. Ugwu mentions what Igbos perceive to be the broad causes of sickness—human and supernatural agents.

The mention of *Ogwu* (magic, sorcery, charm, etc.) and *Amusu* (witchcraft) in the previous chapter come into play when one considers what might have been the causes of one's diseases. These are the human agents believed to be responsible for sicknesses. Many Africans, Igbos included, believe that medicine men who know how to use herbs and manipulate the spirit world to suit their own whims and caprices can be the cause of sickness or misfortune for some other persons. The medicine men are usually either hired by their adherents to cast diseases on other people, or they (the medicine men) willfully do that to show their adversaries or presumed adversaries the extent of the potency of their medicine.

Belief in witchcraft is prevalent in many African societies even though people find it difficult to give explicit definitions.[400] Kofi Asare Opoku defines witchcraft as a manifestation of an aspect of "mystical forces . . . which are neutral in themselves but which can be employed by those who possess the power, for beneficial or evil ends."[401] Harriet Hill throws further light on the understanding of witchcraft thus: "Witchcraft is often categorized in the middle level with spirit beings. In effect, it is not a spirit being, but rather a human psychic power. It does not come from outside of humans, but rather emanates from within their being."[402] Although some westerners had speculated that witchcraft is "a trait of primitive people which will disappear with westernization,"[403] belief in witchcraft is still widespread and cuts across all segments of African people despite the influence of western scholarship and scientific advancement in Africa. This is made clear by Bolaji Idowu, a minister of the Methodist Church of Nigeria and a theologian:

>In Africa today it is "real" that the majority of the people believe that there are witches and there is witchcraft. Witches and witchcraft are sufficiently real as to cause untold suffering and innumerable deaths. . . . When I speak of witchcraft, I am referring to that which is very disturbingly real as to affect the lives of Africans in every walk of life. And by Africans I mean not only the illiterates who carry on with their traditional customs intact, almost as they were received from their forebears; I mean also 'educated' men and women in the civil service, in the mercantile houses, well-known politicians, university professors, university graduates and undergraduates, medical doctors, imams, alhajis, archbishops or bishops and a host of Christian ministers, Muslims and Christians. To most of the persons in these categories, witchcraft is an urgent and very harassing reality; it is diabolical, soul-enslaving presence. . . . I will assert categorically that there are witches in Africa; that they are as real as are the murderers, poisoners, and other categories of evil workers, overt and surreptitious. This, and not any imagination, is the basis of the strong belief in witchcraft.[404]

With such a strong assertion of the reality of witches and witchcraft by no less a person than a reverend minister and professor, one can understand the influential role of the belief in witchcraft in the worldview of many African people, particularly when it comes to finding the causes of diseases and other misfortunes. In fact most of the inexplicable happenings and diseases in most African communities are blamed on witchcraft. "African peoples feel and believe that all the various ills, misfortunes, sicknesses, accidents, tragedies, sorrows, dangers, and unhappy mysteries which they encounter or experience, are caused by the use of this mystical power in the hands of a sorcerer, witch or wizard."[405] The wide range of spiritual entities in Igbo cosmology and the malevolent nature of some of the spirits give credence to their suspicion that spiritual beings cause some diseases.

> The Igbo believe that some sicknesses are due to the actions of some malicious or evil spirits who take delight in inflicting harm on human beings. These may be the spirit of dead wicked human beings, some malevolent spirits like *Akalogeli, Ogbonuke*, and some group-spirits like *Ogbanje*, and some *water spirits*.[406]

Apart from believing that such spirits can and do cause diseases, Igbos also believe that the spirits of the ancestors punish some people for disobeying the tenets of the *Omenani* earlier mentioned. The ancestral spirits punish such people with misfortune, ill-health, barrenness, miscarriages, and physical and mental illnesses.[407] The deities are also believed to be the causes of some diseases.

> The Igbo believe that some deities could punish people if they commit certain crimes in the society. Some people, for example, seek the assistance of some powerful deities or spirits to protect their property. . . . So in the Igbo belief some people can incur the punishment of a deity by meddling with something under the custody of a deity.[408]

With all these numerous possible causes of sickness, when an Igbo falls sick there arises the need to find the cause and seek treatment. The importance of finding a cause does not mean that Africans do not accept the scientific explanations regarding the causes of diseases. Some of the causes are very obvious, but if the circumstances surrounding the disease are unfathomable, some people still go on a cause-finding expedition. Others will also question why the disease did not afflict anyone but him or her. Another reason is to ensure that the calamity will not reoccur.

With a spiritual concept of sickness at the back of their minds, most Igbos (Africans) traditionally rush to consult either a diviner, a sorcerer, or a medicine man to find out the cause of sickness and a prescription for healing. M. M. Green states the important role of the *dibea* (medicine man) in Igbo society, particularly in times of sickness:

What must be stressed, however, is the part played by the *dibea* in the daily life of the Ibo. When someone is ill or overtaken by a disaster, either he or his relations will hurry to a diviner who by the vision he has acquired during his training can see these causes.... The diviner can also be consulted in cases of theft. In addition to all voluntary cases of consultation, if anything habitual can be so described, custom decrees that a diviner shall be consulted in the two fundamental crises of birth and of death.... When anyone dies, kinsmen again must go to ask a diviner, and if need be, several, the cause of death.[409]

Ugwu identifies three stages of healing among the Igbos. The first stage is the diagnosis of the causative factor of the disease. This is done through divination. "Diagnosis, in this sense, does not mean the identification of the disease behind the symptoms, but the identification of the 'force' (spiritual or otherwise) behind the sickness."[410] This stage is very important to most Igbos due to the belief that nothing happens by chance.

The identification of the cause of the disease leads to the second stage—rituals. The expert in this sphere of the healing process is not necessarily the diviner; it is the priest. "The priests are the official intermediaries between the supernatural beings and men."[411] The priests usually ask that a sacrifice or prayers be made to the offended deity so as to mitigate the severity of the healing which might eventually lead to total healing. The motive and importance of sacrifices among the Igbos are stressed by John P. Jordan:

> Every Ibo believed that an invisible universe was in action all around him, and that his term of life was short if he happened to fall foul of its denizens. He felt that it was up to him, therefore, to propitiate them and to treat them with courtesy and deference. That was the fundamental reason why he had such a penchant for sacrifice in all its many forms.... The actual word 'sacrifice'... stood simply for any kind of offering made to the spirits.... To the Ibo, sacrifice was a necessary step towards keeping away adversity and towards propitiating the spirits for some evil committed. The adversity might be ill-health or loss of property or injury or anything indeed that had the stamp of misfortune.... The *dibea* always demanded sacrifice as the only way of escape from the evil machinations of indignant spirits.[412]

The last stage of the healing process among the Igbos is the stage of medication. "This is supposed to be the work of the medicine man. He is supposed to have the knowledge of natural healing agencies like herbs, roots, animal parts, and the like. He also employs the aid of the spiritual forces supposed to make his concoctions effective."[413] Ugwu mentions two different classes of medicine-men in Igbo society. The first are the ordinary medicine men who are believed to have knowledge of the efficacy of herbs. These are called herbalists in some African societies. In western terminology they would be called general medical practitioners. The second class of medicine men is described as "special doctors" or in other words "specialists." They deal with special diseases such as mental illness or those that are believed to be caused by the *Ogbanje, water-spirits* witchcraft.[414]

Healing and Miracles: Some Procedures

From the brief discussion of the Igbo perception of the nature and causes of sickness and the stages of healing, two issues come to the fore when Igbo persons or, for that matter, many Africans, fall sick. The first issue is that the sick person will 'spiritualize' the disease. This means that the cause of the disease will be initially analyzed spiritually. The sick person will take a cursory look at his relationship with neighbors, nature, and the spirit world. He will further take a deep look at the communal relationship between the neighborhood in which he lives and the spirit world, how members of the neighborhood had lived peacefully or otherwise with the spirit world, particularly regarding their relationship with the ancestral spirits.

The other issue is about the type of healing process that will be taken, depending on the religious inclinations of the sick person. If the sick person is not a Christian, he will go through the traditional stages already discussed. If, after going through the stages, the sick person is not healed he will then decide either to seek western medicine or go to see a reverend minister. On the other hand, if the sick person is a Christian the healing process that will be decided on will depend on his denominational tradition in the Christian faith. He will either seek western medicine or depend solely on faith healing. If the Christian is a member of a western mission-founded church there is the likelihood that when the disease defies treatment at the western-inclined hospitals and clinics, that person will turn to faith healing as a last resort. This practice is an open secret asserted by many people. "The simple truth is that members of the historic churches also often resort to African Independent Churches in periods of crisis."[415] If the person belongs to a faith-healing tradition, depending either on his maturity in that tradition or his intellectual influence, he will decide to depend on God and Western medicine concurrently for his healing. Unlike the sick person who is not a Christian, hardly will a Christian go through the already-stated traditional stages should the sickness persist. The worst action the Christian might choose, in this regard, is to seek the services of an herbalist.

From the foregoing discussions, which are real in Africa, in most cases, it is evident that the patronage of western-inclined hospitals and clinics is not considered a first priority for many Africans in times of sickness. This is true because of the spiritual perception of sickness by Africans. How can a medical doctor tell a patient the spiritual nuances of a disease? As a result, most Africans have a strong belief that not all diseases can be treated by western medicine or by using scientific methods. It can be concluded, therefore, that before someone who is not a Christian seeks faith healing, the person might have gone through different kinds of healing processes and tried different kinds of medications. This is also similar to a Christian who is not a member of a faith-healing tradition; the only difference is that he will not go through the tedious traditional processes of healing. Nevertheless seeing the faith healer is usually a last resort.

Healing and Miracles: the reality

It is in this regard that one must perceive the assertion of members of Christ Holy Church who claim to have become members as a result of being healed in the church. With the exception of the few whose parents were already members of Christ Holy Church International, sick people who were brought to the church for healing came after trying many other processes of healing. This implies that the nature of the diseased persons deteriorates till they go to the church to seek healing. The phrase, "I tried many medicine men and went to different hospitals without any success," is, as a result, like a musical refrain on the lips of people who claim to have had their healing in Christ Holy Church International.

The church has three core beliefs about healing. The first is that all diseases can be healed by God, but not all diseases are healed instantaneously; the healing of some diseases does take some time. There is, however, no consensus over why some diseases are not healed. Three main reasons were suggested—either the one praying did not have enough faith, the one being prayed for does not have enough faith, or it is God's will that healing does not take place. Members are allowed to patronize western hospitals and clinics, if they wish. The second core belief is that western medicine without prayer can be ineffective; as a result, prayer should, as a matter of priority and at all times, precede the patronage of such medical centers.

The third core belief of the church about healing is that other elements, besides prayer, can be used to heal. Blessed water, oil, and prayer are the three main means of healing in Christ Holy Church. Although the church believes that one can be directed by the Holy Spirit to use other elements besides water and oil, the use of other elements besides the three is considered as extraneous and, as a matter of policy, must be discussed with and approved by a senior minister before being used. This measure, according to the leadership of the church, is to ensure that some members do not do things arbitrarily under the guise of a revelation from the Holy Spirit.

Members are asked to bring water in bottles and containers from home. At the close of the service members are asked to carry their containers of water on their heads. The pastor then blesses the water with a prayer without going near the containers. After saying the prayer the pastor rings a handbell three times. When asked to explain the significance of asking members to carry their containers of water before being blessed and that of ringing the bell three times, Rev. Christian Obiefuna answers:

> We do not want them to bring the water to the small space between the pastor and the members thus making the space crowded; it is for the sake of convenience. The ringing of the bell after blessing the water signifies that we have asked God the Father, Son, and Holy Spirit to bless the water.[416]

The sick are usually asked either to drink or bathe with the blessed water. They are advised to rub parts of their sick bodies with the blessed oil. Healing is at times effected through prayer, without the use of either blessed water or oil.

Diseases that have been named by respondents as having been healed are varied and many. They include blindness, paralysis, poisoning, lunacy, diabetes, infertility, asthma, ulcer, stroke, tuberculosis, dislocation of limbs, hepatitis, hemorrhage, and epilepsy. Some of the healings pull large crowds to become members of the church while others serve as means of conversions for families. The following is an example of the former:

Mrs. Justina Orji-nedo had a daughter called Ebele who was crippled in both legs. Her body looked like a snake, i.e., someone without bones. Her parents were not Christians. They took the child to many hospitals but to no avail. Finally a friend of Justina convinced her to take the child to Mama (Prophetess Agnes Okoh) at the Nkissi stream. In 1963 Justina took her daughter to Mama without the knowledge of her husband, Chief Orji-nedo, since he was fiercely against Christianity and prayer houses in particular. There was a gradual improvement of Ebele's sickness. Though Justina's husband protested his wife's action, she continued taking the child to Mama for prayers, nonetheless. At last the child became so strong that she was able to run to meet her father after Chief Orji-nedo had closed from work. He then admitted the power of God and invited Marius Okoh, the then leader of Christ Holy Church, to establish a congregation at Ihitenansa, his hometown. To show his gratitude, Chief Orji-nedo donated a large tract of land to the Church. When a congregation of the church was established at Ihitenansa, they prayed for Mary Dike, a blind woman. She was totally healed. News about Mary Dike's healing spread like a wild bushfire so the church spread to many outlying villages and towns.[417]

An example of a healing of one person that influenced an entire family to become members of the Church is told by Evangelist Cyril Ofoedu:

In 1967, Mary Ofoedu, my mother, suffered from hemorrhage for six months. She was hospitalized at Iyi-Enu hospital, but she was not healed. Six months later she felt some movement in her body. She was later paralyzed and bedridden for seven years. A member of Christ Holy Church at Abakaliki, then in Anambra State, directed us to the church for healing. We took her there because we had then exhausted all our financial resources at various hospitals. In fact my parents stopped my education because there was no money left to pay my fees. I dropped out of school at Standard Two (tenth grade) as a result. At the church she was prayed for. After the prayer she felt like defecating. While defecating on a pit latrine she claimed an object dropped from her bowel and tumbled into the pit latrine. That was it! She cried out from the pit latrine. When people went there they tried to lift her, but she felt some strength in her legs and began walking. This was what made me and the entire family become members of Christ Holy Church.[418]

Faith stories in Christ Holy Church International are replete with similar narrations of healings that either attracted a whole township or extended families to the church. Unlike many African Independent Churches where healing is synonymous with the name of church leaders, no one particular person is credited with accounts of healings in Christ Holy Church International. Members of the church do not refer those who are sick to some particular pastors of the church for healing, as is the practice among some African Independent Churches.

The gift of healing is said to abound in the church to the extent that it is very difficult to identify those with that gift. When one hundred pastors were asked to list three spiritual gifts with which they have been endowed, sixty percent listed healing. Many of them were themselves healed, including five of them who were healed of insanity. Rev. Pastor Charles Obalum, formerly insane, remembers the tree stump to which he was chained after his relatives put him into a car and brought him from northern Nigeria to Christ Holy Church International, Nteje Station. With references to numerous biblical instances, members have been thoroughly taught that God can use anyone who believes in Christ to do things beyond their expectations. Pastors and members of the church have, for that reason, a strong belief in the immutability and omnipotence of God. "Here in Christ Holy Church, the Lord has revealed that, as he was a healer in the Bible days, so he is today."[419]

Miracles[420] are closely connected to healing, but miracles are not always related to healing, as, for example, the bringing back of a dead person to life. Miracles, undoubtedly, attract many people to Christ Holy Church International. Emphasis in this section will be on miracles that have no relation to healing.

A miraculous act is a happening or deed which can be effected by no natural cause, being above the settled and recognized laws of nature; and which can hence only be attributed to God, the creator and lord of nature, for example, the resurrection of a dead body.[421]

Much as the above definition will be disputed by scholars who have a different views on miracles, this definition will be used to state what is meant by miracles in this chapter. The claim of giving back life to a dead person by a pastor is very common in Christ Holy Church. An example of such a claim is said to have made the Very Rev. Isaac Afunwa famous:

The Lord of [the] vineyard called I. O. Afunwa to the ministry as a catechist some thirty-eight years ago. He responded. He was a catechist when the Lord used him at Ogbunike in present Anambra State to raise the dead. He was returning from his morning visitation prayer session when he saw young men carrying a corpse for burial, but behind them wailing was a middle-aged widow who had now lost her only son, her only hope. Like Christ and remembering Christ's authority unto his believers and disciples, Afunwa halted the corpse bearers. On the road there he rang his bell, raised his Bible up, lifted his face towards heaven, and called upon his master Jesus, and instant miracle or raising the dead, who till this day is alive, happened.[422]

Such a miracle and others like commanding the lame to walk, healing the blind, and restoring sanity to lunatics reported to have been performed by a cross section of pastors of the church attract people to the church. Emmanuel Alamanjo, who claims to be an eye-witness of many miracles and had, himself, been an object of several miracles, states the reason miracles happen in the church:

> The point is that we in Christ Holy Church do not see miracles as anything strange. Jesus Christ, during his earthly ministry healed every sickness and every disease among his people, and he said, "He who believes in me, the works I do shall he do even greater works than mine because I go to my Father." So when Jesus ascended to heaven he did not ascend with his miracle power; he dropped it here on earth for those who believe in him, and it is the same power for those who believe in him in spirit and in truth. Christ Holy Church was founded on love, faith, and miracles.[423]

When asked by *Glad News* to reflect on the miracle of healing two lame sisters through prayer in 1963, Enoch Okonkwo concurred the assertion by Alamanjo by stating *inter alia*, "Miracle is not new to us in CHC."[424]

Teaching

The motherly role of Prophetess Agnes Okoh and the respect accorded to mothers in Igbo communities facilitated the teaching role of the prophetess. Though not literate enough to read and exegete the Bible, she made great use of analogical, repetitive, and exemplary pedagogies to pass on her knowledge of the Bible and her cumulative experience in Christian leadership to her followers about God, Jesus Christ, the Holy Spirit, and faith. The remembrance of the emphasis of the prophetess, in an oral culture, is ample evidence that the teaching of the prophetess has been firmly etched in the minds of her followers.

The establishment of a catechist training school in 1963 by the Rt. Rev. Marius Okoh decentralized teaching in the church. It enabled the teaching of the Bible to be done on a wider scale. All the catechists were trained to study and teach the Bible so Bible teaching was done in almost every congregation, not only by the prophetess to a privileged few.

The introduction of adult Sunday school teaching and the publication of Sunday school manuals by the church have brought a big wave of interest in the teaching of the Word of God. Members of the church have been equipped to study and teach the Bible. The teaching ministry in the church has, accordingly, been shifted from being leadership-centered to membership-participation.

The scope of teaching has also been enlarged. Contents of the Sunday School Manual (Vol. 1, January—July, 2002) for instance, include: Origin of man; God's Perfect Purpose for Man; Sin: Man's Greatest Problem; A Redeemer Needed; A Redeemer Promised; Redemption Fulfilled; Waiting for God's Promise; Leading People to Christ; and many others.[425] Members of the church, as a result, study a wide range of topics on any given Sunday. Each lesson begins with a topic, a main text that will be exegeted, a memory verse, supporting texts, and an outline.

The members are urged to study the manual before they go to church. "Those who are not able to read are grouped into special classes with a teacher who reads and interprets for them. The members devote their time to help the less literate ones outside the school period to make sure they understand the contents."[426] Tuesday evenings are also used to teach the Bible. The pastor may choose to give further explanation to the topic of the previous Sunday or introduce a new one.

The teaching of the Bible as a church growth tool is unique, because a structured system of studying the Bible is rare in African Independent Churches. Secondly, a greater number of the members of Christ Holy Church who were formerly members of some western mission-founded churches claim that the teaching of the Bible was not taken seriously in their former churches. The other members who were either born in the church or were not Christians prior to becoming members are equally fascinated by the way the Bible is taught in the church. They feel proud to invite their friends to worship with them on Sundays. Most of the invited guests, having seen the difference, most often remain in the church. No wonder when members of the church were asked to state some reasons for their continued membership in the church the three most recurring reasons, in their order of priorities, were: "I am growing in the Lord," "I like the teaching programs," and "I am healed whenever sick."

Minor Factors of Growth
The Role of Individuals

Apart from the major factors of growth there are some other factors that contribute to the growth of the church, though not on as large a scale as those previously mentioned. First, the role of individuals in the spread of the church will be discussed. How the church fared during the civil war will also be highlighted. Lastly, a discussion on the qualitative nature of the growth will end this chapter.

The testimonies of individuals who claim to have experienced healing or some kind of miracles in their lives are one of the factors influencing the growth of the church. The comparison of their former state of health to their present state of health convinces others that the church is an organization worth belonging to.

Many pastors of the church have untold stories of planting or initiating the planting of churches before the leaders of the church were notified. Some planted the congregations amidst threats of being hacked to death. Rev. John Ekweoba narrates a typical example of his experience in the Niger State of Nigeria:

> At Katangura in Niger State, the chairman of the Local Government gave me three plots of land. The next day I went there to clear the bush, but the emir of that locality came with some young men to attack me. When I saw them coming I knelt and prayed, "Lord, please have mercy on me." Their anger abated when they saw me praying. After telling them how I possessed the land they went away to the Local Government chairman. Later they asked me to pay some extra money so as to own the land again.[427]

Church Growth During the Biafran War (1967-1970)

The three-year Biafran civil war in Nigeria had a great effect on the growth of Christ Holy Church since the war was fought in Igboland, the heartland of the Church. The relocation of the headquarters of the Church from Onitsha to Arondizuogu and the refugee status of most of the members hampered the growth of the Church. The Church had to suspend plans to plant congregations in areas beyond Igboland. The civil war, ironically, promoted the growth of Churches in Igboland. Peter DomNwachukwu quotes Hilary Achunike addressing some of the effects of the civil war, states how some African Independent Churches were perceived as having solutions to the plight of the refugees:

> Before the civil war the established churches had attained stability, but they began to lose grip of their members who moved from one town to another due to the pressures of the war. There were many refugees in this war period. Many people went into hiding in the thickets. Thus hardship, social tensions, dreadful sicknesses like kwashiorkor, refugee lifestyle, and psychological problems to which the mainline churches could not offer solutions, diverted the response of many Igbo towards the Aladura churches and prayer houses which were springing up at an alarming rate at this time; and promised to offer solutions to some of the problems mentioned above.[428]

Some of the fleeing members of Christ Holy Church International regrouped at their refugee centers and continued their practice of worshipping twice daily. Other refugees went to them with their spiritual and emotional needs. Making use of their spiritual gifts and faith in God, they were able to offer solutions to some of the spiritual needs of the other refugees. As a result, seventy-five new congregations were planted at their places of refuge. Two of these congregations are Ihembosi in Anambra State and Oguta in Imo State.

News about the new congregations which were without pastors and the plight of some members who bore the brunt of the war prompted the leadership of the church to appoint a three-man coordinating team—Marius Okoh, Enoch Okonkwo, and David O. U. Nwaizuzu—to provide supervisory leadership, as much as they were able, to the self-appointed leaders of the refugee congregations. During the civil war the leadership of the church divided eastern Nigeria into Biafra One (the present Anambra State) and Biafra Two (the present Imo and Abia States). Enoch Okonkwo and David O. U. Nwaizuzu were given the task of meeting the spiritual and emotional needs of the members of the church in Biafra One. Daniel Okoh states the role of Marius Okoh during the civil war:

> As a courageous and gallant soldier of the cross, Rev. Marius Okoh was not discouraged during the Nigerian civil war. For those three years he defied the sound of bullets and

bombs and continued to travel to different locations where members and ministers were staying in order to motivate them, to give hope to the hopeless and comfort to the aging in the name of Jesus Christ. Even at this time he led ministers of God to open more stations. Many attempts were made on his life by soldiers who were fighting on both sides, but God Almighty delivered him from their hands.[429]

Despite the addition of new congregations, church-planting activities in some areas were inhibited by the intensity of the war. Some of the properties of the church were destroyed while soldiers of both sides occupied some of the worship centers of the church. The three-man supervisory team of Marius, Okonkwo, and Nwaizuzu nevertheless managed to secure the gains of the church during this traumatic time. Efforts to plant congregations did not end with the war; rather, leaders of the church, intensified their church-planting efforts to plant more churches in northern, midwestern and western Nigeria. This was done despite the negative feelings for Igbos by non-Igbos.

Paradigms of Qualitative Growth in the Church

Unity

Unity: An Appreciative Background

The factors of growth stated above are clear indications that members of Christ Holy Church International have been growing steadily for the past fifty-five years in quality and in large numbers. One feature of qualitative growth which is evident in the church is the demonstration of unity in the church. This is antithetical to the schismatic nature of most African Independent Churches. In fact their history is replete with multiple schisms which happen as rapidly as the popping of popcorn in a microwave. The following historical account of the Zionists and Apostolic churches in South Africa is typical of schisms in African Independent Churches:

> The seeds of division did not take long to germinate. One of the Zulu Zion leaders, Daniel Nkonyane, had seceded from the AFM [Apostolic FaithMission], possibly as early as 1910, forming the Christian Catholic Apostolic Holy Spirit Church in Zion. . . . In 1917, Elias Mahlangu . . . founded the Zion Apostolic Church of South Africa. From Mahlangu's church, Edward Motaung . . . seceded in 1920 to form the Zion Apostolic Faith Mission (ZAFM). . . . Engenas Lekganyane's Zion Christian Church (ZCC) seceded from ZAFM in 1925. . . .[430]

Reasons leading to schisms in African Independent Churches are many. These include personality clashes (as in the case between Tunolase and Abiodun)[431] and issues regarding succession of deceased leaders (as between the Shembe brothers—Londa and Amos—in the AmaNazaretha Church).[432] Major A. B. Lawrence, who led one of the early schisms of the Cherubim and Seraphim Society (C&S), claimed that "he had been ordered by God to quit the C&S."[433]

The results of some of the schisms leave a sour taste in the mouths of many. Alan Anderson describes the results of the schism after the death of Johannes Galilee Shembe, second leader of the AmaNazaretha Church thus: "On Galilee's death in 1976, a fierce and acrimonious schism resulted, with court cases, violent clashes, and even killings between the two factions."[434]

The example of secessions cited above is not peculiar to South African Churches. Nigeria, the locus of our study, has had its fair share of divisions. Among African Independent Churches in Nigeria, schisms in the history of the Cherubim and Seraphim Society are perhaps the most dramatic. Members of the society lived in peace for barely four years after its establishment. There were six secessions from 1929 to 1938.[435] There have been numerous schisms since then. Commenting on the schisms in the movement, Ayegboyin and Ishola have observed that:

> Today, there are hundreds of splinter groups scattered all over the country, each claiming to be the headquarters of the Cherubim and Seraphim Society of Nigeria. There is probably no sect in Christendom that has suffered so much splintering as this movement. . . . The schisms that rended the church in its formative years have continued. Each succeeding year gives birth to multiple splinter groups within the movement.[436]

The Cherubim and Seraphim Society is not the only African Independent Church in Nigeria that has experienced constant schisms and legal battles. The Celestial Church of Christ,[437] the Christ Apostolic Church,[438] Christ Army Church,[439] and many others have also suffered from dissent. S. Onuvughakpo describes the ease with which Nigerian Christians secede from one denomination to establish their own:

> To found one's own branch and headquarters is as simple as winking an eye. The procedure is first to procure for yourself the power of vision and prophecy. . . . The next step is to approach an apostle or bishop to receive the order of

apostleship. As you settle down in a neighboring or far-away town, your parlor becomes the cathedral church and your room the headquarters.... Your house becomes consulting chamber for all sorts of people: boys and girls anxious about love, students wishing to pass their examinations, clerks and executive officers seeking promotion . . . and the poor and destitute seeking wealth.[440]

Onuvughakpo's description seems sarcastic, yet it cannot be disputed when one considers the innumerable schisms in the history of Nigerian African Independent Churches.

Unity: An Appreciative Reality

The essence of the unity of members of Christ Holy Church which epitomizes their qualitative growth must be seen in the context of the spate of secessions among African Independent Churches in Africa and particularly in Nigeria.

Secondly, there are certain tendencies in the church that could have been used as stimuli for secession—tendencies like the use of prophecies to appoint and retire leaders of the church as was the case of the appointment of Marius Okoh as the head of the church, the retirement of Samuel Ejiofor at the young and vibrant age of forty-two, and Gabriel Chiemeka stepping down for Daniel Okoh to become the head of the church. Any of these could have been good reasons for secession in the church. Considering Onovughakpo's observations, the ability and gift of many pastors of Christ Holy Church to heal and perform miracles could have been other reasons for secessions in Christ Holy Church International, but there has not been any schismatic move in the church for the past fifty-five years. Ekueme's case is not regarded as secession because it did not result in founding a rival church. Members of Christ Holy Church International regard Ekueme's action as that of an angry member who left the church to join another.

Leaders and members of Christ Holy Church International give many reasons for the unity and peace in the church. According to Eugene Ogbonna, the fear of God is the most treasured characteristic of the church. There is, therefore, reverence for what the Bible says and what the Holy Spirit reveals to them through visions, prophecy, and dreams. "Thus saith the Lord" is respected in this church.[441] To leaders and elders of Okigwe Superintendency, honesty and accountability of the leaders of the church are the main preservative factors of unity in the church. "Money is used for the very purpose for which funds are raised. Our leaders do not misappropriate funds; they are eager to hear the word of God before doing things."[442] In Lagos, the Very Rev. Daniel Dike, who acknowledged the Holy Spirit as the leader of the church, gave instances of the exposure of divisive inclinations and imaginations through prophetic utterances. The prophecies, in some instances, were uttered in congregations other than the worship places of such divisive miscreants.[443] To Rev. Pastor Obiemeka, "Mama did not make money off the church; she laid down the principle of service rather than making profit."[444]

Rev. Pastor Emmanuel Alamanjo traces the unity of the church to contentment. "Ministers are content with whatever they have. What brings about a breakaway are discontentment and pride—when people want to lead and not to be led. There is no pride in Christ Holy Church. People are contented."[445] To Rev. Eusebius Iloabuchi, the quality of the leadership training and the leaders' own style of leadership have prevented any division in the church. "Marius made sure that no one was frustrated. He was not an oppressive leader. He did not worry or interfere in the work of any pastor. He allowed God to work. Our leaders were trained very well; it is very difficult to pick a quarrel with them."[446]

These claims and assertions do not imply that there has been perfect peace in Christ Holy Church. As a human institution, disagreements on policies and some mischievous acts cannot be ruled out entirely; that is why a clause in the church's constitution states that: "In cases of misconduct unbecoming a member or Minister of Christ Holy Church International, the senior members of the Central Executive Council with the general superintendent as the chairman, reserves the right to suspend, demote, or terminate the appointment of an offender."[447] The laudable fact about the church is that for the past fifty-five years, members have settled their differences without reference to the Courts of law or resulting in any act of schism.

Stewardship

The deep understanding of financial stewardship is another factor indicative of the qualitative growth of the church. A large percentage of the membership comes from the lower income group. A great number of them do petty trading at the numerous markets in Nigeria. Some of them are civil servants working in government institutions. Very few of them own businesses or are professionals in their respective fields. There are others who are unemployed, looking for jobs. Having enough money to implement all their projected programs is one of the difficulties leaders of the church encounter. Their low income, notwithstanding, members of Christ Holy Church International consider themselves as stewards of their finances and, as a result, make sure they give back whatever they have to God. This concept of stewardship is exhibited in three areas: gifts to the church as an institution, gifts to the pastors and other workers of the church, and help for other members of the church.

Members do not consider the church an institution that is separated from their daily life. They perceive the church as their own property—a property that needs to be sustained not by an outsider but by their own sweat. This explains the reasons behind many of the church's financial policies—the policy of not securing loans from individuals or institutions; the policy of not worshipping in rented facilities; the policy of bearing all the costs of embalmment, burial, and funeral should a pastor die; and the policy of providing free accommodation and payment of utility bills for pastors.

Besides these official policies of care members give to their pastors already discussed is another evidence of the qualitative growth in the church.

When a hundred members were asked to state the activities in the church that they like best, showing love towards one another was the only non-ministerial activity that was mentioned. Carrying one another's burden in the church is a key part of their life. This is particularly shown in times of trouble or during activities marking the stages of life—birth, naming of a child, puberty, marriage, and death. Those who fall into the hands of armed robbers are given money to begin life afresh. Offerings are taken every Tuesday to help widows. An offering is taken every Friday in all the congregations to meet the needs of the poor and needy in the stations. When a person is in need, the church, as a body, offers help while individual members, too, offer whatever help they can afford. For instance, some congregations raise periodic funds for members who lose their jobs. Fasting in proxy for those in need or the sick is also a common phenomenon in the church.

Tithing

One unique practice in Christ Holy Church that epitomizes their qualitative growth is the way tithing is handled. Unlike many African Independent Churches and even some western mission-founded churches where records of tithe paying are kept on membership cards, Christ Holy Church International does not keep records of individual tithing. Members are expected to drop in their tithe in an offering box that is placed at each worship center for seven days a week. Neither tithing envelopes nor cards are provided. In fact there is nothing to determine who paid what. Asked about the reason for this policy, Rev. Nicholas Udemba responded:

> Faithfulness is the core of tithing. Keeping individual records of what one has tithed does not mean the person has been faithful. Being faithful is a matter between the one who is tithing and God. What is important in this church is to teach our members to be faithful in their tithing. We do not use record keeping of individual tithing to intimidate our members to be faithful as some churches in Nigeria do."[448]

During Sunday morning and evening services pastors take some time to explain the meaning of tithing to the congregations. Prayers for those who have given their tithes during the week are made during Sunday services; those who for some reasons could not pay are encouraged to do so.

The generosity of members of Christ Holy Church International is akin to oldtime Christianity in Nigeria as observed by Peter DomNwachukwu, a Baptist theologian and pastor:"Most of the early Igbo seekers of Christianity paid their church and school teachers out of their meager agricultural incomes. They did this proudly."[449] The situation has changed, however: "Unfortunately the tide has changed. Today most people desire what the church will do for them, and not what they will do for the church. It is difficult to offer an adequate explanation for this change of attitude, but the civil war is a factor."[450] The reason members of Christ Holy Church International, a predominantly Igbo church, give money willingly to the church while other Igbo Christians, living in the same context, are stingy towards the church indicates the qualitative growth of the former.

Conclusion

The growth of the church, as noted in this chapter, is not determined by one factor. It is a congregational effort based on their absolute dependence on God, their loyalty to the Lordship of Jesus Christ, and their faith in the ministries and gifts of the Holy Spirit. Members of Christ Holy Church International do not limit the power and love of the Triune God with any human rationalization or philosophies. To them, the God of the Bible, particularly of the apostles, is as powerful, faithful, and loving as they read in the Bible. The mutual respect and honor between pastors and members, and the deep love and concern for one another are like a spiritual fragrance that draws non-Christians to their fellowship.

PART THREE

Theology and Challenges

CHAPTER SEVEN

Theology and Theological Formulation in Christ Holy Church International

The Statement of Faith

The Statement of Faith of Christ Holy Church International expresses the main tenets of faith as found in most evangelical denominations. There are other segments of the statement that reflect their peculiar belief system. This chapter will focus on the belief system, its formulation, and the ministerial aspect of the beliefs of Christ Holy Church. We will look at the development of theology and the attempts that have been made to contextualize theology to suit the thinking of Nigerian Christians. In doing so, a step by step clarification of some aspects of the statement will be mentioned.

The Triune God

Faith in the Triune God is the first article of the statement. The unity and eternal co-equal existence of the Triune God is affirmed. Belief in the Trinitarian doctrine is said to be the foundation of Christ Holy Church International, as Enoch Okonkwo claims: "Our church at our time was built on Almighty God through his Son Jesus Christ and the Holy Spirit as the totality of our abiding faith and deeds. Let the present generation continue likewise, and they shall not be disappointed."[451] God the Father is described as "One who is all-powerful, perfect in love, judgment, grace, and mercy." The mention of the omnipotence of God in the statement is very significant. To a church that believes in miracles, claims to have seen miracles, and therefore expects miracles, the mention of the omnipotence of God in the Statement of Faith is not just a reiteration of what they have read about in the Bible or just a statement on paper. The omnipotence of God, to them, is an experiential phenomenon, hence its mention in the Statement of Faith.

The Bible

All 66 books of the Bible are believed to be divinely inspired and, thus, considered as the "Word of God fit to be the final authority in all matters of doctrines and practices." The emphasis on the Word of God is very prominent in the church. Rev. Enoch Okonkwo recalls the interplay between the Bible and the formulation of the practices of the church during his leadership:

> As a leader of the church my philosophy was that every worker should pursue spiritual wealth from God, abide by the practices of the church which were basically the Word of God as commanded unto us from Genesis to Revelation. . . . All the doctrines of Christ Holy Church are biblical. To abide by the doctrine means to keep the laws of God. . . . There is no other doctrine except that which is in the Bible. So you can understand what we mean when we say doctrines of Christ Holy Church. [452]

The practices in the church, according to Rev. Okonkwo, were directly inferred from the Bible because of the church's belief in the divine inspiration of the Bible. The formulations of the theological positions of the church are, as a result, said to be biblical. Perhaps that explains why the belief in dreams, visions, and prophetic utterances (which we will discuss later) are not played down in the church.

Belief in Salvation

The statement mentions the belief in the "total depravity of humanity as a result of original sin." They thus agree with the reformers that nothing good comes from human beings. To them, the salvation of humanity is by "grace through faith in the Lordship and the finished work of Jesus Christ." Salvation, to members of Christ Holy Church International, does not depend on any meritorious work on the part of the sinner. It rather depends on the once-and-for-all work of Jesus Christ which is vicarious in nature.

As a result of this belief the church invites non-Christians to Jesus Christ, without subjecting them to any extraordinary ritual apart from asking them to see themselves as sinners who deserve to perish but for the vicarious death of Jesus Christ. It is in this regard that when Rev. Okonkwo was asked to admonish international evangelists of the church he states: "Yes, they should hold firm the Word of God. The power in the

Word of God will win souls for them."[453] The humility of the church's leaders should be seen in the context of this belief in the total depravity of humanity.

Christology

The Christological belief of the church is encompassing. The statement mentions belief in the deity, incarnation, humanity, vicarious death, sinlessness, burial, bodily resurrection, the authority and high priestly functions of Jesus Christ. Christology is, thus, very central in the belief system of the church. Unlike many conservative African Independent Churches where there is a conflict of loyalty between their founders and Jesus Christ, the centrality of Jesus Christ in Christ Holy Church International can be attributed to Agnes Okoh's low-key demeanor in the church and her emphasis on Christology.

Belief in the Holy Spirit

The Holy Spirit is believed to be the "teacher and counselor, who regenerates us, enables us, empowers us, and equips us for effective ministry and holy living." When one considers how Agnes Okoh, an illiterate who was surrounded by people who were semi-illiterates with exception of a few, without any theological training, was able to nurture their followers and formulate their theological beliefs, one can not fault them for believing in the various ministries of the Holy Spirit.

Under the enablement and empowerment ministries of the Holy Spirit, mention needs to be made of the belief and uses of spiritual gifts in the church. The gifts of the Spirit are recognized in the church. The church, as a policy, gives recognition to the nine gifts mentioned in 1 Corinthians 12:8-10, though some members claim they have gifts that are not among the nine. Members are, nonetheless, given the opportunity to exercise their gifts whether that gift is among the nine or not. The three most prevalent gifts in the church are healing/miracles, faith, and prophecy. Much has already been discussed about the role of healing/miracles in the church so we will now turn our attention to faith, prophecy, dreams, and visions.

The Gift of Faith

It is common knowledge that without faith no one can become a Christian. For the purpose of distinguishing this common faith that can be found in every Christian and the gift of faith that is peculiar to some Christians, I will call the former object faith—that is, faith that is focused on or has a person as an object. The latter I will call functional faith—that is, faith that enables one to do or imagine the unthinkable or faith that expects some extraordinary results. Calling the latter functional faith does not imply the former does not yield results; those who have the gift of faith exercise it expectantly. The gift of faith, as expressed by members of Christ Holy Church International, leans more towards the latter than the former.

The gift of faith is linked to the performance of miracles and healing. Those with that kind of gift exercise it in anticipation of seeing instant or extraordinary results. It is in recognition of this gift that Rev. Nicholas Udemba is, affectionately called *Ogbu-agu* which literally means "killer of lion." He is known among the superintendents of the church to have accepted most challenges the church has faced, believing that there is no problem that the Lord cannot solve. He is, as a result, said to have ultimately succeeded in dealing with difficult tasks and people. "For 35 years I have never taken any medicine, but I am healthy. I will not take any medicine till I die."[454] This claim by Rev. Emmanuel Alamanjo seems fanatical and unreasonable, all things being equal, but such statements exemplify the beliefs and expectations of one with the gift of faith—a gift that is very common in the church.

Another example of the gift of faith in Christ Holy Church International is the intentional disregard of antenatal care by pregnant women in the church. Since the establishment of the first maternity home in the church in 1963, the majority of women in the church claim never to have taken any antenatal and postnatal medications.

> Women of Christ Holy Church do not go to hospital when they are pregnant; they do not take any medicine. This is because they have faith in God. In case of birth complications the Lord God Almighty does the miraculous. They do not go to hospitals; once the fellow has faith God does everything.[455]

The patronage of the maternity homes is not mandatory for the women of the church according to Antonia Chukwura, self-described a professional midwife who worked in many hospitals before her appointment by the church. She affirms: "There is nothing wrong with going to hospitals."[456] In spite of this belief of the church, even women who live in the cities, apart from not taking drugs during pregnancy, seek maternity services when in labor from the wives of their pastors rather than going to western-style hospitals and clinics.

The Gift of Prophecy

Another gift of the Spirit that is very common among members of Christ Holy Church International is that of prophecy. Prophetic utterances are not only the foretelling of coming events; they are also forth telling. This is a phenomenon that is common in many African Independent Churches, hence their designations as "prophetic movements." Nathaniel Ndiokwere describes the nature of prophecy in the African Independent Churches.

> Prophecy may range from serious warnings and threats against sinful life, to calls to repentance and condemnations of injustice in government circles and in society as a whole. Prophecy includes forecast of wars, famine, outbreak of plagues, and the imminent fall of wicked heads of governments and local leaders. . . . In the independent churches, divine revelation is communicated to prophets in diverse ways, which include visions, auditions, and dreams. Trance—the state of profound abstraction or absorption in the beyond—is regarded as the highest pitch of the prophetic state in which supernormal experiences are undergone. Angels also are regarded as playing an important role in the communication of divine revelation.[457]

Falling into trances and making ecstatic utterances are not prophetic concomitants in Christ Holy Church International. Unlike some African Independent Church members who go to the extent of venerating angels,[458] members of Christ Holy Church International simply regard angels as ministering spirits of God. They neither look to them to mediate prophecies or visions nor accord them any special reverence. Prophecy in the church is usually said in a normal composure, without any drama or hysteria, during a period in the service when they are asked to prophesy in an orderly form.

Dreams and Visions

Dreams are another related phenomenon connected to prophetic utterances. Morton Kesley defines a dream as "a succession of images present in the mind during sleep. . . . From time to time in this period anything from a single picture to an elaborate story may be vividly perceived, which is in no sense a direct perception of the outer physical world."[459] A vision, which Kesley perceives as a third form of dream activity, is defined as:

> The spontaneous image...that appears to a person in the borderland of wake-fulness when a person is not sure whether he or she is awake or asleep. These dreams and visions—they are termed hypnagogic or hypnopompic, depending on whether the dreamer is falling asleep or waking up—are usu-

ally flash pictures focused on a single impression, but in some cases whole scenes, even fairly long stories may appear. At times these images coming on the edge of sleep can seem so tangible that dreamers really do not know whether they are awake or asleep, whether the images belong to the outside world or to the figures of the dream.[460]

The above definition of dreams makes visions integral parts of dreams. The thinnest line is whether the person is fully asleep or fully awake. The definitions, however, have been rightly stated by Kesley as the most common ones. Dreams and visions, as used in this work, go beyond their common definitions; they fit into the psyche of the early church—what is read in the New Testament—and what gradually became the accepted norm in Christianity till the period of Enlightenment. Kesley again puts dreams and visions into the perspective that they are meant in this work:

In the past these spontaneous images and thoughts, distinct from outer physical reality, have been valued as a sign of contact with religious reality. Whether the image was presented in sleep or in wakefulness, whether breaking in unexpectedly or sought and cultivated, it was understood to come from a different world, and nearly all religious groups everywhere have considered that the ability to observe and interpret these images was a religious gift. This was essentially the common Christian tradition from biblical times, through the church fathers, and up into the seventeenth century; in isolated instances it has continued to the present time. In this tradition dreams were significant because they revealed something beyond the human experience that gave purpose and meaning, or warning where spiritual disaster impended.[461]

The perception of dreams and visions among most African Independent Churches, including Christ Holy Church International, fits what Kesley identifies as the perception in "isolated instances [which] has continued to the present time." In fact many African Christians, particularly those of the African Independent Churches, still give recognition to the religious significance and purpose of dreams and visions. It is in this regard that some members of Christ Holy Church International are considered as having the gift of seeing visions even though seeing visions is not listed among the gifts of the Spirit. Such people are thus called "visioners" in the church.

The importance of dreams and visions to members of Christ Holy Church International is seen in the fact that worship leaders and pastors are mandated by the Order of Service to ask members of the congregation, whenever they meet to worship, if anyone has seen visions—the only exception is Sunday mornings. As regards dreams, the worship leaders and pastors are to ask members to narrate their dreams during morning worship services.[462] The belief that the call to pastoral ministry can be mediated through dreams is another fact underlying the importance of dreams in Christ Holy Church International. Speaking on behalf of a group of pastors who were asked to state why the church pays so much attention to dreams and visions, Rev. Aaron Chukwunyelum Eziuzor, the superintendent minister of Owerri Superintendency, stated, "Dreams are revelations of God to his people at night whereby he instructs them what to do and what not to do. God directs us through dreams."[463] The perception of dreams and visions in Christ Holy Church International is, as a result, no different from that of Biblical times, already asserted by Morton Kesley.

Holy Living

Members of Christ Holy Church International do not consider the performance of rituals, mortifications, and self-abnegations as evidences of holy living. They do pray, fast, and read the Bible, but all these are considered results of holy living, not *sine qua non* exercises of holy living. At Owerri when some pastors were asked to articulate their concept of holiness, particularly in light of fasting and prayer, Rev. Ezuizor said: "Fasting does not make one holy, though the church fasts. One can fast and sin at the same time. One who fears the Lord, obeys the Word of God, and makes efforts to abstain from unrighteousness, the one who bears the fruit of the Spirit is the one who is holy."[464]

One of the roles of the Holy Spirit, according to them, is to enable Christians to live holy lifestyles. The Holy Spirit enables those who are obedient to the laws of God, those who depend on his directions and act accordingly to live holy lives.

Part of the Statement of Faith mentions *sanctification of all believers in Jesus Christ* and the need *to live like Christ*. Holy living and Christlike lifestyles are, therefore, synonymously linked together in the Church's concept of Christian life. One can, therefore, sense a Trinitarian formulation regarding Christian lifestyle in Christ Holy Church International—the Holy Spirit enabling Christians to obey the laws of God so as to live like Christ.

Signs and Wonders

The church believes that "the Holy Spirit baptizes believers with signs and wonders following." The signs and wonders can take any form;

any thing that overwhelms the comprehension of human beings is their concept. It is not limited to glossolalic experiences only. Signs and wonders are not perceived as prerequisite to conversion. "On Friday evenings we call upon the Lord to come down with his Spirit as the disciples did in the Acts of the Apostles. The Spirit of God comes down in the seeing of visions, prophecies, speaking in tongues, interpretation of tongues, and many other miracles."[465] The giving of signs and wonders, according to the church, is the sole prerogative of the Holy Spirit but, the Holy Spirit gives them to those who ask expectantly. Signs and wonders, according to the church, are different from miraculous healing since another aspect of the statement expresses belief in healing and miracles.

Baptism

Adult Baptism by Immersion

"We believe in the sacrament of baptism by immersion in the name of the Father, Son, and the Holy Spirit." Persons who are twelve years and above are the ones baptized in the church. Expressing the reason for adult baptism by immersion, the Very Rev. Nathan Okeke Umeh, the superintendent minister of Jos Superintendency, states: "Jesus Christ was baptized at a reasonable age, in a river, and by immersion. This is the belief of the church. The person must open his mouth and make a confession of faith before being immersed in the river."[466] This concurs with an article on baptism by the Rt. Rev. Marius Okoh who defines baptism as, "To immerse or dip" and states its symbolism to mean publicly "burying the old and sinful nature in the water in the name of the Father, the Son, and the Holy Ghost; and rising again in the newness of life unto the glory of the Father; accepting ONLY Jesus Christ (and none other) as the Saviour."[467] He further explains why the church does not baptize infants:

> The scriptures made it clear to understand that teaching Christ, believing in him, and repentance from sin precede baptism. But a baby cannot be taught Christ: for it has no sense of comprehension and as it cannot comprehend the teaching of Christ, it can neither believe in him nor repent from a sin it knows not. The baby therefore cannot be baptized. Likewise, any child below the age of accountability needs no baptism; rather they are being dedicated. Luke 2:22. Logically, the Bible rules out infant baptism. [468]

He debunks the practice of bringing godparents during baptism: "Thirdly we have learned from these portions [of scripture] that neither Jesus nor the Ethiopian eunuch was asked to bring sureties or godparents before having the baptism. . . . Therefore, it would be counted a sordid heresy and unruly for anyone to appear and stand a surety for another in the question of belief or confession when one is to be baptized."[469]

Though the church believes in adult baptism, not every adult is baptized since Marius makes a distinction between converts and baptismal candidates. He states that, "only converts and NOT candidates should be baptized."[470] Those who are qualified to be baptized are those who have repented from their sins and made a public proclamation of their belief in the lordship of Jesus Christ. Pre-baptism lessons are, therefore, taught before baptism takes place.

Rt. Rev. Marius Okoh's illustration of the importance of immersion is interesting and worth noting:

> When Achilles was young, the mother thought of making the body of her son invulnerable in order to fortify him from wounds of enemies; maybe, he was the only son. One day she took the child to the Styx (one of the rivers of Hades) and dipped him therein; holding tight the heal [heel] whereon the mother held him. The child grew up as a hero and could not be wounded on the body by any human weapon. Achilles felt that he was completely invulnerable until one day when he was mortally wounded during an encounter with Paris, the son of the King of Troy. Therefore, till today, the vulnerable heel of Achilles remains a parable or metaphorical expression. This Greek hero would have lived longer if no part of his body was left undipped in the styx. So is any type of baptism beside immersion.[471]

The teaching on the need and importance of baptism by immersion by the Rt. Rev. Marius Okoh with profuse quotation from the Bible and an illustration of Greek mythology have sunk deep into the minds of members of Christ Holy Church International. As a result, the church is thoroughly Anabaptist; she rebaptizes anyone who has not been baptized by immersion prior to becoming a member of the church. The person's prior experience, maturity, and position in Christianity are counted as nothing in this regard.

Baptismal Services

Baptismal services of the church are held along the banks of rivers. It is a joyous occasion characterized with music provided by the members at the riverside. Those to be baptized change their clothing and wait in a line, with the male going ahead of the female. They walk into the river and stand knee-deep before the officiating minister. In the river the minister asks the following questions: "Do you believe in Jesus Christ? Do you believe that Jesus is your Savior? Do you reject Satan and his works?" After the one to be baptized has answered in the affirmative to all the questions, then the minister asks the person, "What is your name?" On mentioning the name, the minister repeats the name and says, "Because of your confession of faith I baptize you in the name of the Father, Son and Holy Spirit." Then the person will be immersed in the river. Witnesses of the baptism ceremony either pray for those baptized at the riverside, asking God to baptize them with the Holy Spirit, or say the prayer with them at the worship center the same day depending on prevailing circumstances at the riverside.

Renouncing the Work of Satan

The practice of renouncing Satan and his evil works by people who are to be baptized has some religious significance. Firstly, it is an indication of the church's belief in the reality of Satan and his mischievous activities as stated by Jesus Christ in John 10:10, which is also the thematic message of Prophetess Agnes Okoh. Secondly, it is meant to nullify some pre-Christian covert experiences and covenants with some deities by those to be baptized.

The activities of medicine men, witches, wizards, and some malevolent deities, already discussed in this work, make some people seek protection from many mishaps. The protection is achieved through many means. John Mbiti touches on some means of acquiring protections in the traditional African religion:

> Another important duty of medicine men is to take preventive measures. We have just pointed out that people experience suffering as being caused by mystical forces applied or used against them by their enemies or by those who hate them. This is often magic, witchcraft, sorcery, "evil-eye," or bad words. The medicine men must therefore supply people with counter measures. These are generally in form of charms, performing rituals at the homes or fields of those in need, or applying medicines that are swallowed or rubbed into the body.[472]

In the process of giving out such preventive measures the medicine men usually act as liaisons between the gods and the seekers. Clients are made to believe in the power and trustworthiness of the deity behind the medicine. For a surety of sustainable protection by the deity, the seekers are usually convinced to enter into a blood covenant with the deity. The place of the body where an incision will be made to extract the blood for the covenant is, more often than not, the place where medicines are applied. The application of the medicine to the body, consequently, serves as the conclusion of the blood covenant. The scars always remind the person of the covenant.

Seekers of sustainable protection are at times asked to make a verbal pledge of allegiance to the deity. The pledge of allegiance usually ends with a self-pronounced curse in case of showing the slightest sign of disloyalty. The charms and other protective elements one receives from traditional priest or medicine man, on the periphery, look like common protective elements. They are actually, however, means of establishing a bond of allegiance between the seeker and the shrine. Many African societies believe that one can even contract such acts of bondage on behalf of one's children and children's children; its effects, it is believed, can be applicable to generations yet unborn.

Another reason for the public renouncement of Satan and his works by those who are to be baptized by Christ Holy Church International is the spate of cultism in Nigeria. Cultic activities on Nigerian campuses of higher learning have become rampant since the 1970s. Barnabas Otoibhi quotes newspaper reports about the spread of cultic associations:

> According to the newspaper report, these data given above are contained in security reports made available to authorities of the nation's universities at a meeting held with intelligence agencies in Abuja, the federal capitalof Nigeria on July 9, 1997....A breakdown of the type of institutions said to be cult-prone, had 27 universities, 19 polytechnics/colleges of technology, and 16 colleges of education/agriculture. This list only excludes schools in the far north. But it includes those from other parts of Nigeria.[473]

According to Otoibhi, students are either lured or coerced to become members of the cultic groups. The craving for power, dominion, protection, and association with elitist groups on campuses are some of the basic baits used to lure members into the cults. Intimidation comes into play when prospective candidates refuse to go through the process of initiation. "Former cultists were quoted as confessing that they had the problem of frustration, intimidation, oppression, insecurity, hunger, inferiority complex, and family lineage which informed their decision for involvement with cults."[474]

The cultists constitute themselves into secret and sinister pressure groups on Nigerian campuses. Their activities include "raping, killing, robbery, arson, and other heinous activities." These activities are heightened when two rival cults engage each other on a campus. Their activities disrupt academic activities and instill fear in students, faculty, and staff alike.[475]

Otoibhi identifies three stages in the process of initiation. The first stage is that of observation, where the general behavior of the prospective member comes under strict scrutiny by members. After this stage comes what is termed as "inter-talk," a by-word for "intellectual soundness interview." This includes an interview and physical fitness drilling in a military style. So intense is the military drill that the effects on some weakling applicants are disastrous; some even die.

The final stage, which is the initiation proper, culminates with the initiatee being made to kneel behind a coffin with a human skull, bones, axe, or sword displayed on top of it. The one to be initiated is given a short but vivid lecture on the consequences of being a member—expulsion from school, losing one's eye, hand, leg, or even one's life. The candidate is then given some time to decide whether to become a member or not.[476]

> If any one's decision is in the affirmative, then curses would be rained on them, telling them that it would not be easy but interesting. They would then be told to recite the creed of the association. . . . After the recitation comes the blood oath. At this point, the candidates will be compelled to close their eyes while the blood oath lasts: with a sharp razor, a mark would be made on the hand of each candidate in order to extract blood from him; the blood from each is smeared on a piece of roasted meat, and every candidate would be given the piece smeared with his fellow brother's or sister's blood to eat. . . . The initiation ceremony is capped with the drinking of some alcoholic beverage, called "brew."[477]

People who go to the extent of professing allegiance to wicked deities in times of need and cap it with self-imprecation and those who willfully comply with initiation rites which are coupled with curses and blood oath of cultic associations become naturally afraid of what will happen to them when they sever ties with the gods and cults in preference to Christianity. This fear is also prevalent with all other people (secret society members and traditional title takers) who might have covenanted with some deities and shrines. Some shudder to think of the probable effects of their covenanted dealings and the results of their disdained allegiance to the gods and secret societies.

Assuring such people of the protection of the Triune God on becoming Christians does not seem enough to them. Christ Holy Church International, as a result, gives such people the opportunity to recant their former beliefs and pledges of allegiance in public. Doing that in a baptismal river, in front of a crowd of witnesses, is believed to be very significant since such recantations are believed to extricate the person from the bondage of former spiritual overlords.

Holy Matrimony

Concept of Marriage

The second sacrament of Christ Holy Church is Holy Matrimony. Belief in marriage as a sacrament is an influence from the Catholic background of Agnes Okoh and many of the leaders of the church. The concept of marriage will be understood when put into an African context. Kwame Gyekye defines an African concept of marriage:

> In Africa . . . marriage is not merely an affair between two individuals who have fallen in love and plan to spend the rest of their lives together. It is a matter in which the lineage groups of both the man and the woman are deeply interested. . . . A marriage might seem to be between two individuals, but in fact the marriage contract is between two families. The man and the woman are both warned straightaway that they are not being married to an individual but to a family.[478]

Marriage, therefore, is a communal affair—a union that binds two families together forever. Africans take it for granted that marriage is a union between a man and a woman. Same sex marriage is unheard of, unimaginable, and considered an abomination in African communities. "Homosexuality is considered taboo and would be outlawed on moral as well as social grounds, because the continuity of the family and, indeed, of the human species would be most seriously affected if homosexuality were practiced."[479]

Monogamy and Polygamy

Two main types of marriage are practiced in Africa—monogamy and what is popularly called polygamy, while in actual fact polygyny is what is meant.[480] Monogamy is marriage between one man and one woman at a time. Polygamy, a form of marriage that allows one man to keep two or several wives contemporaneously, is quite popular among many Africans. The first wife in a polygamous marriage is considered to be the principal wife. All the others are considered extra wives. Many African Independent Churches practice polygamy. In Nigeria, the Celestial Church of Christ,[481] the Church of the Lord (Aladura),[482] Cherubim and Seraphim,[483] and many others see nothing wrong with polygamous marriage.

Polygamy is, in principle, abhorred in the church even though pre-Christian polygamists are accepted into membership. The church denies pre-Christian polygamists any position of authority in the fellowship despite the fact that they enjoy every other privilege that is open to members. Post-Christian polygamy is interpreted in the church as concubinage, a result of concupiscence. Post-Christian polygamists are, consequently, summarily excommunicated from the church. They are accepted back into fellowship only after they have gotten rid of the concubine and confessed the sin.

Customary (Traditional) Marriage

Marriage in Africa, whether monogamy or polygamy, is, first of all, contracted to suit the traditional norms and rites of either the bride or the groom. This is so because of the communal interest in marriage. Elders of the families of the bride and groom follow some traditional rites and requirements to bring the would-be couple together. Such rites are, more often than not, established rules in the traditional religion. For example, concerning traditional Igbo marital rites, Basden mentions a day of feast which is characterized by "copious supplies of gin and palm wine."[484] Some Christians, consequently, do not perceive traditional marriage as something acceptable to God due to the cultural ramifications. Such Christians go a step further by blessing their marriage, after it has been traditionally contracted, in a Christian context. This is popularly called church wedding. Other Christians, nevertheless, consider traditional marriage legitimate and properly contracted; consummation, for that reason, becomes a *de facto* affair.

Church Wedding

Christ Holy Church International has no authority over how parents should give their children in marriage. The church, therefore, accepts traditional marriage at face value, but does not recognize it as a satisfactory marriage because of the traditional religious nuances associated with it and the unwillingness of some family members to make any amends in the rites to suit Christian norms. The church, accordingly, perceives traditional marriage as *in loco parentis*, leading to holy matrimony. In view of the church's position on traditional marriage, the blessing of a marriage that has already been contracted in a traditional way is not considered as holy matrimony in the Statement of Faith. Members are, therefore, required to bless their marriage in the church. Another reason for the church's insistence on the blessing of marriage before being recognized as such is the belief that marriage is a sacrament, an act that must be performed within a Christian worship context.

According to Rev. Emmanuel Aniago, for a marriage to be blessed in Christ Holy Church International, the couple will have to declare their intention of blessing, in writing, to the local pastor. The local pastor will help the couple to forward the declaration of the intention to the superintendent minister through the district pastor, if the applicants are not members of a district congregation. The district pastor will be assigned to investigate the authenticity of the marriage. This is a check against polygamy or wife inheritance. After the district pastor is satisfied that the marriage is in line with Christian norms, he and the couple will sign the church's register in which all marriages that are to be blessed are recorded. The register will be forwarded to the superintendent minister to signify the successful end of the investigative exercise.

A bann is published and read to the congregation for three successive weeks. When the couples are not both members of Christ Holy Church International, an arrangement is made so that the banns will be published in the congregation of the other. The banns will be published in the hometowns of the bride and groom respectively before the day of blessing. An example of the banns in the church's Order of Service is:

> I publish the Banns of Marriage between James Uchendu Okeke of Ogidi in Idemili Local Government and Victoria Akuabia Okonkwo of Enugu-Ukwu in Njikoka Local Government. If any of you know cause or just impediment, why these two persons should not be joined together in holy matrimony, ye are to declare it.[485]

The announcement is made on three successive Sundays. The announcer is required to remind the congregation the number of times the announcement has been made, for example, "This is the first time of asking."[486] The minister then minutes the announcement form and mails it to the superintendent minister, signifying that there is no impediment to blessing the marriage. After this process the groom sets the date, venue of the wedding, and the officiating minister of his choice. Premarital counseling precedes the blessing.

The couple are free to wear any clothing of their choice. The church does not prescribe any paraphernalia associated with western weddings. The only thing that the church requires from the couple is a Bible. Marriage vows designed for use in the Anglican Church are what the church members use with some modifications. The most significant change in the marriage vows is that the church leaves out the ring as part of the vows. Instead of saying, "With this ring, I thee wed," the church substitutes it to read, "With this Bible, I thee wed." When asked for the reason behind the substitution of the ring, Rev. Emmanuel Aniago says: "We believe that the words in the Bible are more abiding than a ring."[487] Wearing rings to signify a marital status is, therefore, optional. The women, nevertheless, love wearing wedding rings while the men scarcely do. Certificates of marriage are signed and given to the married couple after the ceremony.

Divorce

Divorce is said to be very rare in Christ Holy Church International. When a marriage is in crisis the church appoints people to mediate and settle every misunderstanding. In case of obstinacy and in the absence of credible evidence of unfaithfulness, the obstinate one is excommunicated from the church. Members of the church who were interviewed do not remember if any member has ever defied the mediation of the church elders and as a result sought the services of the law courts to dissolve a marriage.

The Lord's Supper

The third sacrament in Christ Holy Church International is the Lord's Supper. Going strictly by the name of the meal, the sacrament is held in the evening. "It is called the Lord's Supper, not the Lord's breakfast or the Lord's lunch."[488] The supper is taken on the last Sunday of every month. Only ordained pastors are qualified to administer the sacrament.

Three days of teaching precede the administration and participation of the Supper. The teaching covers topics like the incarnation, lifestyle of Jesus Christ, sin, the death of Jesus which is seen as a supreme sacrifice, holiness, repentance, and confession of sins. After the three-day pre-communion lectures, members are given the opportunity to "examine themselves" in fulfillment of the biblical injunction in 1 Corinthians 11:26. Confession of sins to the pastors follows the self-examination. There are certain people who are not given the privilege to participate in the prerequisite preparation of self-examination and confession of sins. The church excludes polygamists, extra wives of the polygamists, those who are not baptized, those who have not had their marriage blessed, and those who do not attend all of the three-day teaching leading to the supper. Non-members of the church who attend all the three teaching sessions and have examined themselves are qualified to partake of the supper. Adult children from polygamous marriages who fulfill all the pre-communion preparations ironically, are allowed to participate in the sacrament.

The church prepares her own yeast-free bread and unfermented wine from grapes. Preparation of wine from grapes forms part of the training of pastors in the church. The vessels in which the wine and bread are kept are usually new and set apart for that purpose only. On the evening of the Lord's Supper, those who have complied with all the pre-communion requirements assemble at the place of worship to pray, sing, and listen to a sermon. When it is time to take the supper, all communicants are called to kneel in front of the pastor. At this stage all doors are closed to keep away late-comers and other outside distractions. Windows are, however, not closed so as to satisfy the curiosity of non-members. The elements are blessed by the pastor and given to the communicants with the instructions: "Take and eat; this is the body of Christ that has been given to you." The instruction which goes with the giving of the wine is: "Take and drink; this is the blood of Christ given to you in remembrance." The serving of the elements is done very solemnly with the singing of hymns. After serving the elements the pastor says a thanksgiving prayer while the communicants are kneeling. The Lord's Supper service ends with the saying of a benediction by the officiating minister.

Belief in Healing and Miracles

"We believe in the healing of physical and spiritual diseases and the reality of miracles in the name of Jesus Christ—the name that is above every name." Numerous references to healing and miracles are cited in this work. The content of this belief statement indicates that members of Christ Holy Church International perceive two kinds of diseases—physical and spiritual. They also see Jesus Christ as the core of healing and miracles. Their Christology is not different from the early Christians in New Testament times who brought to Jesus people with all kinds of sicknesses in expectation of a miracle. They, consequently, go to Jesus Christ not only to worship him but also with expectant faith to receive healing and miracles. By so doing they make a distinction between healing and miracles that occur through the power and faith in Jesus and other healings and miracles that are devoid of faith in Jesus. They do not doubt the reality of healing and miracles through means other than Jesus Christ; they, however, do not believe in such.

If they consider the name of Jesus as the foundation of healing and miracles, why do they use oil and water to heal? They cite James 5:14 as their biblical basis for using oil as an element of healing. (Is anyone among you sick? Let him call for the elders of the church, and let them pray over him, anointing him with oil in the name of Jesus). In responding to the use of water as an agent of healing, they again appeal to the Bible. Rev. Christian C. Obiefuna says:

> Paul used handkerchiefs to heal people; Elisha used water to heal a leper; Jesus used water to perform miracles. When Jesus got to the pool of Bethesda, he did not condemn the use of water to heal. Even if there are no evidences of water being used to heal in the Bible, the Holy Spirit has the right to reveal what can be used to heal. The Holy Spirit revealed to Mama to use water to heal. It is the power behind the element that matters, not the element itself.[489]

Their argument is based on the omnipotence and unlimited actions of God through Jesus Christ. Writing on the use of water in the Celestial Church of Christ (CCC) Afe Adogame stresses the importance of the green water (*omi agbara*):

> *Omi agbara* (green water) is a special type of concoction (liquid) peculiar to the CCC among the other Aladura churches. The recipe and the composition is believed to have been revealed by the Holy Spirit to the pastor-founder. Though it is made from a mixture of blue sulphur (alum), water, lime juice and sanctified water, the preparation remains the exclusive preserve of the pastor.... Owing to the efficacy which members attach to it, the green water is kept under the exclusive custodianship of the pastor or the shepherd by virtue of his status as the pastor's representative in the respective parishes.[490]

Members of Christ Holy Church International, unlike those of the Celestial Church of Christ, do not consider the water to be blessed as medicinal or different from all other water. They claim that there is nothing supernatural about the water in its pre-blessing state; the application of the name of Jesus in the prayer of faith is to them, what matters. The efficacy of the blessed water in healing all kinds of diseases is a further reason why the Statement of Faith links miracles to healing. This is why they always exhort their members to put their trust in Jesus solely.

Belief in the Sufficiency of God

"We believe in the sufficiency of God, the Jehovah—Jireh, who supplies all needs, both known and unknown, of his faithful children who worship him in faith, obedience and contentment." Total dependence is one of the hallmarks of the lifestyles of members of the church. Mention has already been made of depending on God for land and money to begin a congregation and for direction to the destination of establishment of a congregation. We will call that institutional dependence. Perhaps that is the reason the church, as an institution, does not raise loans from any individual or bank to finance projects. The Statement stresses individual dependence, expecting God to supply tangible and intangible needs of his children. The church, however, believes that such provision is distributed on condition of one's relationship with the Triune God. One's faithfulness to God, reflecting on worship, and one's obedience and contentment are the conditions. It is, therefore, no wonder that *contentment* was mentioned as one of the reasons for unity in the church. In Nigeria, like many other African countries, where there is unfair distribution of national wealth which has resulted in abject poverty, being content with what one has and depending on God for one's needs are essential ingredients for survival.

Eschatological Beliefs

"We believe in the physical, personal, unexpected, sudden, and glorious Second Coming of Jesus Christ." The Second Coming of Jesus Christ is one of the pivotal beliefs of Christ Holy Church International. This is seen in the fact that, as a matter of policy, pastors of the church are mandated to preach about the Second Coming of Jesus Christ at every Friday morning service. The Return of Jesus Christ, according to the Statement of Belief will culminate "the resurrection of the body, final judgment, eternal reward and punishment, final defeat of Satan, and the establishment of the new heaven and the new earth."

According to the Very Rev. Obiokoye, belief in the return of Jesus is not the most important doctrine in the church despite the oft-recurrence of the theme in their sermons. He, nonetheless, stated that the Second Coming of Jesus Christ explains all other Christian doctrines. "Without a better understanding of the Second Coming of Jesus," he said, "Christians will not know why they are different from non-Christians and why they (Christians) are expected to live an exemplary life." [491] Members of the church are, as a result, reminded to be steadfast to Christ, no matter how serious their conditions are, so as to receive rewards from Jesus Christ.

Tools for the Formulation of Theology in Christ Holy Church International

Earlier in this work we asked the question of how theology is formulated in a church that is led by an illiterate woman with a team of pastors who are likewise without seminary education. The Statement of Faith, already discussed, is for all intents and purposes, in line with mainstream Christian doctrines. How the doctrines were formulated is the topic of this segment of the chapter. Three influences of theological formulation will be discussed. They are Traditional Religion and Culture, the Bible, and Previous Denominational Experiences.

Traditional Religion and Culture

African traditional religion, unlike Christianity, Islam, and other well-known religions, is a religion that has no scriptures in which one can find a set of beliefs and practices. Mbiti makes this fact clear: "A great number of beliefs and practices are to be found in any African society. These are not, however, formulated into a systematic set of dogmas which a person is expected to accept."[492] The beliefs and practices are passed on from one generation to another through oral tradition and are observed by the people of the group only. The insistence of the elders of African society to preserve and observe the dictates of the religion has been the continuity of belief for the religion.

Due to the many different cultural groups in Africa there is no unanimity of beliefs and practices in the religion; that is why some scholars, like John Mbiti, call for a plurality of religions instead of a singularity: "We speak of African traditional religions in the plural because there are about one thousand African peoples (tribes), and each has its own religious system."[493] In spite of the fact that there are uncountable people groups in Africa with differing views on what is religious or not, there are many similarities in what they believe and practice.

> Africa is so vast and has such a large number of different societies that one runs the risk of generalization when one speaks of traditional African religion. And yet there is a common thread in indigenous values, views, and experiences which shows a large measure of uniformity. Out of this emerges the African concept of the supernatural, ideas about man, society, and nature.[494]

It is for these reasons that Kofi Asare Opoku and other scholars discuss African traditional religion as a unified one. Whatever position one takes, either singularity or plurality, there are some common beliefs in African traditional religion; the main ones are belief in God, ancestral spirits, supernatural entities or lesser deities, totemism, mystical powers, charms, amulets, and talismans.[495] Beside these main beliefs in the religion, there are many differing beliefs.

African religious beliefs and practices are portrayed in proverbs, myths and legends, names and attributes of the Supreme Being, art, craft, political system, and indeed in every aspect of African life.[496] Many early European writers, as a result, depicted African religion as animistic, paganistic, polytheistic, fetishism, and ancestral worship.[497]

Despite the inaccurate definitions of African traditional religion by early European authors because they did not comprehend the dynamics of the religion, many Africans got to know God through the traditional religion. The names of God in many African societies are indicative of their knowledge of the Supreme Being. The names of many Africans exemplify the attributes of God. Opoku gives instances of such names among the Igbos:

> The Ibo have *Chukwuneke* or *Chukwukolu*, "God creates;" *Chukwunyelu*, "God gave;" *Chukwuma*, "God knows;" *Chukwumaijem*, "God knows my steps or my journey;" *Chukwuka*, "God is greater;" *Chukwunweike* or *Ikechukwu*, "power is with God;" *Chukwuka-Odinaka*, "it is all in God's hands;" *Ifenayichukwu*, "nothing is impossible with God;" *Chukwuemeka* or *Olise meka*, "God has done much;" *Kenechukwu*, "thank God;" *Arinzechukwu*, "thanks to God, (i.e. were it not for God);" *Ngozichukwu* or *Ngozi*, "Blessing of God;" *Chukwumailo*, "God knows my enemies;" *Chukwuzoba*, "God saves;" and *Chukwuagbanarinam*, "may God not be far from me." [498]

The meanings of these Igbo names are not different from what classical Christian theology calls the sovereignty, omniscience, omnipotence, infinity, salvation, and imminence of God. One, therefore, does not have to take the African through the basics of Christian doctrine before the African can be said to be theologically inclined or theologically knowledgeable. Jenkins cites the experience of Diedrich Westermann, who in 1926 wrote: "The African, apart from his magical practices, believes in God. He is not a tribal God, but Lord of the universe, and the Christian missionary can in most cases introduce himself as ambassador of the God the African knows."[499] Bishop Shanahan took advantage of the Igbos concept of sacrifice to explain the significance of the Catholic Mass to them:

Father Shanahan noted three points of great importance about sacrifice: first that all Ibos felt the need of it on account of evil or sin or impending disaster; secondly that it was offered by some one specially set apart for that work; thirdly that after it had been offered, the people generally showed their belief in its reconciliatory effects, by inviting the spirits to join them in a common feast. He utilised this knowledge in bringing an understanding of the Mass before the people. He pointed out that the Mass was a sacrifice to propitiate God on account of sin; that a deputed priest was the right person to offer it; and that Holy Communion at the end was a spiritual feast partaken of only by those who had fully reconciled to God through forgiveness.[500]

Philip Jenkins is not wrong, therefore, to assert that "The traditional religions should be seen as a *preparatio evangelica*, a preparation for the gospel."[501]

The role of traditional religion and culture as agents of formulating theology is prevalent, as well, in Christ Holy Church International. The Igbo cosmology, already discussed in this work, is an important factor in their belief in God not only as the Supreme Being but as the healer as well. If among the Igbos some people are called *Ifenayichukwu*, meaning "nothing is impossible with God," then it will not be difficult for them to trust God to heal and perform miracles. The belief in spiritual diseases, as stated in the Statement of Faith, is also not far-fetched when one considers the activities of malevolent spirits and the cruel medicine men already discussed. The generosity of the members resonates with their cultural practice of offering kola nuts to their guests. Now they substitute kola nuts with other tangible gifts. Another example is the giving of titles or appellations to some distinguished pastors and elders of the church. "Titles are given by the traditional ruler in cooperation with the community leaders to respected citizens they hold in high esteem due to their contributions to the progress of the community or to the country or world in general."[502] It is no wonder that many pastors of the church have been given titles (appellations) that spur them to work assiduously to help the church. There are many other beliefs and practices in the church that are nuanced by the traditional religion and culture—time and space will not permit the explication of them all.

To conclude this section one must not be mistaken to think that it is the traditional African religion and culture that dictate what the Church should believe or not. If that were so Christ Holy Church International would have included issues such as the veneration of ancestors in their Statement of Faith, and consequently, would venerate both Agnes Okoh and Marius Okoh. They have, however, tried as much as possible to eliminate some traditional religious elements that contradict plain biblical teaching.[503]

The Bible

Pastoral respondents to some questions posed by the author regarding their reading and interest in certain people in the Bible give some underlying understanding to their theological formulation. Answering a question on which of the testaments they read more, fifty percent of the respondents replied that the question was not necessary since both the Old and New Testaments constitute the Bible. Of the other half who answered the question, ninety-five percent read the New Testament more than the Old Testament. Of the respondents, fifty-five percent have read through the Bible once or twice. The most widely read books in the Bible by the respondents are the Gospel of John, the Gospel of Matthew, and the Acts of the Apostles. The two most admirable biblical characters, apart from Jesus Christ, are Paul and Peter. The love, humility, and obedience of Jesus Christ are what the pastors admire most.

These responses give an understanding of the reason for the prominence of New Testament theology in their Statement of Faith; for example, the centrality of Jesus Christ, the deep faith in eschatology, and the non-encouragement of polygamy. The Matthean account of the life of Jesus draws heavily on the fulfillment of biblical prophecy, while the Acts of the Apostles is replete with activities that are common in Christ Holy Church International—visions, dreams, healing, hearing of voices, prophecy, miracles, caring for the poor and needy, giving of personal testimonies, pointing of people to Christ instead of the other human agents, and selfless communal life among the believers.

The mention of the love, obedience, and humility of Jesus Christ as the most admired character traits explains only there is unity and empathy in the church. The mention of Paul and Peter as the two most admired characters in the Bible sheds more light on the reason for belief in miracles in the church and the boldness to proclaim the Bible no matter the circumstances. The Bible, therefore, serves as an important agent in the formulation of theology in Christ Holy Church International.

Previous Denominational Background

The third most prevalent tool in theological formulation in Christ Holy Church International is the previous denominational experiences of the leadership of the church. About seventy-five percent of the pastors of Christ Holy Church International were either Catholics or Anglicans prior to becoming members of the church. There are, as a result, a lot of Catholic and Anglican inferences in the theology of the church. There are also heavy theological influences of Christ Apostolic Church in the church due to the early association of Prophetess Agnes Okoh with some leaders of Christ Apostolic Church.

The theology of pastoral ministry is one example of this influence. The role of women in the church is a reflection of the theological positions of these three denominations. Although leaders of the church have some biblical backing for not ordaining women, one can infer the influence of Catholicism, Anglicanism, and Christ Apostolic Church in shaping that theology since none of these churches ordain women.[504] Agnes Okoh's first contact with Christianity was Catholicism. Her mentor, Prophetess Ozoemena, did not consider herself a pastor. Agnes was also heavily influenced by Babajide and Babalola. None of these denominations ordain women into the pastoral ministry. Christ Apostolic Church gives some liberty to women to exercise their spiritual gifts without necessarily ordaining them. With some biblical backing, it is, thus not surprising that Christ Holy Church International allows women to exercise their gifts and have created Christian Mothers positions for women in the Church even though women are not ordained.

Another influence of Catholicism is in regard to marriage. With the Catholic background of most of the leaders it is no wonder that holy matrimony is deemed a sacrament.[505] It is also a well-known fact among Western mission-founded churches in west Africa that those in polygamous marriages are not allowed to participate in the Lord's Supper. This has been a contentious issue among African theologians.[506] Christ Holy Church International, likewise, subscribes to that policy even though they are aware that some African Independent Churches do accept polygamists and do not put any liturgical impediments in their way. The tolerance of polygamists and the use of the Lord's Supper as a means of demonstrating their dislike for that lifestyle are influences from the three churches already mentioned since the New Testament does not debar polygamists from coming to the Lord's Table; it only prohibits them from holding leadership positions in the church.

Confession of sins to priests is a practice among Anglicans and Catholics. In fact, it is one of the seven sacraments in Catholicism—the sacrament of penance. Members of Christ Holy Church International also confess their sins to their pastors, a clear theological influence from

Catholicism and Anglicanism. It is ironic that confession of sins is not regarded as a sacrament in Christ Holy Church—an indication of the church's freedom to make choices.

Conclusion

The Statement of Faith of Christ Holy Church International has been the main concern in this chapter. We have seen a step-by-step documentation of the belief system of the church. We have observed the uniqueness of the statement in the sense of its uniformity with evangelical beliefs and the fact that not many African Independent Churches have a systematic documentation of their beliefs. Their theological beliefs were formulated through three main tools of theological formulation: traditional religion and culture which act as the *preparatio evangelica*, the Bible which serves as foundational hub, and the role of past denominational experiences which serve as an unconscious influence. These factors give a better understanding of the theological disposition of the church.

CHAPTER EIGHT

The Challenges of Ministering in Nigeria: The Experience of Christ Holy Church International

The Challenge of Being Accepted by Society

The church is a congregation of people who have been called out of the world to profess faith in the Lordship and vicarious death of Jesus Christ, resulting in worshipping the Triune God and living in the world according to the dictates of the Bible, while hoping for the second coming of Jesus—an event that will culminate the realization of its hope. The above definition of the church makes it a people-oriented divine institution which requires the acceptance of society.

Establishing and administering a church in a multi-faceted Nigeria obviously has its own challenges. The nature of the challenges depends on factors such as the linguistic composition of the members, the tribal composition of the church, the widespread nature of the church, the dominant religion in the area where the church is functioning, the attitude of the members towards people of other faiths and cultures, the social status of the members of the church, socio-political infrastructure in the areas that the church functions, the political situation of the country, and the traditional perception of the type of the church. For instance, there are respective societal perceptions of the following types of churches: western mission-founded churches, charismatic churches, and African Independent Churches. All these factors and many others determine what churches perceive together challenges of Christian proclamation in Nigeria. The challenges, as a result, may be similar or distinct from one church to another.

The challenges of being accepted by society is two-fold (1) it applies to the church as an institution and (2) to some members in the church. While society initially rejected the church, some members in the church still find it extremely difficult to accept social outcasts in the church. Though the challenges will be centered on Christ Holy Church International, examples of other African Independent Churches in Nigeria will be cited to buttress some points.

The challenges under this section will include persecution, skepticism, and the acceptance of social outcasts in the church.

Persecution

Christ Holy Church International, like other African Independent Churches, has had her fair share of persecution in Nigeria by non-Christians and Christians. Adherents of traditional religion saw the church as rivals-in-trade since many people consulted the traditional priests and spiritualists for the solution of their spiritual needs prior to the establishment of Christ Holy Church International. The switch of allegiance from the traditional medicine men to pastors of the church served as good reasons to persecute the church. Initial persecution of the church by adherents of traditional religion took the form of offering evil forests to them, an offer that was meant to obliterate them from the various towns in which they wanted to establish congregations.

One other reason for persecution is the rejection of some traditional norms which members of the church deem contrary to Christian principles. For instance, in the 1960s, community leaders of the Eziawa in Orsu Local Government Area in Imo State passed a law forbidding members of the town becoming members of Christ Holy Church International. The refusal of some women in the church to sweep the masquerade grounds in the town, which were considered holy grounds by adherents of the traditional religion, was the reason for the action by the community leaders. The outbreak of the civil war brought the injunction to an end. The persecution, in certain instances, helped the church to grow as the following incident indicates:

> In 1971 some pioneer evangelists of the church went to preach at Ihembosi in Ekwusigo Local Government Area, Anambra State. As custom demanded, they had to seek permission from the chief of the town before preaching. The chief accepted them warmly but asked them to rest in a forbidden room since nightfall was approaching. The room was believed to be the dwelling place of evil spirits who kill all

those who slept in it. If anybody was to be punished in the town, the person would be put in that room and by the following morning the person's corpse would be dragged out of the room. Unknown to the evangelist team, they swept the room, prayed, and slept. Many people gathered at the premises of the chief at dawn the following day because there were rumors that some people who called themselves missionaries had been given the forbidden room to sleep in. They were, therefore, expecting to see the corpses of the so-called missionaries.

When the evangelists opened the door, they were surprised to see a big crowd of people in the chief's palace. It was then that they were told of the nature of the room in which they had slept. Rev. Clement Okoye, the leader of the evangelists, took advantage of the presence of the crowd and their shock of seeing people coming alive from the room to speak to them about the power of Jesus Christ and what Jesus can do for them if they put their trust in him instead of being afraid of evil spirits. The people believed, and many signs and wonders happened that morning. As a result the chief asked for forgiveness and became a member of the church. He later donated land for the church to build a worship center.[507]

Adherents of African traditional religion were not the only ones who persecuted members of the church. Rev. Samuel Ejiofor alleged that Roman Catholics and Anglicans ganged up in the 1960s to mock the church by calling them "Alleluia Church" because of the constant shouts of "Alleluia!" during worship services of Christ Holy Church International. "They mocked us because we sang Igbo praises and danced to the tunes of traditional musical instruments. They said we were occultic. Once we got into a town, it was announced that Alleluia people have come; do not join them.'"[508] Members of the church claim that in the early 1960s it was a common practice of head teachers of Catholic and Anglican schools to flog school children on Mondays for not worshipping with either Catholic or Anglican churches on Sundays. Worshipping at Christ Holy Church congregations was not recognized by the Catholic and Anglican schools' authorities, hence the flogging of those who did so..

The intensity of the persecution enabled the church to stick together as a worshipping community. Hated by the more established churches and in some cases by the traditional leaders, members of

Christ Holy Church International had no recourse but to lead careful lives and love one another, thus, constituting a close-knit Christian community.

Skepticism

Many non-African Independent Churches Christians have expressed doubts over the motives of those who establish those churches. DomNwachukwu admits the growth of African Independent Churches in Igboland but states that "the motives for the founding of these churches are mixed."[509] He later quotes a pastor he interviewed to support his skepticism of the motives of their leaders:

> Two things are responsible for this. Number one is name and money. Some people want to make money with the Bible, as they hide under the umbrella of God's call. Eighty percent of them are not called. On the other hand, there are those who are called like myself.[510]

This quotation, no doubt, is based on unsubstantiated data, yet a popular perception among many non-AIC religious observers regarding the motives of establishing African Independent Churches.

Ndiokwere sees the acquisition of wealth as one of the motives for founding African Independent Churches in Nigeria. Quarrels over money are said to be one of the common factors of schism. He cites the example of one John Mmuo-Nso of the Holy Chapel of Israel Church who is alleged to have made "a lot of money out of his church business."[511] Moral decadence is another indictment of Nigerian African Independent Churches. Ndiokwere quotes prophet John Ezekwe's perception:

> Most of them are places of immorality, where men and women, even though they call themselves brothers and sisters, are free to do what they like, provided they contribute to the running of the cult, and these are places where immorality is never mentioned as sin, since the 'prophets' themselves take the lead.[512]

In his conclusion, Ndiokwere states, "Whatever the case may be, it should not be forgotten that we are dealing with 'false' prophets. There is no doubt that in the independent churches there exist responsible religious leaders who are convinced of their divine call."[513] Such mixed feelings are prevalent in Nigeria although it is debatable why many Nigerians see the African Independent Churches as the only place where religious miscreants function.

These perceptions have had negative effects on almost all African Independent Churches in Nigeria. Doubts over the veracity of their ministries, particularly as regards their claim to heal, perform miracles, and prophesy accurately, are very common. There are some who flatly reject such claims while those who see the reality of the miracles are quick to attribute the efficacy of their power to powers other than God's. The skeptics do not keep such suspicions to themselves; they at times openly cast a heavy shadow on the ministries of others. DomNwachukwu expresses that concern:

> In some cases preachers denounce other churches and condemn their leaders. They use their pulpits to promote their own churches and condemn others. They concentrate so much on the negatives that non-Christians and weak ones find excuses to keep distance from deep commitment to the Christian faith.[514]

Agnes Okoh was equally concerned with such rejection of the power of God by skeptics. Victoria Njoku, a house helper of Agnes Okoh, reveals this concern in a conversation with the prophetess:

> She once asked me this question. One morning at 9.00 a.m. sometime in July 1978, she told me that some people were saying that she was not a human being, but since I had stayed with her at Asaba, Arondizuogu, and then Ndoni and know her relations, what then should I answer anybody who makes such remarks? Then I told her that I can answer from all I have seen. She asked me whether I had discovered any image of any sort in her cupboards, wardrobe, parlor, kitchen, or other places in her compound, since I usually sweep the house. I said, no. Secondly she told me that some people said she was doing *wayo*. She asked me whether I had seen her as a deceiver; I said, no. So she began to tell me her life history.[515]

The dialogue between Victoria Njoku and Prophetess Agnes Okoh indicates how deeply the rejection of her ministries effected her. Even after the death of the prophetess, leaders of the church are periodically compelled to address the issue of skepticism:

> There is a misunderstanding by some people claiming that all prophesies are false. That is not true. Christ said that if we repent, we shall receive the Spirit of God. He also said that all the people he will convert into the fold in the future, that they shall equally prophesy and see visions and perform miracles.... In Mark 16:15, 18, Christ said that if you believe in

him, you will heal the sick, cast away demons, and, if you drink poison it will not kill you.[516]

Trying to overcome the rejection of their ministries by both non-Christians and some non-African Independent Churches in Nigeria poses one of the greatest challenges facing members and leaders of Christ Holy Church International, although they know that they are ultimately accountable to God.

Therefore, leaders of the church have instituted some measures to safeguard their own integrity. Some of the measures are the recording of prophetic sayings, miracles that have taken place, and some visions purported to have been seen by members. The content of such utterances are compared to what the Bible says concerning the theme of the prophecy, vision, or dream. They then wait for other prophecies from other congregations to confirm previous ones. There are times when they run seminars for prophets and prophetesses (popularly called "visioners"). Participants at such seminars pray for the confirmation or otherwise of some prophecies that have not been fulfilled. People who utter false prophecies are either suspended from making further pronouncements in the church for a period or summarily excommunicated from the church, depending on seriousness of the deception.

To ensure that people who claim they are called by God are aware of the implications of pastoral ministry, they need to undergo a long period of observation before being ordained. After expressing conviction of being called by God to the pastoral ministry one is trained to be a pastor but observed for a period not less than 15 years before being ordained. Very Rev. Isaac Afunwa emphasizes the circumspection with which the selection of those to be ordained is done:

> Recommendations for the promotion to pastors come from the superintendencies to the board of Superintendents. The board then screens those recommended, and a final list is drawn. You have to note that before a worker gets to the rank of senior evangelist he would have been in the ministry for 15 to 20 years. During this period he would have worked in nearly all the superintendencies and therefore will be well known to all the superintendents. It is the responsibility of the superintendents to observe the character, conduct, ability, and spiritual gifts of the workers under them—those who have the gift of administration, evangelism, pastoral duties etc. The superintendents know the weight and gravity of the office of the pastor and therefore seek the guidance of the Holy Spirit

in making their recommendations and in screening the candidates.[517]

These measures and the others are painstakingly taken to ensure that the church does not give skeptics cause to confirm their suspicions. The only exception to the policy of being observed for a long period is when people in different congregations prophesy (at various times) that someone under observation should be ordained.

Accepting Social Outcasts in the Church

The challenge of accepting social outcasts in the church can be understood with a brief account of slavery among the Igbos. Trade in slaves was common in early Igbo society. Narrating the dynamics of the slave trade in Akokwa, a village group northeast of Orlu, Mbagwu Ogbete states:

> As I heard from our father, our people participated in the slave trade. Our major slave buyers were Ndizougu and Arochukwu. Nkalu brought their slaves down to Akokwa for sale. They were famous in the trade. People could be kidnapped from their houses at night, children could be stolen while playing, travelers were kidnapped, and captives in war were all sold as slaves. Immoral people were also sold away. When we grew up we were told how people were sold like goats.[518]

There were two different kinds of slaves in Igbo land—*oru* and *osu*. The *orus* were slaves who were owned by men while the *osus* were slaves owned by gods. It will be worthwhile to spend some time to write about the *osus* due to the challenge Churches in Igboland face over what to do with negative societal attitudes toward the *osus*.

"The word osu means a 'slave,' but one that is distinct from an ordinary slave (*oru*) by the fact that he is the property of a god; in plain language 'a living sacrifice.' Once devoted to a god, there is practically no prospect of such a slave regaining freedom."[519] There were two ways, according to Basden, of becoming an *osu*. The most common was the offering of a boy or girl to a public deity either to gain favor or in obedience to such a request from a native priest. The reasons for such offerings were numerous.

The second way of becoming an *osu* was to voluntarily flee to a shrine and request protection. Whichever way one became an *osu*— either voluntarily or involuntarily—one is considered the bonafide property of the deity. All children born by the *osus* and free men who have sexual intercourse with an *osu* automatically become *osus*.[520] Igbo society is now made up of three groups—the *oru*, the *osu* and the *diala*. The *dialas* are the free people.

The *osu* system is said to be an integral part of Igbo religion which prior to the trade in slaves among the Igbos was regarded as honorable, because the *osus* were held in high esteem.[521] The honor and dignity of being dedicated to a deity has, however, vanished over the years. As a result the *osu* has become a caste society with many humiliating social sanctions and restrictions in the Igbo society. The *osu* caste system was formally abolished on 10 May 1956 by Nnamdi Azikiwe's government of eastern Nigeria,[522] but the stigma and humiliation are still prevalent in the Igbo society because Igbos sadly enough believe that "a slave is always a slave."[523] Victor E. Dike states the social humiliations the *osus* endure:

> Being an *osu* (an ascribed status) in a community dominated by the *diala* means that you are always relegated to the background. The *diala* would not take an *osu* person seriously, no matter how plausible his or her opinion might be in any public forum. They are often belittled in public. . . . In some communities the *osu* class ostracism is operated in such a way that any *diala* who talks to or greets an *osu* pays a fine. In a community such as the Oruku town in Nkanu East Local Government area of Enugu State where the system is revered, the *osu* has its own village market; and it is very difficult for the *osu* to be appointed to any position of authority in local churches. The *diala* is traditionally and socially abhorred and forbidden to marry an *osu*; intermarriage with *osu* is an abomination.[524]

These social sanctions are not peculiar to the *osus*; they apply to all people of slave descent. According to Rev. Obiemeka, a father can place a curse on the head of a son who marries an *osu* in defiance of the traditional norm; also an *osu* is not allowed to take a title in Igbo society no matter his influence.[525]

Churches in Igboland face the challenge of enforcing the abolition of the entire discriminatory caste system and according *osus* all the rights and privileges denied them by society. Basden, himself a minister, states the popular view about the church's attempt to obliterate the osu caste system in Igboland: "In this respect, the Christian element has failed miserably and, to its shame, has done little to obliterate the inequalities or to purge out, once for all, the stain of slavery."[526]

Christ Holy Church International, like the other churches, considers the *osu* caste system to be a very sensitive issue, one that could shatter the unity of the church in a short time if not handled circumspectively. The Most Rev. Daniel Okoh expresses the difficulty the church faces in trying to dissuade her members from believing such traditional norms:

> The main problem arises during marriage; when family elders of the respective spouses investigate the lineage of each other. . . . When you want to tell them about the unity and oneness of all Christians in Christ, people find it difficult to accept, particularly when it comes to marriage. Even if there is a revelation that "such a person should be my spouse," some elders [in the church] will not doubt the revelation but they will not accept it either when they find out that the spouse is either *osu* or *oru*. Then you will have to go through the rigorous process of convincing people that all such beliefs do not matter any longer in Christianity. Some people have accepted our position but others do not.[527]

The church has, consequently, adopted an unofficial "don't ask, don't tell" policy regarding the issue. As a result, all members are treated equally and fairly without regard to how society perceives them. Pastoral and other positions are open to all members. To the leaders of the church, one's giftedness and a clear sense of God's call in one's life are more important than one's genealogy and its societal perceptions. Members in the church who delight in tracing the roots of *osu* and *oru* people have been cautioned and, in some instances, excommunicated if they disregard the church's admonition.

The Challenge of Theological Education and Documentation

Theological Education and Training

Providing theological education for leaders and members of African Independent Churches has been a need observed by their leaders. Paul Makhubu echoed the need in Kenya during a conference. "Many AIC leaders are men of wisdom but without education. . . . Most of our leaders have very little education and no training at all. . . . Untrained leaders cannot guide the people of God."[528] Sam Babs Mala reiterated that need at a conference in Zaire (now Democratic Republic of Congo) six years after Makhubu had expressed his concern:

Many African Independent Churches have no particular training program; neither do they possess Bible schools, colleges, or seminaries to train both the clergy and the laity.... With the trend of affiliation of the mission-oriented seminaries with the universities to become degree-awarding institutions, the African Independent Churches might soon discover that for the second time in their existence, they would have to rely heavily on other churches' seminaries to train their leaders.... In short, there is a crying need among African Independent Churches for a well-planned and concerted effort to develop their own theological institutions.[529]

The reason behind the need for theological education and training for African Independent Church leaders has been stated succinctly by Makhubu: "In Africa things are changing fast politically and economically. The indigenous churches have a responsibility to meet these needs. The people are looking to the church for answers to questions affecting their local problems such as crime, educational needs, unemployment, poverty."[530]

The need for theological education has also been noted by leaders of Nigerian African Independent Churches. Ten African Independent Church denominational Bible colleges and seminaries have, as a result, been established in Nigeria.[531] Regarding the quality of the Bible colleges and seminaries, Mala observes:

As of now, none of these seminaries are well-developed, fully-equipped and adequately staffed to cater for the demands of the members. All the seminaries merged together cannot qualitatively match any one of the seminaries of the mission churches, in terms of physical structures, library facilities, staff, and curriculum. Unfortunately, even the curriculum is the imported one. No one is making an effort to interpret, indigenize and contextualize it to suit the needs for future development of AICs. The illiterate African Independent Church clergy have not succeeded in bringing the enlightened laity to appreciate the necessity for developing theological education. [532]

The observation of Mala depicts the enormity of the challenge and the task of offering qualitative theological education that is suitable to the needs of African Independent Churches.

Marius Okoh Memorial Seminary (MOMS) of Christ Holy Church International is the only center for theological education for all the pastors and other workers of the church. The situation at MOMS is not different from the observation of Mala except for the fact that the leadership of the church has been organizing seminars and conferences to let both laity and clergy appreciate theological education. The Catalogue of MOMS states:

> The academic qualifications of our lecturers are important especially when it comes to the school's accreditation. The government and other affiliating bodies require that lecturers have the minimum of arts degree and maybe with a diploma in education. However, the ministry of teaching in the body of Christ is clearly also a gift of the Holy Spirit. So if those who have the gifts are to lecture the student body, it should be made clear that academics is a subsidiary function of the seminary and not its primary function. The primary consideration of choosing lecturers is faithfulness. The lecturer's life must measure up morally.[533]

As a result of the above policy the highest academic degree of the nine full-time lecturers who are all members of the church is a bachelor's degree. The basic educational qualification for all students is a secondary school certificate. The duration of the training is one academic year, after which students are awarded a certificate in Biblical studies and church policies. Courses offered are: Biblical Studies (Genesis—Revelation), Basic Christian Beliefs (with emphasis on beliefs about God and eschatology), Church History (with emphasis on the seven church ages—Ephesus to Laodicea, and history of African instituted churches), Bible Geography, Christian Education, English Language, Research and Reporting, Greek 101, Church Polity, Accounts, Chorus, Hymns, Music Theory, and Music Instrument.

The administration of MOMS is aware of the inadequacy of the courses offered so the last pages of the catalogue lists 33 courses they intend to offer. The courses include West African Church History, Christian Doctrine, African Christian Theology, Hermeneutics, Cross-cultural Evangelism, Discipleship, Pastoral Counseling, Advanced Greek, Introduction to Sociology, and French, Hausa, Yoruba, and Ewe languages.

An adequate infrastructure that enhances teaching and learning is another challenge facing MOMS. One big classroom is the only space for teaching an average student population of 82 who are all residential. A library of 1,100 books and one journal also serves as the administrative office of MOMS. Lecturers are given monthly stipends. The church, however, pays for their accommodation and utility bills. Tuition at the seminary is free; students, nevertheless, are expected to take care of themselves. The church, at times, gives the students free foodstuff.

The church faces the challenges of providing further training for the lecturers, payment of salaries instead of stipends, improving dormitory facilities for students, offering educational programs for those already holding pastoral positions, teaching languages that are widely spoken in Nigeria, and meeting the aspiration of offering degree programs in response to the rising rate of literacy among the clergy in Nigeria.

In a country where inter-denominational castigation is a common phenomenon, a thorough training of pastors is a necessity. The challenge for the church has even become more enormous with the establishment of congregations in Ghana, a country with different kinds of languages and cultures.

Christian Education and Training

Christ Holy Church International faces the challenge of educating segments of her members. With the exception of having adult Sunday school, there are few educational programs for other members. There are no regular and sustainable educational programs for the men, women, married couples, youth, and children. In fact it was not until the dawn of 2000 that children's and youth programs were instituted in the church. Leaders of the church were, nevertheless, aware of the importance of the programs but were hesitant to send their members to be trained by non-African Independent Church institutions for fear of their members being poached, a fear based on the experiences of other African Independent Churches. The challenge, therefore, is not an apathetic attitude toward addressing the need to intensify Christian education in the church; it is rather apprehensive. "Due to inter-denominational mistrust in Nigeria, one needs to find an institution that teaches members of other churches without necessarily indoctrinating the students to secede from their churches. As a result we try as much as possible to educate our members as much as we can."[534]

Educating women, for instance, reflects the church's efforts to use limited resources to educate members. Following the footsteps of Prophetess Agnes Okoh, women of the church receive individual counseling from the wives of pastors and elderly women in the church. The women meet periodically at district levels, but there is not a regular educational program for all the women at all stations. The church has been organizing annual women's conferences since 1998. The conference is a time when women leaders from all stations gather at one place to think about their improvement. A three-fold purpose of the conference has been stated as:

(1) focusing on the problems and needs of Christian women as wives and mothers in nation building,

(2) designing programs and projects that enhance the moral and spiritual integrity, virtuousness and social importance of Christian women and the church of God,

(3) empowering and encouraging women to improve their economic well-being and the welfare of their families.[535]

The church has, in the past, drawn on the experience of women educators among their womenfolk and international speakers from the Women's Department of the Organization of African Instituted Churches. Other speakers from Ghana and Australia had been invited to address the annual conferences.

Formulation and Documentation of Theological Beliefs

In the previous chapter, the models of theological formulations in Christ Holy Church International were discussed. Churches do not function without some theological presuppositions or theological beliefs. African Independent Churches, therefore, cannot be said to be without theological beliefs. After formulating their theology they face the challenge of putting theology into a theological language or framework which will be understood by the wider church. The lack of documenting theological beliefs is one of the reasons theologians of western mission-founded churches struggle to understand the belief system of African Independent Churches. Gilliland expresses this concern:

> The problem is that historical Christianity seems not to be able to tell who the independent churches are and what they believe. It is rare to find anything systematic written within a given movement that will help us understand the view of independent churches regarding the Bible, the place of Christ, and their thinking about ecclesiology and the church universal.[536]

Where theology is documented, it is done with only the African Independent Church members in mind, disregarding the wider church, perhaps not deliberately. This makes it difficult for a non-member to know offhand the beliefs of the church; it also impedes theological dialogue and finally breeds some false sense of superiority on the part of theologians. In a few instances when the beliefs are documented, the documentation lacks theological phraseology.

The most popular form of theological documentation among African Independent Churches is in a catechetical form—question and answer. E. Olu Coker's doctrinal questions in the context of the Cherubim and Seraphim illustrate this point.

Q. How shall I overcome the world?
A. Colossians 3:1-6; 1 John 5:4, 5; Gal. 1:4
Q. Why do Christians have so much trouble in the world?
A. 1 Corinthians 11:32; Psalm 94:12; Hebrew 12:6-11 etc.
Q. What is sin against the Holy Ghost?
A. Mark 3:28-30; Hebrew 10:28-29; Acts 8:18ff.[537]

Unlike the Cherubim and Seraphim Society, Christ Holy Church International does not document their theology in a question and answer form. Prior to formulating their Statement of Faith in a creedal form the beliefs of the church were not stated theologically. The beliefs were imprinted in their memories through teaching and admonitions and some periodic exegesis by leaders of the church in *Good Tidings*, the church's news magazine. What came close to stating a coherent document of beliefs was what was written on their old baptismal card:

Rules of Belief

The following is expected of you:

1. A personal Testimony of your Salvation in Christ. Acts 4:12; Rom. 10:9

2. Your acknowledgement of and obedience to the Order and Officers of the Church Apostles, Elders, Deacons, Deaconesses. Heb. 13:17; Eph. 4:11; 1 Cor. 12:28.

3. Your presence in the meetings of the Church and abidance in full Communion, not absent yourself without sufficient reasons. Heb. 10:25.

Rules of Conduct

The following is expected of all members of the Church:

1. Never come to the house of God without praying before coming. Matt. 6:7, Eph. 6:8.

2. Be in your seat at the commencement of the service, you will thus be a good example to those that are late and neglectful. Gen. 22:3; Psa. 108:2, Pro. 8:17; S of S 7:12.

3. Bring your children with you to the House of God. Relatives and servants also have souls. It is your duty and privilege to take care of them. Matt. 11:4;

4. Your conformity with the fundamental Doctrines of the Church as well as the necessary Ordinances 1 John 1: 9; Rom. 6:17, 6:4.

5. That you contribute towards the support of the Cause, as taught unto us in the word of God. Gen. 14:20-28; 28:22; Lev. 27:30; I Chron. 28:14; I Cor. 16:2; Matt. 23:23; Heb. 7:8-17.

6. That you keep the counsels of the Church within the Church. Matt. 7:6

7. That you pray for and help every member in the remembering that we are joint members in the body of Christ. Heb. 10:24; 1 Cor. 12:25-26 Tim. 3:16-17. 1 Tim. 2:1; Gal. 6:2

8. Endeavouring to keep the unity of the Spirit in the bond of peace. Eph. 4: 3.

Exo. 20:10; Acts 10:24; John 1: 41-46; Gen. 18:19.

4. Make the pastor your personal friend. His sympathy, support and counsel are needed by you. Constantly pray for him. 1 Thes. 2:7; Joel 2:17; Matt. 2:7; Rom. 15:30; II Cor. 6:19; Heb. 13:17.

5. Make the Church your Spiritual home. Acts 2:46-47.

6. When conversing in the home never speak disrespectfully or criticisingly of God's Servants or their ministrations in the presence of your children. Gal. 6:7; Prov. 22:8; Hos. 8:7.

7. Take your Bible with you to the House of God. Psalm 1:2; 119:16; Rom. 15:4; 2

8. Enter reverently, pray fervently, listen attentively, give praise from a grateful heart and worship God in the beauty of holiness. Eccles. 5: 1; Rom. 12:11; James 1:19.

The beliefs and expectations stated on the Baptismal Card of the church could have been skillfully crafted into a theology of the ecclesia, sacraments, stewardship, spirituality, pastoral support, and many others had they been trained theologically.

The lack of theological documentation does not mean members of the church are not theologically inclined. Our discussion of the nature and growth of the church and the Statement of Faith clearly indicates the interplay of these beliefs in the lives of the members and of the church, but from a theological standpoint a non-member would say (prior to the writing of their Statement of Faith and Mission Statement) that the church was not theologically inclined.

Overcoming this challenge is, perhaps, what prompted the leadership of the church to invite the faculty of Good News Theological College and Seminary to help structure their beliefs into a Statement of Faith. The church still has the challenge of developing their theology of using water, oil, claims of hearing divine voices, dreams, seeing visions, and enrolling people who claim to have been called to the pastoral ministry through dreams into theological language. Such theological articulations will enable the church to dialogue with the wider church in a more meaningful manner.

The Cultural Dilemma

African Independent Churches and Culture

Some leaders of African Independent Churches have castigated western missionaries for not studying African culture and thus misconstruing it to be pagan. Many members of western mission churches, on the other hand, perceive the sensitivity of African Independent Churches towards African culture as an affront to Christianity, hence the use of the word "syncretists" to describe some African Independent Churches.[538] The cultural dichotomy between African Independent Churches and western mission-founded churches is not different in Igboland as DomNwachukwu has observed: "The mission churches have deep roots in Euro-American culture, while the indigenous ones see great value in the Igbo culture and endeavor to create an indigenous Christianity."[539]

With these differing perceptions of what to do with African culture, one would not begrudge the leadership of western mission-founded churches for holding on to the aberration of African culture by their predecessor western missionaries. The problem, however, arises when African Independent Churches are confronted with some aspects of African culture they consider as being contrary to Christian beliefs and practices. Since most African Independent Churches do not have the skill of contextualizing such issues, they are usually faced with the challenge of either accepting the culture in part or denouncing it altogether. They also have the challenge of explaining to their members the reasons behind the church's policies on the acceptance or rejection of a segment of a culture.

Christ Holy Church International and Igbo Culture

Christ Holy Church International has obviously incorporated some of the Igbo culture into their beliefs and practices. Some of the aspects of Igbo culture that are intrinsic in the church are hospitality to strangers, submissiveness of wives to their husbands, respect for elders and people in positions, use of proverbial speaking, respect of law, and the equanimity and industry of Igbos. These cultural tendencies have helped the church in their growth patterns, worship life, and belief systems. Igbos, therefore, feel at home when worshipping in the church.

Not all aspects of the Igbos culture appeal to the leadership of the church. Some aspects of the cultural practices banned in the church are the breaking of kola nuts, taking *orzo* titles, participating in New Yam Festivals, animal sacrifices, snuffing and smoking, masquerading, extensive and expensive funerals, and becoming members of traditional dancing troupes. Time will not allow us to comment on all of these. The breaking of kola nuts and taking of *orzo* titles will be discussed.

Kola nuts

Kola nuts taste bitter, but they are very important in Igbo culture. Basden states the importance of the nut in the culture:

> The Ibo conforms to rules of conduct, and it is useful to have some acquaintance with them in order to be familiar with the proper procedure in certain circumstances. . . . The ancient custom of sharing the kola nut is a typical instance. This was always observed when a visitor called at a house, whether a humble one or a palace. If the owner was too poor or for some other reason was unable to offer the nut, he would always apologize for the seeming lack of courtesy. . . . The welcome is not complete without the sharing of the nut.[540]

The breaking of a kola nut usually goes with either an incantation or with wishful sayings (in a form of a prayer), particularly concerning the issues that led to the convening of the meeting.[541] DomNwachukwu sheds some light on the significance of the kola nut ritual among Igbos.

> The Igbo have a saying which is associated with the giving, breaking, and eating of the kolanut. They say, *"Onye wetara oji wetara ndu"* (whosoever brings kola brings life). For the Igbo, the giving of kolanut to one's house guest signifies acceptance of that guest. Kola is a sign of friendship and goodwill. It signifies love and good neighborliness. It is shared among friends both in Igbo homes and in public social gatherings.[542]

With this significance it is highly offensive not to offer a kola nut or not to chew it when offered at a gathering. Members of Christ Holy Church International are, however, advised against the breaking and chewing of kola nuts. It is a practice that makes them look odd and discourteous in Igbo society, but they insist on what they have been told by their leaders. There are popular beliefs in the church that some of their members were poisoned through the acceptance and chewing of kola nuts, even though they claim that there is nothing fetish about the offering and breaking of kola nuts. For a similar reason, members do not drink palm wine. The church, in this instance, finds it difficult to support her position on the ban of kola nuts in a theological context. Till that is done she acts as a protective body, protecting her children from being victims of a seemingly harmless culture that can, however, be abused.

The Orzo title

The love for titles in Igbo societies is so deep that everyone, if possible, would love to be titled. Amadiume gives some examples of titled men in Igboland and states further that:

> The basic and fundamental amongst them is the traditional *orzo* title. It is a societal title taken without prejudice to any religion. It is a title regarded by the people as honourable and conferred only to the people of good character who must speak nothing but the truth always.[543]

Ilogu traces the institution of the *orzo* title, with some difficulty, to the need for traditional priests to supervise ancestral cults and preside over extended family matters. *Orzo* title holders are expected to live holy lifestyles and observe some taboos, religious taboos, ceremonies, and rituals instituted by the gods and goddesses of his community. *Orzo* titled men enjoy numerous privileges, including holding political offices, representing family and lineage groups in village council meetings, being the first to be served during public functions, exemption from menial labor, and many other social privileges.[544]

Taking of the *orzo* title by Christians has been a controversial issue among Igbo Christians. According to Ozigboh, it was hotly debated at a Catholic congress held at Onitsha in 1915:

> The *orzo* was seen as discriminatory, oppressive, and inimical to the Christian principle of humility and belief in beatific vision for all (not just for the titled men)....The problem of *orzo* remained and continued to claim many Catholic victims until the direct intervention of Rome in 1957. In 1960, Archbishop Heerey conditionally authorised the Catholic to take the traditional titles.[545]

Regarding people's reaction to the decision at the Congress and Archbishop Heerey's authority on the *orzo* title, Ugwu comments that "These decisions had never been accepted wholeheartedly by the Igbo till today, but the church tries always to use sanctions to enforce them."[546] One of the reasons some Christians reject the institution of the *orzo* title is its connotation to the spirit world. It is believed that "a title brought a man closer to the *Maw* (Spirit) and insured a good reception afterwards in the *ani-Muo* (land of the spirits)."[547]

The history of the institution of the *orzo* title and its association with some eschatological beliefs of Igbo traditional religion makes it hard to believe Amadiume's assertion that the *orzo* title is "taken without prejudice to any religion." One of the identifying marks of an *orzo* title holder is the use of a walking stick; they hardly walk without it, not because it aids walking but because it is a staff of authority. The pomposity and social elitism that go with the title coupled with some covert idolatrous practices are all perceived by Christ Holy Church International leaders as unacceptable to Christians, hence its abolition in the church.

Cultural Integration

The spread of the church to non-Igbo areas of Nigeria made the church encounter different people groups, languages, and cultures. Under normal circumstances such a challenge is foreseeable, but many Nigerians are so attached to their cultures and language that they find it difficult to let go of that part of themselves which they consider as very important to their identity and livelihood. An example of this challenge in the life of the Celestial Church of Christ (CCC) in Igbo land shows the severity of the issue in doing missions in Nigeria:

> In 1970-72, some soldiers (of Yoruba origin) stationed at Aba reactivated the church in the east as they often gathered to worship. This new group included some Igbo converts. This second attempt at planting the church in this area again proved abortive. One constraint was the claim that the Igbo converts could not completely assimilate the Yoruba mode and style of worship. For instance it was claimed that the Igbo converts found the practice of kneeling and bowing down with heads touching the floor during prayers . . . as strange and uncomfortable.

The Igbo converts requested the translation of CCC Order of Service, songs, hymns, and prayers into their own language, as a way of making them "feel at home" and to actively participate in the ritual services. The failure of the leaders to address this problem at the time also made some members leave. So when the second attempt at planting the church failed in 1972, it took fourteen years for a new parish to be established.[548]

The linguistic challenge is encountered by many African Independent Churches who do cross-ethnic and cross-cultural missions in Nigeria. Meeting the demands of the other ethnic groups is crucial to the survival or extinction of the church.

The spread of Christ Holy Church International among the Yorubas, Efiks, Hausas, Ijaws, Ibibios, Tivs, Igalas, Ntezis, Itsekeris, Urhobos, Ishan, Kalabari, and many others has challenged the church to take a critical look at multi-culturalism in their fellowship. For instance when the church was planted in Jos, Plateau State, some non-Igbo members complained about the use of Igbo language, choreography, rhythms, and the use of Igbo traditional drums.

With his experience in multicultural ministry, the Most Rev. Daniel Okoh has organized many seminars for the pastors of the church on the need to make non-Igbos feel accepted in the church. At such seminars people from different ethnic groups are given the opportunity to express their worldviews and distinctive cultures. Members of the church realize the depth of ethnic diversity in Nigeria and the need to approach people with respect and sensitivity.

As a result of the growing awareness of multiculturalism in Christ Holy Church International, the leadership has made some changes to create a congenial cultural atmosphere for non-Igbos. In Jos and all the other non-Igbo speaking areas the English language is used in worship. In areas where there are diverse languages, the English language is translated into the local languages. Nearly all Igbo choruses have been translated into the Hausa language to enable non-Igbo members in the Plateau State to "feel at home." Among the Yorubas, the church has incorporated Yoruba traditional wedding, talking drums, songs, and child-naming ceremonies into her ministerial life. Members of the church are appointed to positions irrespective of their cultural or linguistic backgrounds.

Administrative Challenges

Administrative Structure

Administration of a church is one of the knotty challenges that face African Independent Churches. Devising an administrative structure that is thoroughly African has been one of their most daunting tasks even though they demonstrate some sense of dexterity in leadership, contextualization, and in motivating their members to spread the Gospel with their limited theological, financial, and pastoral resources. They have, in these regards, proven to be "nobody's puppets" as asserted by Jenkins.[549]

The problem arises when making a decision on an administrative structure and other matters with regard to order. Some African Independent Churches do not have any elaborate administrative system; everything is centered on the leader. This may be due to their inability to devise a structure that is elaborate, perhaps, due to perceived lack of knowledge. Ayegboyin and Ishola, however, see the positive side of such simplistic administrative structure: "The absence of elaborate administrative structures has some positive effects. The leadership is able to give daily spiritual counsel and support to those who have problems."[550]

Dynastic administration structure is another type which is common among African Independent Churches. The running of the church is usually controlled by the family of the founder. At the death of the founder, the son takes over the administration. This type of administration gives the church a sense of ownership, but separating family affairs from church affairs at times becomes very messy as happened between Edward and Engenas Lekganyame after the death of Engenas Lekganyame, the father and leader of the Zion Christian Church.[551]

The administrative structure of Christ Holy Church is similar to that of the Christ Apostolic Church as a result of help Prophetess Agnes Okoh received from some key leaders of Christ Apostolic Church in 1950. Because there is no paradigm of administrative structure in African Independent Churches in Igbo land and because the prophetess was unable to outline an administrative structure for her prayer group due to her illiteracy. The assistance of leaders of Christ Apostolic Church was welcomed, the two churches, as a result, have designated positions of general superintendent, general evangelist, and superintendents.

Another influence on the administrative structure of the Church is that of Catholicism. In spite of the fact that the administration is much the same as Christ Apostolic Church, leaders of the Christ Holy Church International use some ecclesiastical titles akin to Roman Catholicism. Thus the General Superintendent is addressed as *His Grace, The Most Reverend;* the General Evangelist is addressed as *His Lordship, Right Reverend.* The Senior Superintendents are officially designated as *His Eminence, Very Reverend.* The position of *Christian Mother* and *Catechist* are prevalent in Nigerian Roman Catholicism.[552] These are all direct influence of the Catholic and Anglican backgrounds of most of the leaders of Christ Holy Church International.

Administrative Pattern

In most cases a thorough African church administration is nonexistent.[553] Most African Independent Churches, as a result, pattern their administrative structure on western churches depending on what church the founder seceded from or what church influenced the leaders. There are, however, some disadvantages regarding such influences. As regards the history of Christ Holy Church International, the influence of the two clergymen of the Christ Apostolic Church (CAC), Pastor D. O. Babajide and Apostle Joseph Babalola, over Prophetess Agnes Okoh, will clarify the challenges and disadvantages of patterning an administrative structure of one church after that of another church.

In 1950 the prophetess told her members that the Lord had revealed to her that he would send some people from the western part of Nigeria to help her organize her prayer group. Rev. Enoch Okonkwo narrates how that prophecy was fulfilled in the uncompleted house which Prophetess Okoh was using as her prayer house:

> One day she went to her prayer ministry in the evening and saw some people drumming, singing, and dancing inside and around the building. She was astonished but waited outside. She thought in herself those drunkards had taken over her house. But the leader of the group suddenly came, held her hands, and pulled her into the prayer house and told her that they had been searching for her for three months, that God was going to make her a great prophetess and use her to perform great miracles. . . . The leader of those Yorubas was Prophet D. O. Babajide of CAC. . . . He then stayed with Odozi Obodo, and taught her how to conduct service and handle church administration. He usually came to see how Odozi Obodo was faring.[554]

Prophet Babajide was not the only person from Christ Apostolic Church (CAC) who assisted Agnes Okoh in church administration and the rudiments of leadership development. Pastor Egabor was said to have offered secretarial duties to Prophetess Okoh. Apostle Joseph Babalola paid periodic visits to the prophetess and shared his experience in the ministry with her. Rev. Enoch Okonkwo reminisces: "Joseph Babalola was an apostle and head of the CAC; Babajide was a prophet and general evangelist. Babalola was a strong man in the ministry, a real evangelist who performed signs and wonders. He feared God, which was why he became a friend of Odozi Obodo."[555] The prayer ministry of Prophetess Agnes Okoh was for these reasons called Christ Apostolic Church (Odozi Obodo) till 1975 when a new name—Christ Holy Church of Nigeria—was registered.

It is important, at this stage to digress a bit so as to discuss the implications of the name Christ Apostolic Church (Odozi Obodo) and the challenges leaders of Christ Holy Church International faced as a result of patterning her administration after that of the Christ Apostolic Church. There is a belief among some Igbos that Christ Holy Church International is an offshoot of Christ Apostolic Church. Leaders of Christ Holy Church International, however, claim that their church was neither a congregation of nor affiliated to Christ Apostolic Church. They claim that there was an agreement between Prophetess Okoh and the two clergymen from Christ Apostolic Church that leaders of CAC allow the prophetess to use the name Christ Apostolic Church but to distinguish it with "Odozi Obodo" in parenthesis. According to the Very Rev. Clement Okoye:

> It was not a partnership. We did not depend on any church; we were not in partnership with anybody; they [i.e., Babajide and Babalola] came to us as visitors. We did not receive any command from any church. We did not receive any salary from Christ Apostolic Church; they did not transfer any of our pastors; they did not train any of our pastors; they had no authority over us.[556]

When Rev. Obiokoye's attention was drawn to a page in the 1971 yearbook of Christ Apostolic Church (bearing the photograph of Marius Okoh, then head of Christ Holy Church International) titled "Report on Healing and Miracles from our Onitsha District,"[557] he was furious and snapped, "Christ Apostolic Church erroneously called us 'the Onitsha District of CAC.' They did not seek any permission from us. I joined this church in 1958 so I know whatever happened."[558]

Reacting to a rumor that Christ Holy Church International seceded from Christ Apostolic Church because of the former name of their Church (Christ Apostolic Church—Odozi Obodo), the Very Rev. Daniel Dike countered sharply:

> At the time we changed our name to Christ Holy Church of Nigeria, the leaders of Christ Apostolic Church never questioned us. They did not take us to court, and they did not demand any property from us because they knew we all along had been on our own. If we separated from CAC what action did they take? How many workers [i.e. pastors] did they train for Christ Holy Church?[559]

The views of the leader of the church, the Most Rev. Daniel Okoh, are compelling:

> There was an unwritten partnership, because in those days things were done in trust not in documentary form. All

properties that were bought were receipted without deference to CAC. Our documents bore our name. I still have documents to prove it. The fact that CAC never raised any objection about the change of name, either legal or mutual, although many of their leaders lived many years after the change of name, exemplifies the fact that they never regarded us an integral part of them. In fact Pastor Egabor of CAC, who served as Mama's secretary, visited Mama several times after the change of the name. There was never a quarrel between leaders of the two churches.[560]

The claim of the leaders of Christ Holy Church International could be understood in the light of the activities of Christ Apostolic Church in Urhoboland, also in Nigeria. Samuel Erivwo wrote about the activities when recounting the history of pentecostalist churches in Urhoboland. According to Erivwo, some evangelists of American World Christian Crusade, led by R. Cock, evangelized the Urhobo in 1954 but with no express intention to plant churches. Erivwo continues:

> The thousands of converts made were not initially constituted into a separate church, but were asked to join denominations of their choice. Apostle J. A. Babalola from Efon Alaiye, who followed this movement to Sapele, seized this opportunity to establish his own churches (Christ Apostolic Church) all over Urhoboland, using the myriads of converts made by the crusaders.[561]

According to Erivwo, some of the converts went to the hinterlands of Urhoboland and congregated themselves into independent churches hoping that the Americans would take them as their congregations, but they did not. "Thus, on coming to any of such congregations, Babalola explained what the Christ Apostolic Church (CAC) stood for and, if the congregation accepted his leadership, they became his members."[562] This evangelistic strategy of making a church from people who have already been evangelized by someone else yielded bountiful results for CAC according to Erivwo. "In this way Babalola's CAC spread throughout Urhobo and became particularly strong in Okpe area.... CAC members also grew up in Ephron, Agbarho, and Ughelli areas."[563] Some congregations, however, refused to be coaxed into CAC membership. Some, like Prophetess Agnes Okoh, as claimed by leaders of Christ Holy Church International, had some kind of agreement but never intended to be linked permanently to CAC. Others were, nevertheless, "converted" to Christ Apostolic Church:

Other congregations who preferred to be unattached continued their independent existence. . . . In Isoko there were also a number of Faith Tabernacle churches from 1938 onwards; but they were converted to Christ Apostolic Church by an Ijo revivalist in 1948, and acquired by Apostle Babalola in 1955 during his itineration of that area.[564]

Erivwo's historical account seems to confirm the assertion of the leaders of Christ Holy Church International. Whatever the motive of Babajide and Babalola, their immense influence over Prophetess Agnes Okoh in laying the administrative structures of the prayer ministry cannot be overemphasized. As a result, the administration of Christ Holy Church International is quite similar to that of Christ Apostolic Church. The only exception is the position of *president* in CAC.[565] Other positions like channel and evangelist and structures like districts, superintendencies, etc., are common to CAC administration. The help, however, did come with its own apprehensions and suspicions after the death of those who made the agreement.

Liturgical Challenges

The challenge of evolving a liturgy that is thoroughly African is also yet to be overcome by African Independent Church leaders. Apart from inculcating some African liturgical elements, what usually happens fits the following description of the liturgy of the Church of the Lord (Aladura), an African Independent Church founded by Josiah Ositelu who was formerly a catechist in the Anglican Church. "The church preserves a substantial part of Anglican Church practices. All the Anglican's Lent, Easter, Whitsun, and Palm Sundays are observed."[566]

Despite the Catholic and Anglican backgrounds of most of the leaders of Christ Holy Church International, they do not burn incense, light candles, use rosaries, pray to Mary, or use any iconoclastic image to aid their spirituality. They neither use lectionaries nor observe any liturgical calendar with its attendant observation of some days like All Saints and Ash Wednesday. They observe Good Friday, Resurrection Sunday, and Christmas.

Christ Holy Church International's solution to the liturgical challenge is a policy of picking and choosing various elements of other traditions. The liturgy of the church is, therefore, a potpourri of Christian traditions. The pastors wear suits with clerical collars. Senior ministers, at times, wear white cassocks with colorful stoles. Their worshippers sing hymns from *Ancient & Modern* (an Anglican hymnbook), *Sacred Songs and Solos* (originally used by Anglicans and Methodists), *Method-*

ist Hymnbook, Hymnal Companion as well as some hymns translated into the Igbo language—all prepared to be used primarily by western mission-founded churches. Choristers clad in robes, with surplices, stoles, and mortar boards, sing canticles and western anthems in addition to African songs. The songs are usually accompanied by pianos, organs, guitars, and local musical instruments. From the traditional religion comes dancing, clapping, drumming, and shouting. Prophetic utterances and periodic speaking in tongues with interpretations also remind one of the worship settings of charismatic/pentecostal churches. The policy of picking and choosing from various traditions, according to Rev. Udemba, is to enrich the liturgical life of the church and also to give members of the church who came from other denominations a reminiscing taste of their former churches.

The Challenge of Providing Social Services

The provision of social amenities and services in most African countries, particularly sub-Saharan African countries, was begun by western missionaries. Even after gaining political independence, many churches have not left the provision of social services to their national governments. Churches supplement the efforts of the national governments by establishing schools, hospitals, clinics, leprosaria, and relief centers in times of disasters. Provision of such services has, as a result, become one of the social expectations of churches in Africa. Western mission-founded churches in Africa still have the privilege of relying on the resources of the west to continue living out what has become a legacy for them.

The enormity of the challenge facing African Independent Churches in meeting the non-religious expectations of the communities they serve can be appreciated when one considers three facts: (1) that the African Independent Churches minister to most countryside communities in areas where these services are virtually non-existent; (2) that the provision of such services requires a lot of money; and (3) that African Independent Churches do not have foreign partners who will fund such projects. A typical example of this challenge happened in Igboland during the Nigerian Civil War. DonNwachukwu writes:

> Though the leaders of Aladura churches and prayer houses established their centers of worship close to most refugee camps, they did not necessarily outdistance the leaders of the established churches in the work of evangelism. Baptist groups conducted evangelistic outreaches from one safe town

to the other.... J. B. Durham directed the relief efforts of the World Council of Churches (WCC). He was a Southern Baptist missionary to Nigeria. The Catholics, the Anglicans, and a few other churches were also meeting people's physical and spiritual needs through the distribution of relief materials and evangelistic efforts.... The Baptist people did not rest during the war. They went from village to village, distributing relief materials, building sick-bays, and establishing churches in many villages. These efforts resulted in more than 100 new churches.[567]

DonNwachukwu's account clearly states that both the African Independent Churches and the Western mission-founded churches were at par in providing the spiritual needs of the refugees. African Independent Churches, however, were in a disadvantageous disposition in providing the tangible needs of the refugees. The advantages of having contacts with foreign agencies because of denominational affiliation and of having a resource base in the West gave members of the Western mission-founded churches an advantage over the African Independent Churches.

Christ Holy Church International also faces the challenge of meeting these expectations and the difficulties that go with it. The most common answer given by some members when they were asked to suggest what they would like to see the church doing apart from proclaiming the gospel was the desire to see the church building more schools, from primary to tertiary levels. This desire does not mean members are unaware of the church's primary school at Ndoni and the construction of another school at Amaigbo in Imo State. The building of two maternity homes at Ndoni and Onitsha where patients pay nothing in return for the services and the mass training of pastors' wives in midwifery also underscore the church's sense of the need to meet the social needs (with their limited resources) of the communities to which they minister. Society, nevertheless, expects more from the church.

The Challenge of Coping with Instability

Political Instability

The thirty-three-year-old political instability in Nigeria (1966-1999) had posed a number of challenges and apprehensions for churches in the country, Christ Holy Church International not excepted. Even though leaders of the church expressed their joy at the freedom of worship prevailing in Nigeria, some laws of the federal government are seen as inimical to the spread of churches. The Most Rev. Daniel Okoh cites an example of the government's policy on land acquisition:

Just before 1976 land was in the hands of the local people so they could freely give land or sell it to whomever they wished. But the federal government passed a land decree in 1976, and since then you have to go through the process of acquisition from the government agencies. You can still go to the family people, but sometimes they only give the land to you through the power of attorney meaning that you hold the land in trust for them. In places like Abuja, it is no longer easy for churches like us to get an allocation from the federal government, to get land to buy in the center of the city. If one wants to buy land in a central area of Abuja one has to pay a lot of money to buy the land from a second party. This policy has actually affected church growth in Nigeria.[568]

With the church's policy of buying lands before beginning a congregation one can imagine the difficulties and frustrations the leaders endure before getting land to buy. The poor public perception of African Independent Churches, the low percentage of intelligentsia among their members, and their resultant lack of an advocacy group with federal government officials leave them with little or no influence on government policies.

Religious Unrest

Christians and Muslims in Nigeria have hardly lived in peace. There have been many clashes between the two. Cyril Imo traces some of the causes of the unrest to the discouragement of social and religious mixing between Muslims and non-Muslims, lack of adequate exposure of Muslims to the principles of dialogue, the use of religion for the reinforcement of power and politics by Nigerian politicians, and the misuse of freedom of speech by both Muslims and Christian enthusiasts.[569] The situation was heightened with the official adoption of *sharia* law—an Islamic moral code that directs the everyday life of orthodox Muslims—in most of the States being ruled by Muslim politicians and clerics.[570] Though the *sharia* is intended to apply to Muslims only, Christians are, more often than not, harassed and intimidated for breaking it.

The *sharia* is not the only phenomenon that sparks religious unrest in northern Nigeria. Simeon Nwobi traces the causes of religious unrest in northern Nigeria to the Islamization campaign of Ahmadu Bello (the Sardauna of Sokoto), the head of the government of northern Nigeria, in the early 1960s. The Sardauna of Sokoto, who claimed to have converted 60,000 non-Muslims in five months, built several mosques and made a rule that the Islamic religion be taught in all schools in northern Nigeria.

He also built a Koranic Teachers Training School and opened an Arabic faculty at the Ahmadu Bello University. He established the *Jama' at-el-Nasr-el-Islam* (the Society for the Victory of Islam) a missionary society for Muslims in 1961 and mandated every Muslim to be a member.[571]

Of course some of these associations turned out to be anti-non-Muslims. Later on, the *Jama' atu Nasril Islam* degenerated into what is known today as the "Kaduna Mafia." The era of Sardauna of Sokoto was the era of religious consciousness, both among the Muslims and Christians alike, in the sense that it forced both sides to fight and defend their religions.[572]

Provocative utterances by some Christians under the guise of evangelism and the lack of respect to Islam as another worldwide religion are other causes of religious unrest in northern Nigeria. As a result, Nwobi claims that "There has been at least one religious riot every year especially since 1980s."[573] Such hostilities are either between Islamic groups or, in most cases, against Christians. The riots result in the loss of lives and destruction of properties. Worship places are specifically targeted and burned down, thus causing a lot of financial burden for Christians. The Very Rev. Umeh, the superintendent minister of Jos Superintendency, tells some of the experiences of Christ Holy Church International in northern Nigeria:

> Muslims do attack Christians irrespective of denominations. At Sokoto we bought land, but as soon as the Muslims heard that the land was to be used for a church, they refused to register it. So we were compelled to build a school instead. In Edo State I went to do evangelism and went to Malam Naseru, a friend, but they stoned me. In 1997, at Kafanchan in Kaduna State, we bought land and started building, but they ordered us to demolish the building or they would order their boys to demolish it. A member of our church provided an alternative land in another town for us to build.[574]

The establishment of a congregation of Christ Holy Church in Kano, a predominantly Muslim city in northern Nigeria, was abandoned in 1992 as a result of an attack on Christians in the city. Many southerners were killed. Leaders of the church, Pastors Ebuziome and Ejiofor, went into hiding for two weeks before they were able to travel to the south. A second attempt was begun in 1996. The church now has three congregations in Kano, but the congregations are all centered in Sabon-Geri, a segregated part of the city reserved for non-Islamic activities. Ministering in northern Nigeria, therefore, entails fear, insecurity, death threats, financial loss, intimidation, destruction of properties, and restricted pastoral functions. All these impede the growth of the church. Members of Jos Superintendency, as a result, claim that the hostile Christian—Muslim relation up in Nigeria . . . is the most challenging aspect of ministry in northern Nigeria.

HIV/AIDS

The HIV/AIDS pandemic has caused death and social instability in many African countries. According to estimates in CIA World Factbook in 2001, 3.5 million people live with the disease in Nigeria. Every year 170,000 people die of AIDS. The adult prevalence rate is estimated at 5.8 percent[575] Compared to the population of Nigeria, the figure seems insignificant, something that should not warrant any serious attention, as has been the position of many churches in Nigeria. The social stigma that goes with the disease is another factor that promotes reticence to spread information on the disease.

Notwithstanding the apathetic attitude of some churches about the need to create awareness of the disease, Christ Holy Church International, in conjunction with Interfaith HIV/AIDS Council of Nigeria and Youth Development Initiative, have organized two seminars[576] on HIV/AIDS at Onitsha, the headquarters of the church. Prior to the seminars, the YDi prepared a manual (with instructions on how to create awareness and provide care and support for AIDS victims) for the pastors of the church.

The first seminar was attended by 543 youth, and 800 women participated in the second one. The church intentionally chose to organize the seminars for youth and women since they are considered the most vulnerable ones in the society regarding the spread of the disease. Explaining further the church's decision to organize the seminars, the Most Rev. Daniel Okoh says:

> As nation builders we saw this as another responsibility to teach and spread the Good News of our Lord, which could be seen as care and support borne out of his nature and compassion. We even saw that as an African instituted church we were well-positioned to reach out to the grassroots of the society. The purpose is not only to talk about the dreaded disease but also to educate, create awareness, destroy the myth that people build around it, and offer care and support.[577]

The church has specifically targeted the villages of the southeast and the Niger Delta where many are ignorant, less educated, and consequently at the mercy of oil workers who flaunt their wealth to woo them into sexual intercourse resulting in being infected by the virus that causes

AIDS. The church has made her two maternity homes available to help expectant mothers who are already infected. The church has in addition acquired land at Iyiowa, near Onitsha, to develop a resource center for the training of care givers and the support of HIV/AIDS victims.

The Challenge of Self-Sufficiency

The understanding of stewardship in the church; the policy of not worshipping in rented facilities; the caretaking of pastors, widows, and the needy in the church; the policy of not borrowing from any person or institution; and the offering of free education for pupils in their schools are all laudable policies that have enabled the church to achieve a certain modicum of self-sufficiency. The generosity of the members and their willingness to donate towards the needs of the church is another contributory factor to the relative self-sufficiency in the church even though, like many Nigerians, the majority of the members are traders and workers who barely make a sustainable income.

The church still struggles to meet evangelistic and developmental targets, notwithstanding the generosity of the members. The most common response to the question,"What are the challenges facing the church?" was "Money to preach the gospel." When answering that question, the Very Rev. Daniel Dike said:"Money to spread the gospel to the nooks and corners of Lagos. We are expecting to open not less than 50 to 60 additional congregations in Lagos, an overpopulated city. Plots of land are sold at exorbitant prices. Publicity of events is inadequate."[578] Leaders of the church perceive ministry in Nigeria to be competitive among charismatic churches, western mission-founded churches and other African Independent Churches. Their method of surviving the competition is to upgrade the educational standard of their seminary and run many seminars for the laity. The church plans to go into radio and television ministries. "In the 70s and 80s many churches used microphones to preach on the streets and corners, but the federal government has banned that practice. The richer churches make use of TV and radios to spread the Gospel. This requires a lot of money."[579] A church that thrives on the generosity of its members runs the risk of not meeting all projected objectives and goals. For a church whose *raison d'être* is evangelism, self-sufficiency is imperative.

CHAPTER NINE

Concluding Observations

The Unfinished Task

This work examines the history of Christ Holy Church International for a 55-year period. A brief review of the emergence, typologies, revivalism, and contributions of African Independent Churches—particularly the African Independent Churches in Nigeria—has been done. A description and analysis of the work of Western missionaries and some African missionaries who worked with Western mission agencies (such as Samuel Crowther) have been made to serve as a background to the emergence of African Independent Churches. The ministry of Christ Holy Church International has been put in the context of the history of Christianity in Nigeria and the cosmology of the Igbos.

The history, ministry, and growth of Christ Holy Church International have brought to the fore many new dimensions to the study of African Independent Churches. The African Independent Churches can be said to be one group of Christians that has attracted the attention of more researchers than any other group of Christians. Judging from the voluminous work that has been assembled on African Independent Churches, one would be tempted to think that there is an appreciable understanding of them. The most recurrent observation in this work is the fact that studying African Independent Churches remains an unfinished task. Many African Independent Churches are still not known. To all intents and purpose, this work has demonstrated that there are still many more African Independent Churches and unsung African Independent Church leaders who have contributed to the growth of African Christianity yet have not caught the attention of scholarly analysis. Some of them may be as small as one congregation while others may be as big as Christ Holy Church International.

The voluminous yet selective nature of scholarly work on African Independent Churches ultimately creates some stereotypical knowledge about them instead of a broader one. The knowledge of African Christianity can, as a result, be said to be incomplete judging from the fact that the African Independent Churches, of which much is yet to be known, form about one-third of African Christianity. It can be conjectured, in this regard, that there are many qualities as well as challenges in African Christianity which are yet to be revealed.

The Agnes Okoh Factor

Apart from women who jointly established African Independent Churches in West Africa with men, there are those who single-handedly founded their own prayer houses or denominations, as did Mrs. Lucy Harriet Harrison who founded the Church of Christ the Good Shepherd in Nigeria in 1946 and Mrs. Theresa Effiong, who founded the Holy Chapel of Miracles in 1947, also in Nigeria. Although African Independent Churches founded solely by women outnumber those jointly founded by a female and a male, the former, in most cases, hardly grew in greater proportions. Concerning the growth of Mrs. Lucy Harrison's church, Rosalind Hackett observed in 1987, 41 years after its establishment, that: "The church had remained small, never exceeding more than a few hundred members, its branches in Lagos, Port Harcourt, Calabar, Enugu and Sierra Leone."[580] The trend of growth of Mrs. Theresa Effiong's Holy Chapel of Miracles was no different after 40 years of existence. "Since Calabar became the headquarters of the church in 1956, the Holy Chapel of Miracles has made little effort to develop new branches."[581] A similar growth pattern can be said of African Independent Churches solely founded by women in other West African countries. It is no wonder Isichei observes that "there are vast numbers of women healers and prophets, each with a single congregation."[582] It is in this regard that the role of Prophetess Agnes Okoh in the growth of Christ Holy Church International is very significant. The extensive growth of the church marks her as one of the few sole female founders of African Independent Churches in West Africa (if not the only one) who was able to organize men and women to advance the proclamation of the gospel under very difficult conditions and to many towns and villages.

Regarding the motives of establishing African Independent Churches, Isichei echoes a popular suspicion: "One possible response to unemployment is to found and lead a church."[583] Agnes Okoh's action of selling all her textile merchandise and giving the proceeds to the poor and needy (being a widow at that time) before beginning her itinerant evangelistic mission and her initial claim of divine injunction on accepting gifts debunked any selfish motive of establishing the church. Her philanthropic activities toward her members and non-members further buttress the fact that founding the church to serve her own interest was neither her initial nor ultimate ambition.

Nigeria is a country where the love for ecclesiastical titles by church leaders, whether male or female, is a common phenomenon. For instance, Lucy Harrison was addressed as "Most Reverend Spiritual Mother" or "Big Mamma Prayer" while Theresa Effiong was addressed as "the Blessed Spiritual Mother."[584] Agnes was officially titled "Holy Prophetess of God" but popularly addressed as "Mama" or "Mama Odozi Obodo." Agnes could have taken a more sophisticated title than simply being called "Mama."

The egalitarian nature of the administration of the church, unlike that of many Aladura churches and other African Independent Churches where leaders/founders are nearly deified, is another of Agnes' contributions to the governance of African Independent Churches. Prophetess Agnes Okoh's leadership was different from that of some African Independent Church leaders who are deified (while alive or posthumous) due to claims of efficacious results of their gifts. To avoid any attempt at being deified, whether implicitly or explicitly, she directed her adherents' attention to Jesus Christ while receiving the honor and respect mothers of African societies deserve. Her ability to avert a conflict of allegiance between her and Jesus Christ is noteworthy.

The mutual parting of ways between Agnes and Prophetess Ozoemena is ample evidence that leaders of African Independent Churches can advance the cause of proclaiming the gospel without necessarily being engaged in acrimonious tussles as had sadly been the case between many African Independent Church leaders. Even though women are perceived to be more temperamental than men, Agnes proved that in proclaiming the gospel of Jesus Christ what matters most is attention to the love of God through Jesus Christ, not one's personal ambitions.

Women who established healing homes and prayer houses lived in their towns of ministry, receiving guests, praying, and healing those who came to them. This had been the traditional roles of such leaders. Prophetess Agnes Okoh, however, reversed the traditional role and began itinerant evangelism. Her ability to combine itinerant evangelism with a centralized prayer center was unprecedented in female leaders of African Independent Churches in Nigeria and perhaps other parts of Africa.

The contribution of Prophetess Agnes Okoh to the growth of African Christianity, therefore, simply cannot be overlooked.

The Contribution of Christ Holy Church International to the Study of African Independent Churches

Christ Holy Church has used her ecclesial independence to broaden the dynamics of African Christianity.

The Church's policy of blessing marriage in the church while not insisting on the paraphernalia of Christian wedding which in fact are fraught with western culture—wedding gowns, maids of honor, etc.—epitomizes the ingenuity of Nigerian clergy when given the liberty to contextualize theology. To use the Bible as a symbol of completeness in marriage instead of a ring and asking the couple to say, "With this Bible, I thee wed," is a hallmark of laying a sound foundation in Christian marriage since Christians use the content of the Bible to authenticate their concept of marriage. The wedding ring, to an African, is not as significant as the Bible in marriage. These innovations make marriage in the Christian context very simple, less expensive, and more meaningful.

The church's policy of preparing her own bread and wine for the Lord's supper gives members of the church a renewed understanding of the significance of the Supper. By so doing the church, again, has exercised her independence by getting rid of westernism in Christianity and to a certain extent preserving their hardearned money by not using imported wafers and communion wine, thus, improving the economies of the west to the detriment of Nigerian economy.

Many African Independent Church leaders are suspicious of the effects of theological education on their pastors and members. The practice of certain rituals, such as blood sacrifices, and the taking of some theological positions which lack clear-cut biblical support make some leaders apprehensive that a thorough education in theology may result in dividing the members and/or in weakening their authority. Some of them, as a result, use the results of their spiritual gifts to explain away the importance of theological education and, in so doing, covering up their fear. Others establish what they call Bible colleges and seminaries which, at times, do not measure up to their names in terms of qualified teachers and facilities. The schools are also, in most cases, a means of avoiding any meaningful theological education which will ultimately bring the beliefs and practices of the church into a biblical spotlight.

Seeking the help of the Good News Theological College and Seminary to put the doctrines of the church into a theological framework, writing a Mission Statement and training her members to write Sunday school study manuals is an example the church has set for other African Independent Churches facing similar problems—an example that could get AICs out of their theological quagmire without necessarily being afraid of the influence of some theological positions that may be deemed strange to their core beliefs. By introducing a regular Sunday school educational program, the church has taken a bold step that seemed unimaginable in African Independent Church studies some years ago. Christ Holy Church International has demonstrated how African Independent Churches can integrate spirituality with academic excellence without any hint of undermining growth, whether spiritual or academic.

African Independent Churches are known for offering practical solutions to the spiritual needs of their adherents and society. The traditional method of attracting people, however, has been that of praying for people who are more often than not introduced to the leaders. That is why they are called "pray for me churches" in many West African countries.

Outdoor evangelistic campaigns had for a long time been the preserve of pentecostal/charismatic churches. Such campaigns expose the homiletical and hermeneutical skills or vulnerability of the church leading the campaign. That is one reason many African Independent Churches do not engage in that type of evangelism. Another reason is the perceived poor image of the AICs in Nigeria. Many African Independent Churches prefer doing things that will not bring them to public scrutiny as a result of these poor social perceptions.

By organizing outdoor evangelistic campaigns, Christ Holy Church International took up the challenge of engaging public scrutiny—with all her limitations, vulnerabilities and strengths—disregarding negative perceptions of African Independent Churches in Nigerian society. The church has, accordingly, not allowed herself to fit into societal pigeon holes. She has broadened the dimension of missionary methods and, by so doing, has narrowed the differences in missiological methods between African Independent Churches and charismatic churches. The church has combined the traditional African Independent Church missiological method (expecting people to come to receive prayer and healing) with a method that had hitherto been considered as the prerogative of non-African Independent Churches. By so doing, the church has proven that even though missiological methods may differ from one cultural and geographical group to another, with prayer and dependence on God no method can be said to be peculiar to a certain group of churches or people.

Proclaiming the gospel in Nigeria is no doubt difficult. The study of Christ Holy Church International affirms the difficulties but has also proven the ingenuity, flexibility, equanimity, and integrity of its leaders. With the disintegration of African Independent Churches into smaller congregations and an ever-growing list of schisms within African Independent Churches, the unity in Christ Holy Church International is a significant contribution. The church has demonstrated that unity and leadership integrity are two of the ingredients of church growth. With the fifty-five year peace in the church, leaders have been able to plan and pray together for its expansion. The study has also affirmed God's desire to use people who have not had the privilege of formal seminary education and the application of scientific methods to advance the gospel. The church has given ample evidence that peace and unity can be veritable qualities of African Independent Churches.

Endnotes

[1] The names *Christ Holy Church* and *Christ Holy Church International* refer to the same church and will be used interchangeably.

[2] The words "Igbo" and "Ibo" in this document mean the same and are used interchangeably. They describe a group of people who inhabit the South Eastern side of Nigeria. The Biafran war or Nigerian civil war (1967-1970) was fought in the heartland of the Igbos.

[3] In her survey of African Independent Churches in Calabar, in the southern-eastern Nigeria, Rosalind I. J. Hackett mentions *Christ Holy Church* and describes it as "*a church of Ibo origin (Aba and Onitsha), whose founder the Holy Prophetess of God (Odiono Obio) is not resident in Calabar.* This is the closet reference to the central theme of this work even though the leader was not called Odiono Obio. Rosalind I. J. Hackett, "Women as leaders and Participants in the Spiritual Churches," in *New Religious Movements in Nigeria*, Rosalind I. J. Hackett, ed. (Lewiston: Edwin Mellen Press, 1987) 197.

[4] See works by some West African scholars on AICs: Christian Baeta, *Prophetism in Ghana* (London: SCM Press, 1962), Nathaniel Ndiokwere, *Prophecy and Revolution* (London: SPCK, 1981), J. Akinyele Omoyajowo, *Cherubim and Seraphim: a history of an African Independent Church* (New York: NOK Publishers International, 1982), Deji Ayegboyin & S. Ademola Ishola, *African Indigenous Churches: an historical Perspective,* (Lagos: Greater Heights Publications, 1997), John S. Pobee and Grabriel Ositelu II, *African Initiatives in Christianity* (Geneva: WCC Publications, 1998), Afeosiemime Adogame, *Celestial Church of Christ*, 1999.

[5] Scholarly works about the African Independent Churches has been done by missiologists, Church historians, Theologians, Sociologists, Priests, and many people with different interests and professions.

[6] Bengt G. M. Sundkler's *Bantu Prophets in South Africa* (Oxford: Oxford University Press, 1976) was one of the first extensive works on AICs. It was first published in 1948. Other regional work on AICs include, Ephraim Anderson, *Messianic Movements in the Lower Congo*, Uppsala: Almqvist & Wiksells Boktryckeri AB, 1958, Ane Marie Bak Rasmussen, *Modern African Spirituality: The Independent Churches in East Africa 1902-1976* (London & New York: British Academic Press, 1996).

[7] These include Allan Anderson, *African Reformation: African Initiated Christianity in the 20th Century,* Asmara: African World Press, 2000.

[8] See for instance, Marie-Louise Martin, *Kimbangu: An African Prophet and his Church* (Oxford: Basil Blackwell, 1975).

[9] See Gordon M. Haliburton, *The Prophet Harris: A Study of an African Prophet and his Mass Movement in the Ivory Coast and the Gold Coast 1913-1915* (London: Longman, 1971).

[10] By 1 August 1945 Bengt Sundkler listed 848 AICs in South Africa alone. In a footnote he added "On May 30 1947, a list with 123 new names of churches was sent to me by the Secretary for Native Affairs. These churches are not included in the list published here. Bengt Sundkler, *Bantu Prophets in South Africa*, 354-374.

[11] Turner wrote many articles and books on AICs. The most popular book is *The Church of the Lord (Aladura)* Vols. 1 & 2, (Oxford: Clarendon Press, 1967). The church was founded by Josiah Oshitelu in 1930. Turner later established the *Centre for New Religious Movements*, a Research Center of AICs, at the Selly Oak Colleges, University of Birmingham, UK.

[12] See Turner, *Religious Innovation in Africa*, 92. This definition seems to be popularly accepted by most scholars. To Jenkins, African Independent Churches are "...African churches with African leaders for African people." Philip Jenkins, *The Next Christendom: The Calling of Global Christianity* (Oxford: Oxford University Press) 52.

[13] Allan Anderson gives a detailed review of such typologies in his article, "Types and Butterflies: African Initiated Churches and European Typologies" in *International Bulletin of Mission Research* (July 2001) 107-113.

[14] Ibid., 108-110.

[15] I used to be a member of an AIC from 1968 to 1988. I have since worked with, interacted with, brain-stormed with, taught and worshipped (periodically but not infrequently) with AICs for more than a decade.

[16] "Visions" in this context is the seeing of some events, in a quasi-active mood, purported to have been revealed by a Supreme Being or a deity. See detailed definition in Chapter 4, footnote 15.

[17] Anderson, *African Reformation*, 18, 19.

[18] Ibid., 19.

[19] Alan Anderson, *African Reformation*, 109.

[20] H. L. Pretorius, *Historiography and Historical Sources regarding African Indigenous Churches in South Africa* (Lampeter: Edwin Melles Press, 1995) 23.

[21] Examples of other works that preceded Sundkler's were: C. Loram, "The Separatist Church Movement" in *International Review of Missions,* (1926) 476-482. See also, R. H. W. Shepherd, "The Separatist Churches of South Africa" in *International Review of Missions* (1937) 453-463.

[22] Ayegboyin and Ishola, *African Indigenous Churches,* 15.

[23] Paul Makhubu, *Who are the Independent Churches?* (Johannesburg: Skotaville Publishers, 1988) 3.

[24] David Barrett and T. John Padwick, *Rise Up and Walk,* (Nairobi: Oxford University Press, 1989) 12.

[25] Bengt Sundkler, *Bantu Prophets in South Africa,* 3.

[26] Bolaji Idowu, *Olódùmarè- God in Yoruba Belief* (London: Longman, 1962) 212.

[27] Ratovonarivo, "The Independent Churches in Madagascar: A Brief Survey" in *African Independent Churches in the 80s.* Sam Babs Mala, ed. (Lagos: Gilbert, Grace and Gabriel Associates, 1983) 47, 48.

[28] For more information on the causes, nature and results of AIC persecutions, read Harold Turner, "Prophets and Politics: A Nigerian Test-case" in *Bulletin of the Society for African Church History* Vol. 2, no. 1, (1965) 97-116. Ayegboyin and Ishola, *African Indigenous Churches,* 55, 56, 58. The Church of Jesus Christ on Earth through the Prophet Simon Kimbangu, "The attributes of Papa Simon Kimbangu, Founder of the Kimbanguist Church" in http://www.kimbanguisme.com/e-option 1 a.htm (accessed 20 April 2001). Elizabeth Isichei, *A History of Christianity in Africa: from Antiquity to the Present* (Grand Rapids: William B. Eerdmans, 1995) 200-201. Frank Botchway, "The Ossamadih Church – Church of Light" in *Journal of African Christian Thought* Gillian Bediako, ed. Vol. 3, no. 2, (2000) 3. Wyatt MacGaffey, *Modern Kongo Prophets* (Bloomington: Indiana University Press, 1983) 40. David A. Shank, *Prophet Harris: the Black Elijah of West Africa* (Leiden: E. J. Brill, 1994) 11-14. Bengt Sundkler and Christopher Steed, *A History of the Church in Africa* (Cambridge: Cambridge University Press, 2000) 2000.

[29] For a detailed typology of churches in Africa, see Harold Turner, *Religious Innovation in Africa,* (Boston: G. K. Hall & Co., 1979), 79-108. To facilitate further exploration of African

Christianity,Turner, Cameron Mitchell and Hans-Jürgen Greschat compiled a comprehensive *Bibliography of Modern Religious Movements* (n.p.: Northwestern University Press. 1966).

[30] Ibid., 83, 84. Examples of Neo-primal movements cited by Turner are: The National Church of Nigeria, now called Godianism, the Church of Orunmila, also of Nigeria and the Church of the Ancestors, in Southern Malawi.

[31] Ibid., 84. Turner further divides the Hebraists into two movements – 'Israelitish' and 'Judaistic.' He defines the Israelitish as "African movements which reject idolatry and magic, and now feel that the one God of the Scriptures is loving and helpful and speaks to the community through its founder or successor prophets, commanding faith in himself alone, together with various forms." Ibid., 85. He describes the Judaistic type who emphasizes on laws, rituals, taboos, baptisms, purifications and festivals. They are exclusivistic "and may appear in hostility to the white race..." Ibid., 85. God's Kingdom Society in Nigeria is counted as an example of the Judaistic type.

[32] Philip Jenkins, *The New Christendom*, 43.

[33] These include, Anglican, Baptist, Congregational, Lutheran, Methodist, Presbyterian, Roman Catholic, Salvation Army and other interdenominational societies, Sudan Interior Mission and Worldwide Evangelization Crusade. Harold Turner, *Religious Innovation*, 86.

[34] Ibid., 92.

[35] David Barrett, *Schism and Renewal in Africa: an Analysis of six thousand contemporary Religious Movements* (Nairobi: Oxford University Press, 1968) 3.

[36] Ibid., 3. The entire book is about schism/separatism. Evidence in this work will, however, prove that not all AICs are schismatics.

[37] This does not mean every one recognized AICs as legitimate Christian churches. There were still some skeptics.

[38] Bengt Sundkler, *Bantu Prophets in South Africa*, 297. Italics not mine.

[39] Nathaniel Ndiokwere, *Prophecy and Revolution* (London: SPCK, 1981) 274.

[40] Jenkins, *The New Christendom*, 57.

[41] Dempster, "Leap of Faith" in *Focus on African: BBC Magazine* (Jan-Mar. 2001) 46.

[42] ZCC stands for the Zion Christian Church, an AIC in founded in South Africa. It has grown from 920 members in 1925 to over 8 million members in 2001. It is said to be the largest African Independent Church. The site of their pilgrimage is also known as Moria. See Dempster *Leap of Faith*, 44-46.

[43] Jenkins, *The New Christendom*, 68.

[44] Dempster, *Leap of Faith*, 46.

[45] http://www.kimbanguisme.com/e-option2a.htm The church has congregations in the Republic of Congo, the Democratic Republic of Congo, Angola, Gabon, Central Africa Republic, Zambia, Zimbabwe, Rwanda, Burundi, South Africa, Nigeria, Madagascar, Spain, Portugal, France, Belgium, Switzerland and England.

[46] John S. Pobee and Gabriel Ositelu II, *African Initiatives in Christianity* (Geneva, WCC Publications, 1998) 52.

[47] Three AICs worship in the Twin cities of St. Paul and Minneapolis, Minnesota. One of them, Mount Sinai Cherubim and Seraphim Church, USA, worships at the premises of Central Baptist Church, 420 North Roy Street, St. Paul.

[48] Ndiokwere, *Prophecy and Revolution*, 280. The last sentence is noteworthy regarding evangelistic methods of AICs.

[49] Ibid., 281.

[50] For the history of Good News Training Institute, read Edwin & Irene Weaver, *Kuku Hill: among indigenous Churches in West Africa* (Elkhart: Institute of Mennonite Studies, 1975) 132-160.

[51] Pobee and Ositelu, *African Initiatives in Christianity*, 5.

52 Ibid., 4.
53 Anderson, *African Reformation*, 4.
54 Kwame Bediako, *Christianity in Africa: The Renewal of a Non-Western Christianity* (Edinburgh: Edinburgh University Press, 1995) 113.
55 Andrew Walls, *The Cross-Cultural Process in Christian History* (Maryknoll: Orbis Books, 2000) 129.
56 Lamin Sanneh, "World Christianity and the new Historiography" in *Enlarging the Story: Perspectives on Writing World Christian History*, Wilbert Shenk, ed., (Maryknoll, Orbis Books, 2002) 109.
57 Pobee & Ositelu, *African Initiatives*, 5.
58 Prior to the acceptance of the two churches into the WCC had rejected applications for membership by many AICs including Cherubim and Seraphim of Nigeria in 1960, Eglise Harrist of Ivory Coast in 1966. Barrett and Padwick, *Rise Up and Walk*, 55 -90.
59 Dean Gilliland, "How 'Christian' are African Independent Churches?" in *Missiology* 14, no. 3 (1986) 260.
60 Ibid., 262 - 264. Gilliland cites five factors (ignorance, unconcern, pride, history and fear) as reasons for the chasm between African members of Western mission-founded churches and AICs.
61 David Barrett (ed.) "Who's Who of African Independent Church Leaders" in *RISK*, 7, no. 3, 1971, Victor Lamont, Guest Editor. 186-190.
62 Ibid., 23 - 34. Some of the leaders were animists, who have had no prior contact with missionary churches.
63 Ibid., 24.
64 Ibid., 24.
65 Discussing the causes of the emergence of African Independent Churches seem like putting the work of Western missionaries on trial or castigating the ministries of Western missionaries. That is not the intention of this work, as the four-fold latent factors that follow indicate. Though Western missionaries had their own shortcomings, being humans as they were, they had their merits as well. John Baur lists some of their merits as, "their religious motivation in coming to Africa, their heroism especially in the early times, their renouncement to many commodities of their home country even later on." See John Baur. *2000 Years of Christianity in Africa* (Nairobi: Paulines Publications Africa, 1998) 422. The passion and toil of Western missionaries in Africa can be reiterated in the words of Bishop Daniel Comboni "This time I am writing only a few lines because I am broken by fever, by difficulties, by weariness and by heartache. The only way God's work can thrive is at the foot of Calvary. But although I am broken in body, I feel by God's grace fresh in spirit and resolve to suffer everything and to give my life for the redemption of Africa." Quoted in Walbert Buhlmann, *The Missions on Trial* (Maryknoll: Orbis Books, 1979)114. In spite of the commitments and sacrifices of some Western missionary, one cannot help but to touch on their shortcomings when one is writing about the genesis of African Independent Churches.
66 Quoted in Walbert Bühlmann, *The Missions on Trial*, 79.
67 Quoted in Bühlmann, *The Missions on Trial*, 83.
68 John Baur, *2000 Years of Christianity in Africa*, 413.
69 Note: The success of philology in Africa cannot be attributed to westerners only. Apart from the unknown Africans who acted as the missionaries' language teachers, informants and linguists - teaching them the fundamentals, etymologies, and syntax of the various languages, - the works of some African philologists and Bible translators need to be mentioned. Samuel Ajaye Crowther, the first African to be ordained a bishop in the Anglican community, published Yoruba vocabulary and grammatical structure. The Yorubas live in Nigeria. He translated the Book of Common Prayer into Yoruba. He and J. F. Schon set up a language study base at the Fourah Bay College in Sierra Leone. He is also noted to

be the leading influence in the translation of the Bible into Yoruba. He studied the Temne and Nupe languages. He wrote the first book about the Igbos, also in Nigeria, in 1882 and in fact translated the Bible into the Igbo language. He began compiling a dictionary in the Hausa language but had to ask J. F. Schön, a German missionary, to complete it due to his numerous other duties. For more information about the literary achievements of Crowther, read Andrew Walls, *The Cross-cultural Process in Christian History*, 155-164. See also, Lamin Sanneh. *West African Christianity* (Maryknoll: Orbis Books, 1983) 169-178. On his achievement as head of the Niger Mission, Ajayi mentions: increase of trade, increasing prosperity of emigrants and Crowther's own Consular status. J. F. Ade Ajayi, *Christian Missions in Nigeria 1841-1891: the making of the Elite* (London: Longmans, Green and Co. Ltd., 1965) 215.

[70] Bühlmann, *The Missions on Trial*, 107.

[71] Ibid., 108. Note: Kwame Bediako adds "periodicals" to the work of Christaller. He states that Christaller collected 3,600 proverbs. Cf. Bediako, *Christianity in Africa*, 52.

[72] Anderson, *African Reformation*, 31.

[73] Bediako, *Christianity in Africa*, 110.

[74] Ogbu Kalu, "Anatomy of an Explosion," interview by an anonymous interviewer. *Christian History*, Issue 79, Vol. 22, no. 3(2003) 8.

[75] Not only policies; the lifestyles of some of the missionaries was measured in terms of Biblical injunctions. In the Gold Coast, now Ghana. David Barrett states: "The first secession occurred over a century ago in 1862 near Cape Coast, when a small teetotal group among the Fanti tribe seceded from the Wesleyan Methodist Mission to form the short-lived Methodist Society." This is in protest against the Missionaries' laxity on drunkenness and in fact the drunken lifestyles of some of the missionaries. Barrett, *Schism and Renewal*, 18.

[76] Many African Independent Churches see nothing wrong with Polygamy. They use the Bible to support the practice. To them if God used Jacob, David, Solomon on others who were polygamists then they see no reason why God will not use 20th Century polygamists. According to C. G. Bëeta, *Prophetism in Ghana*, 154. The Musama Disco Christo Church (MDCC) in Ghana "believe that (as an African Church) polygamy is not a moral sin." . The MDCC, thus, adds another dimension to the practice – being an African Church. Paul Makhubu states how a text in Genesis 35:29 "Isaac died and was gathered to his father's …" agrees with African concept of life after life. Paul Makhubu, *Who are the Independent Churches?* 61.

[77] Psalm 68: 31 (NKJV).

[78] According to Makhubu, the Ethiopian churches "were the first AICs in Southern Africa. Today their existence is obscure to many because there is usually nothing eye-catching that makes them too different from mainline churches." Makhubu, *Who are the Independent Churches*, 5.

[79] Walls, *The Cross-Cultural Process*, 91.

[80] The ordinations of Philip Quaque, J. E. J. Capitein and a few other Africans were exceptions. See Hans Debrunner, *A History of Christianity in Ghana* (Accra: Waterville Publishing, 1967) 66.

[81] For an extensive work on Bishop Samuel Crowther, read J. F. Ade Ajayi, *Christian Missions in Nigeria 1841-1891: The Making of a New Elite* (London: Longmans, Green and Co. Ltd., 1965). See also Andrew Walls, *The Cross-Cultural Process*, 155-164.

[82] Walls, *Cross-Cultural process.*, 164.

[83] Jenkins, *The Next Christendom*, 41.

[84] David J. Bosch, *Transforming Missions: Paradigm Shifts in Theology of Mission* (Maryknoll: Orbis Books, 1991) 291.

[85] Ibid., 293.

[86] Ibid., 294.

[87] Makhubu, *Who are the Independent Churches?*, 22.

[88] John Calvin, *Calvin's Commentaries, 1 Corinthians*, Translated by John Fraser, David and Thomas Torrance, eds., (Grand Rapids: Wm. Eerdmans Publishing Co. 1960) 270.

[89] Baur states that missionaries frowned on the belief in witchcraft because a similar belief in the late 17th century medieval Europe was counteracted by the development of natural science. He apparently conjectures the missionaries' mind and asks, "should Africa not be liberated from them and enjoy the same progress?" Baur, *2000 Years*, 417.

[90] Pobee & Ositelu, *African Initiatives*, 29.

[91] For an analysis of this view of miracles, read Ernst & Marie-Luise Keller, *Miracles in Dispute: a Continuing Debate* (Philadelphia: Fortress Press, 1969) 29-39.

[92] Pobee & Ositelu, *African Initiatives*, 42.

[93] See for example Ajayi's chapter on "Civilization Around the Mission House." Ajayi, *Christian Missions in Nigeria*, 126-167.

[94] As a matter of fact, many scholars considers AICs as "renewal movements." See, for instance, Ndiokwere, *Prophecy and Revolution*, 276.

[95] Williston Walker, et. al. *A History of the Christian Church* (New York: Charles Scribner's Sons, 1985) 596, 597.

[96] The giving of Bible and Western names to Africans was made to look like a sacred phenomenon. Mobley quotes Nana Annor Adjaye complaining about that practice: "I cannot understand, for example, why our names are changed when we become Christians...I believe when we go to heaven every nation shall exhibit her glory. If this is correct why would the European missionary wish to see Kwesi Mensah in heaven as John Menson. Mobley, *The Ghanaian's Image*, 131.

[97] Quoted in Pobee, *Toward an African Theology*, 62, 63.

[98] Omoyajowo, *Cherubim and Seraphim*, 3.

[99] Andrew Walls likens the AICs' radical Biblicism, ecclesiological concepts and their various types to that of the Radical Reformers in European church history. Walls, *The Missionary Movement in Christian History*, 116.

[100] M. F. Perrin Jassy, "Women in the African Independent Churches" in *RISK*, Vol. 7, no. 3 (1971) 48, 49.

[101] Kimpa Vita, also known as Dona Beatrice, is known to be the first African woman to attempt Africanizing Christianity (See Allan Anderson, *African Reformation*, 47-51). David Barrett briefly discusses the ministries of Gaudencia Aoko of Legio Maria Church, Alice Lenshina Mulenga of the Lumpa Church, Christina Mokutudu Nku of St. Paul Apostolic Faith Church, and Maria Mtakatifu of Maria Legio of Africa Church. Barrett, *RISK*, 7, no. 3 (1971) 24, 29, 30. The ministry of prophetess Nonetetha Nkenkwe can be read in Robert Edgar and Hilary Sappire, *African Apocalypse* (Johannesburg: Witasterand University Press, 1999). The contribution of West African AIC leaders will be discussed later in this work.

[102] The first part of the song is in Pidgin English while those aligned against is an English translation by Pobee & Ositelu. Notice how Satan is personalized and addressed in the first person singular in the song. This throws some insight into African Independent Churches' theology of demons. Satan is perceived as an evil doer but Jesus is the conqueror of Satan and the restorer of what had been damaged by the devil. Human responsibility is less talked about in AIC doctrine of demonology. Pobee and Ositelu, *African Initiatives*, 36, 37.

[103] Lamin Sanneh, *Translating the Message: The Missionary Impact on Culture* (Maryknoll: Orbis Books, 1990) 152. Although Walls, *The Missionary Movement in Christian History* 92. translates "Aladura", to mean "praying people," I find Sanneh's translation to be more authentic since he links it etymologically to the Arabic word, *al-du'a* which literally means "supplicatory prayer." Ibid. 152. According to Ayegboyin & Ishola, state that, "In Ghana, especially among the Akans, these churches are described as Mpaebo Kuo. Ayegboyin and Ishola, *African Indigenous Churches*, 16.

[104] Sanneh, *West African Christianity*, 191.

[105] Thomas Oduro, "The History of the Good News Training Institute (Accra)," in *Ministry in*

Partnership with African Independent Churches, David A. Shank, ed. (Elkhart: Mennonite Board of Missions, 1991) 132,133.

[106] Many AICs have broadened the theology of healing, particularly on elements used to heal. According to Anderson, some AICs use blessed water, ropes, and strings, staffs, salt, wood, and sand to heal. Anderson, *African Reformation*, 199, 200

[107] Pobee and Ositelu, *African Initiatives*, 49.

[108] Oduro, *The History of the Good News Training Institute*, 134, 135.

[109] Makhubu, *Who are the Independent Churches*, 29.

[110] Solomon Zvanaka, "African Independent Churches in context." in *Missiology*. 25, no. 1, 1997, 71-72.

[111] Odhiambo W. Okite, "The Politics of African Church Independency" in *RISK*, 7, no. 3, 1971. (Victor Lamont, guest editor), page 45.

[112] Omoyajowo, *Cherubim and Seraphim*, 51.

[113] Adogame, *Celestial Church of Christ*, 41.

[114] Ibid., 42, 43.

[115] Apart from some quick references to some leaders and names of some AICs in Nigeria, a detailed history of the establishment of AICs in Nigeria can be found in the next chapter.

[116] Gordon M. Haliburton has written a detailed account on Harris in his book, *The Prophet Harris* (London: Longman, 1971). On Garrick Braide, read Frieder Ludwig's article, "Elijah II: Radicalisation and Consolidation of the Garrick Braide Movement 1915-1918" in *Journal of Religion in Africa* Vol. 23, Fasc. 4 (Nov. 1993), 296-317.

[117] Omoyajowo, *Cherubim and Seraphim*, 24. Italics not mine.

[118] G. O. M. Tasie gives credit to "self-consecrated evangelists", "native teachers", and "native interpreters" who contributed to Harris's success. He did not even state the gender of Harris's feminine co-evangelists let alone mention their names. G. O. M. Tasie, "Christian Awakening in West Africa, 1914-1918: A Study in the Significance of Native Agency." in *The History of Christianity in West Africa*. O. U. Kalu, ed. (London: Longman, 1980) 293-308.

[119] Baeta: *Prophetism in Ghana*, 28-67.

[120] Elizabeth Isichei, *A History of Christianity in Africa*, 285.

[121] Ayegboyin and Ishola, *African Indigenous Churches*, 107, 108. See also Allan Anderson, *African Reformation*, 77. Baeta attributes the founding of Twelve Apostles to Grace Tani and John Nackabah. See Baeta, *Prophetism in Ghana*, 9.

[122] Thaddeus Ihejiofor, Lawrence Nwokorah, James Okoye, Vincent Nwosu "Prayer Houses and Faith Healing" in *Nigeria* (Onitsha: Tabansi Press, 1971) 8 - 52.

[123] Elizabeth Isichei, *A History of Christianity*, 291.

[124] Jenkins, *The Next Christendom*, 51.

[125] Quoted in Pobee and Ositelu, *African Initiatives*, 68.

[126] Rex Niven, *The War of Nigerian Unity 1967-1970* (Ibadan: Evans Brothers Ltd., 1970) 36. Italics not mine.

[127] BBC NEWS/ WORLD/ AFRICA/COUNTRY PROFILES/Country Profile - Nigeria. http://news.bbc.co.uk/1/hi/world/africa/country-profiles/1064557.stm (accessed 16 January 2004).

[128] CIA - The World Factbook http://www.cia.gov/cia/publications/factbook/geos/ni.html (accessed 16 January 2004).

[129] Ibid., (accessed 16 January 2004).

[130] Patrick Johnstone and Jason Mandryk, *Operation World: 21st Century edition* (Carlisle: Paternoster Publishing 2001) 488.

[131] Some of the kingdoms and empires were Borno, Oduduwa, Benin, Warri, and Calabar.

[132] Helen Chapin Metz, ed. *Nigeria: a Country Study*

[132] http://lcweb2.loc.gov/cgi-bin/query/r?frd/cstdy:@field(DOCID+ng0028) Federal Research Division, Library of Congress (accessed 14 February 2004).
[133] Ibid., http://lcweb2.loc.gov/cgi-bin/query/r?frd/cstdy:@field(DOCID+ng0029) (accessed 14 February 2004).
[134] Ibid., http://lcweb2.loc.gov/cgi-bin/query/r?frd/cstdy:@field(DOCID+ng0030) (accessed 14 February 2004).
[135] Niven, *The War of Nigerian Unity,* 31. A fourth region, Midwest, was created in 1963.
[136] Toyin Falola, *Violence in Nigeria: the Crisis of Religious Politics and Secular Ideologies* (Rochester: University of Rochester Press, 1998) 52, 53.
[137] Ibid., 53.
[138] Niven, *The War of Nigerian Unity,* 72.
[139] Ibid., 79.
[140] Ojukwu's declaration of the Republic of Biafra is documented by Kirk-Greene, *Crisis and Conflict in Nigeria:A Documentary Sourcebook July 1967- January 1970* Vol. II (London: Oxford University Press, *1971)* 104.
[141] Niven, *The War of Nigerian Unity,* 107.
[142] Read Lt. Col. Effiong's address in Kirk-Greene, *Crisis and Conflict in Nigeria* (Vol. 2) 451, 452.
[143] Falola, *Violence in Nigeria,* 65, 66.
[144] Andrew Walls, *The Cross-Cultural Process,* 105.
[145] Johnson and Mandryk, *Operation World,* 487.
[146] Elizabeth Isichei, *The Ibo People and the Europeans: the Genesis of a Relationship – to 1906* (New York: St. Martin's Press, 1973) 18.
[147] Solomon Amadiume, *Igbo Tradition and Philosophy* (Enugu:Aritiz Communication, 1998) 5-14.
[148] G. T. Basden, *Among the Ibos of Nigeria* (New York: Barnes and Noble, 1966) 31.
[149] Isichei, *The Ibo People and the Europeans,* 18-26.
[150] G. T. Basden, *Among the Ibos,* 28.
[151] Daryll Forde and G. I. Jones, *The Ibo and Ibibio-Speaking Peoples of South-Eastern Nigeria* (London: Oxford University Press, 1950) 28-60.
[152] Ibid., 9.
[153] Ibid., 9.
[154] Chinnyelu Moses Ugwu, *Healing in the Nigerian Church:A Pastoral-psychological Exploration,* (Bern: Peter Lang, 1998) 35. The sources of knowledge of Igbo Religious beliefs and practices reflected in this work are mainly from Ugwu and Edmund Ilogu, *Christianity and Ibo Culture* (Leiden: E. J. Brill, 1974). Ugwu admits that there are differences in the belief systems of different Igbo communities. Ugwu, *Healing in the Nigerian Church,* 39.
[155] Ibid., 40. Ilogu mentions only Chukwu and Chineke. Ilogu, *Christianity and Ibo Culture,* 34.
[156] Ibid., 34, 35.
[157] Ibid., 53.
[158] Dualism is explained by Millard Erickson as: "Dualisms propose that there are not one but two ultimate principles in the universe: God and the power of evil. This evil is generally thought of as uncreated, simply a force that has always been present. There is therefore a struggle between God and this evil power, with no certainty as to the ultimate outcome. God is attempting to overcome evil, and would if he could, but he is simply unable to do so." Millard Erickson, *Christian Theology,* 2nd ed. (Grand Rapids: Baker Books, 2001) 440.
[159] Ugwu, *Healing in the Nigerian Church,* 41. Ilogu specifically asserts that the concept of Ekwensu, an Igbo equivalent of the Christian Satan, was borrowed from Christianity. He supports this view with the claim that there is neither any known authentic traditional

Igbo proverb that refers to *Ekwensu* nor an Igbo name that alludes to *Ekwensu*. Ilogu, *Christianity and Ibo Culture*, 38, 39.

[160] The problem of evil evolves around the omnipotence and goodness of God as against the reality of evil in the world. Erickson puts the problem in a thought-provoking way: "For if God is great, then he is able to prevent evil from occurring. If God is good, he will not wish for evil to occur. But there is rather evident evil about us. The problem of evil then may be thought of as a conflict involving three concepts: God's power, God's goodness, and the presence of evil in the world." Erickson, *Christian Theology*, 437.

[161] Quoted in Ugwu, *Healing in the Nigerian Church*, 47.

[162] Ibid., 48.

[163] Ibid., 50, 51.

[164] Ibid., 51.

[165] Ibid., 51.

[166] Ibid., 53. Ugwu claims that the belief in witchcraft is not prevalent in all Igbo communities. It is however strong in the riverside Igbo communities. Ibid., 54.

[167] Ibid., 29, 30.

[168] Ilogu, 39.

[169] Sanneh, *West African Christianity*, 36. Pages 36 – 52 give examples of the policy.

[170] Ibid., 38.

[171] Ibid., 47, 48, 51, 52.

[172] Sanneh mentions four types of freed slaves who were settled in Sierra Leone. They were: (1) The Black Poor, i.e., slaves in England who proclaimed their freedom after the favorable ruling in the Somerset Trial in England in 1772. The self-proclaimed freed slaves left the homes of their slave masters without any prior provision for their sustenance. They became poor as a result; (2) the Nova Scotian Settlers, slaves who fought alongside with British army during the American War of Independence. They were settled in Nova Scotia after the war and finally settled in Sierra Leone; (3) the Maroons, they were off-springs of some Africans and Indians escaped into the bush lands of Jamaica; (4) the Recaptives, slaves who were recaptured by British Naval men on the high seas and set free. The Recaptives came from many parts of Africa. Lamin Sanneh, *West African Christianity*, 68-74.

[173] Ajayi, *Christian Missiions in Nigeria*, 10. Italics mine.

[174] Quoted in Ajayi, ibid., 10, 11.

[175] According to Ajayi, "Buxton adopted the slogan from Read, a missionary in South Africa. Read had said: 'We take the plough with us, but let it be remembered that in Africa the Bible and the Plough go together.'" Ajayi, *Christian Missions in Nigeria*, 17.

[176] Nicholas Omenka, "The role of the Catholic mission in the development of vernacular literature in eastern Nigeria," *Journal of Religion in Africa*, 26, fasc. 2, 1986, 121-137.

[177] Ibid., 125.

[178] Elizabeth Isichei, *The Ibo People and the Europeans*, 101, 102.

[179] Ugwu, *Healing in the Nigerian Church*, 106.

[180] Ugwu describes such religious practices as "obnoxious." Ibid., 94. See also Ilogu, *Christianity and Ibo Culture*, 103. The banning of such practices was initially not easy. Ilogu gives an account (recorded in the Journal of Rev. Solomon Samuel Perry, a C.M.S. missionary from Sierra Leone of Igbo parentage, stationed at Onitsha) of how some traditional rulers at Onitsha attacked some C.M.S. members for saving the lives of some twins born to a convert. In an ensuing attack two Christians were killed and the mission house was looted. Ilogu, *Christianity and Ibo Culture*, 64, 65.

[181] These achievements were not possible without the active involvement of local members of the Western mission-founded churches. Ugwu acknowledges the great contributions of the laity who were trained to be Catechists/teachers who were considered as "new missionaries." He quotes Ozigboh to elucidate the activities of the Catechists/teachers:

"They catechized. They conducted Sunday services in the outstations. They examined the candidates for the sacraments (Baptism, Holy Communion and Confirmation); often they did this as preliminary to the priest 'public examination' of the same candidates: They made home-visitations in the village to instruct and to baptise those in danger of death. They acted as liaison and as public relations officers for the missionary. They interpreted for the priest when the latter was on a visit to the station. In fact, the local church of the village station grew around the catechist." Ugwu, *Healing in the Nigerian Church*, 100, 101. Isichei records that: "In 1906, the Holy Ghost mission had ten priests, five lay brothers, and thirty-three African catechists." Isichei, *The Ibo People and the Europeans*, 150.

[182] Felix K. Ekechi, *The Medical Factor in Christian Conversion*, 294 -296.

[183] Ibid., 294.

[184] Ibid., 296.

[185] Some of the new converts sought protection from the Christian God, not necessarily healing. This is so because a non-Christian soothsayer, during the smallpox epidemic, told the people of Onitsha that unless they listened to the missionaries they would be wiped out by the epidemic. Ilogu, *Christianity and Ibo Culture*, 86, 87.

[186] Ugwu writes at length about this religious concept and practice by the Igbos. Ugwu, *Healing in the Nigerian Church*, 108-113.

[187] Ibid., 105, 106. Augustine Radillo, a Baptist deacon, for instance, changed his name to Chukwuma, which means, "God knows." Isichei, *The Ibo People and the Europeans*, 92.

[188] Jordan, *Bishop Shanahan of Southern Nigeria*, 77.

[189] Kirk-Green, *Crisis and Conflicts in Nigeria*, 412 - 414.

[190] Ogbu U. Kalu, "Color and Conversion: The White Missionary Factor in the Christianization of Igboland, 1857-1967" *Missiology* 18, no. 1 (1990) 63.

[191] Ibid., 61-70.

[192] Quoted in Ajayi, *Christian Missions in Nigeria*, 126.

[193] Ajayi, *Christian Missiions in Nigeria*, 130.

[194] Sanneh, *Translating the Message*, 148.

[195] Anthony O. Nkwoka. "The Role of the Bible in the Igbo Christianity of Nigeria" in *The Bible in Africa* (Leiden: Brill, 2000) 326. Dennis was an Anglican clergyman.

[196] Ben Fulford, "An Igbo Esperanto: A History of the Union Bible 1900-1950," *The Journal of Religion in Africa*, Vol. 32.4 (2002) 477.

[197] Ugwu, quoting from other sources, narrates two incidents about the dissimilarity of Igbo dialects that embarrassed Rev. J. Friederich Schön, a German missionary who was a genius in linguistics. "In July 1841, the expeditions sailed from Freetown and in a month's time was sailing up the Niger through the Igbo country. At a stopover, Schön tried to communicate in Igbo with a people he met at Aboh. But to his utter disappointment the people did not understand him clearly. So he lamented his wasted efforts in the following words...'the dialect of the Ibo language on which I had bestowed so much labour in Sierra Leone differs widely from that spoken and understood in this part of the country. It never escaped my observation, that a great diversity of dialects existed; but I must blame myself for the present occasion.'" The other incident occurred when Schön was addressing the Obi (King) of Aboh in Igbo. The Obi, after being impressed by Schön's pronunciation and intonation, got bored and had to stop him midway in his address. Ugwu, *Healing in the Nigerian Church*, 86.

[198] Ben Fulford, *An Igbo Esperanto*, 472.

[199] Sanneh, *Translating the Message*, 149.

[200] Nkwonka claims that the Union Ibo remained "unchallenged as the most used and influential translation among the Igbo." Nkwoka, *The Role of the Bible in Igbo Christianity*, 327. Perhaps the size of the Bible also merited its description as "monumental." Nkwoka further states that "When I was a boy, the Roman Catholics used to taunt us by offering us '*aju*' to help us carry this Bible on account of its volume (1,075 pages)..." Aju is described as a

cushion-like object made from old soft clothes or banana leaves used to carry heavy loads on the head in Igboland. Nkwoka, ibid., 326.

[201] Omenka, *The Role of the Catholic Mission*, 124.

[202] The new orthography was devoid of the distinctive local characteristics of the Igbo language. It was, consequently, received with much prejudice, albeit accepted in the long run. Omenka, ibid., 123.

[203] Ajayi, *Christian Missions in Nigeria*, 130. ("Today," i.e., cannot be said to be a period beyond 1965 when the book was published).

[204] Anthony Nkwoka, *The Role of the Bible in Igbo Christianity*, 327.

[205] Ibid., 326, 334.

[206] Ben Fulford, *An Igbo Esperanto*, 476.

[207] Amongst other examples, such a transition can be seen in the case of the Yoruba, where the word "Yoruba" was originally a Hausa term not used by the Yorubas. It was taken up by Samuel Crowther to denote the language of the people he and his colleagues were trying to reach; Crowther was indeed the first Yoruba to call himself such. Through Bible translation, missionary work, and missionary schemas of native history, a generation of the Yoruba came to use that term for themselves, as they forged an identity with the tools of Crowther and other CMS missionaries and agents had equipped them. Ibid., 491.

[208] Johnstone et al. *Operation World*, 488. Nigeria ranked second to South Africa, which had 4,589 AIC denominations in 2001. Ibid., 577.

[209] See also the figure of AICs in Nigeria as compared to that of the total figure of AICs in Africa. Ibid., 21.

[210] Ibid., 488.

[211] Ayegboyin and Ishola, *African Indigenous Churches*, 34 - 42.

[212] Sanneh, *Translating the Message*, 147 - 151.

[213] One of the churches founded in this era was Christ Apostolic Church which began as a prayer group called Precious Stone or Diamond Society in St. Saviour's Anglican Church at Ijebu-Ode. This was in response to the influenza epidemic in 1918. Acting on a vision seen by Sophia Odunlami, the prayer group began using blessed water to heal. The precious stone prayer group got in touch with Faith Tabernacle, an American Pentecostal group, which influenced them on the efficacy on prayer, the importance of personal holiness, healing, the millennial return of Jesus Christ, and adult baptism. These new teachings set a head-long collision course between members of the prayer group and the Anglican authorities. A split became inevitable. The prayer group later was turned into an Apostolic Church. It is now known as the Christ Apostolic Church. Sanneh, *West African Christianity*, 184 - 186.

[214] Ogbu Kalu does not regard the Braide's movement as the first Aladura movement in Igboland. He claims that the Braide movement was weak in organization and funding and soon fizzled out. "...the charismatic ministry of his followers could be seen as a precursor of modern Pentecostalism as his influence swept like a 'wave from the rivers' from 1918-1939." To Kalu, it was not until late 1940s that the Aladura movement emerged in Igboland. He, therefore, argues that the establishment of the Faith Tabernacle (a.k.a. Naked Faith People) in Igboland by Pastor E. T. Epelle in 1925 rather was the precursor of both Aladura and Pentecostalism in Igboland. Cf. Ogbu U. Kalu, "Doing Mission through the Post Office: the Naked Faith People of Igboland 1920-1960," *Neue Zeitschrift für Missionswissenschaft. Separat-Abdruck*, 56-2000/4, 263-280. Edmund Ilogu, on the other hand, states that the Braide movement was the "first 'Prophet' Church as well as the first breakaway Church which eventually grew in Iboland. Today the Christ Army Church of Garrick Braide has divided into two: Christ Army Church and Christ Army Church Garrick Braide Connection." Ilogu, *Christianity and Ibo Culture*, 59. Note: "Today" refers to the period leading to 1974 when his book was published.

[215] According to Sanneh, "The water in which he washed was collected and dispensed with spiritual force." Sanneh, *West African Christianity*, 182.

[216] Ibid., 182.

[217] The activities of the healing homes took place at the open compounds of the houses, hence the name "Compound churches." See Rosalind Hackett, *Women as Leaders and Participants*, 195. A proper understanding of the activities and perception of Prayer houses will aid readers to understand the context of the early ministry of Agnes Okoh and the claims of members of her church that they were persecuted by members of some established Christian churches in Igboland.

[218] Ilogu, *Christianity and Ibo Culture*, 61. Another source claims that, "Madam Nwokolo was said to have been cured of insanity in a prayer-house and was advised to set up a family prayer meeting in her home in 1957. In 1958 she affiliated herself with the C.M.S. as a prayer-house (not a church)." Cf. Thaddeus Ihejiofor, et. al. *Prayer Houses and Faith Healing*, Vincent Nwosu, ed. (Onitsha: Tabansi Press, 1971) 26. There were some well-developed AICs from western Nigeria that were operating alongside the healing homes of the Igbo indigenes. Some of these were the Christ Apostolic Church and Cherubim and Seraphim Church. Another AIC, Muyiary-El-Cherubin and Seraphim, was begun in 1971 by an Igbo indigene, one Apostle Peter. Ilogu, ibid., 102.

[219] The Omenma Central Prayer at Omuma in Orlu, The All Christian Prayer Band of Madam Nwokolo in Ufuma, The Cherubim and Seraphim Holy Prayer House of Prophet Caleb Orji in Ufuma, and Christ Healing Sabbath of Mystic Theo. Nwokeocha in Amucha. Ihejiofor, et. al. *Prayer Houses and Faith Healing in Nigeria*, 32-34.

[220] Ibid., 39.

[221] Ibid., 42.

[222] Ibid., 44.

[223] Ibid., 44.

[224] Ibid., 35 – 45.

[225] One-third of the pastors interviewed by the author were formerly members of the Roman Catholic Church. Another third also claim to be former members of the Anglican community in Nigeria.

[226] Ihejiofor, et al., *Prayer Houses and Faith Healing in Nigeria*, 46 – 52.

[227] These measures were quoted in Ugwu, *Healing in the Nigerian Church*, 134. See also G. C. Ikeobi, "Catholic Response to the Challenge of 'Prayer Houses' – Origin of the 'Tuesday Prayer' in Onitsha" in V.A. Nwosu (ed.), *The Catholic Church in Onitsha*, Onitsha, 1985.

[228] Quoted in Ugwu, ibid., 134. The Catholics did not only punish their members for patronizing Prayer houses. They began a similar ministry in 1973. The prayer ministry is now popularly known as the "Tuesday Prayer Group."

[229] Quoted in Ugwu, ibid., 132.

[230] Basden, *Among the Ibos of Nigeria*, 66, 94.

[231] Ilogu, *Christianity and Ibo Culture*, 60.

[232] Ibid., 61. According to Kalu, the Naked Faith people were operating in Igboland by this time. Kalu, *Doing Mission through the Post Office*, 263-280. Agnes Okoh's search for healing in the Prayer houses indicates that there were some prayer houses in Igboland in the early 1940s.

[233] A title that was given to Agnes Okoh. Much will be said about the title in the following pages.

[234] Enoch N. Okonkwo. "Interview with Rev. Enoch N. Okonkwo (Rtd)," interview by Samuel O. A. Ozomah, n.d. *Glad News* 1. no. 2, (n.d.) 12. *Glad News* is a publication of Christ Holy Church. Rev. Okonkwo was healed by Agnes Okoh. He later became a member of the church and subsequently a pastor. He worked with Agnes from 1956 to 1982.

[235] Quoted in Daniel Okoh, "Message from the General Superintendent: Mission Statement of Christ Holy Church." in *Glad News*, 1, no. 1 (2000) 4. Note: Odozi Obodo refers to Agnes Okoh. There will be more details about the title, Odozi Obodo.

[236] Enoch Okonkwo, interview by Samuel Ozomah, n.d. *Glad News*, 1 no. 2. (n.d.) 12.

[237] *New American Standard Version of the Holy Bible*. (Chattanooga: AMG Publishers, 1977).

[238] In her later ministries she wore ordinary clothing, no different from what the ordinary woman wore on the street.

[239] Pidgin English is a street English spoken widely in Nigeria and some Anglophone West African Countries. One does not need to have class room instruction to speak Pidgin English. See footnote 102 for a typical example of a Pidgin English.

[240] Catherine Aso, an Octogenarian elder of Christ Holy Church, Okigwe, Imo State, rendered her recollection of Agnes Okoh's sermon. Interview by author, 11 August 2003, tape recording, Good News Theological College and Seminary, Accra.

[241] The invitation of Gospel messengers to villages and towns and the giving of land as gifts seem to be an old practice among Igbos. Giving a similar example during the days of Western missionaries, Ozigboh recounts: "Several factors determined which missionary society that would be invited... On arrival, the missionary received a tumultuous welcome and gifts to mollify him and make him favourably disposed towards the villagers. The village offered him a piece of land, and readily agreed to the usual conditions for the opening of a catholic station viz: the erection of a school and a catechist's house on the land..." Quoted by Ugwu, *Healing in the Nigerian Church*, 100. Prophetess Agnes Okoh and her followers were not always fortunate to receive a tumultuous welcome and a piece of land from officialdom, as we shall see later, apparently because they were not perceived to have had any social package for their objects of ministry.

[242] A typical example of Agnes' belief in the promptings of the Holy Spirit was narrated by Rev. Okonkwo: "One day she called Mbamalu and Mbaegbu to escort her to Fegge. She did not tell them her mission. At Fegge, she met a man and stopped him. She told the man that she was looking for Mr. Hart. The man said he hoped there was no trouble. She said there was no trouble, that she wanted to meet Mr. Hart. The man said, I am Mr. Hart! She told the man that she was a prophetess and that God directed her to go to Mr. Hart, who will provide a place for her to worship God, and a place for her to live. That Mr. Hart had a lot of houses in Fegge...Mr. Hart was happy because at that time he was in trouble. He had used the wife's name to register a school and the wife had gone to court trying to claim the school...He then took her to the school compound and asked her to choose any building as a place of worship and another for her living place." Enoch Okonkwo, interview by Samuel Ozomah, n.d. *Glad News*, 1, no. 2. (n.d.) 12.

[243] Enoch Okonkwo, interview by Samuel Ozomah, n.d. *Glad News*, 1, no. 2, (n.d.) 12.

[244] Enoch Okonkwo, interview by Samuel Ozomah, n.d. *Glad News*, 1, no. 2. (n.d.) 8.

[245] Daniel C. Dike, Superintendent Minister in charge of Lagos Superintendency, interview by author, 30 August 2003, Lagos, Lagos State, tape recording, Good News Theological College and Seminary, Accra.

[246] Kathleen O'Brien Wicker, "Mami Water in African Religion and Spirituality" in *African Spirituality*, Jacob K. Olupona., ed. (New York, Crossroad Publishing Co., 2000) 199.

[247] Clement Obiokoye, Assistant General Evangelist and Senior Superintendent in charge of Aba Superintendency, interview by author, 25 August 2003, Aba, Abia State, tape recording, Good News Theological College and Seminary, Accra.

[248] Enoch Okonkwo, former leader of Christ Holy Church International, interview by author, 30 July 2003, Onitsha, Anambra State, tape recording, Good News Theological College and Seminary, Accra.

[249] The Church has thrived on donated lands in many cities and villages. There are many instances of people donating land for the Church to build and begin her ministry. An example is the land at Ogidi, donated in 1954 by Mr. Emmanuel Aniagor after being healed by the prophetess. He later became a pastor.

[250] "Evil Forest" in Western terminology is "Haunted Forest."

[251] Samuel Ejiofor, former leader of Christ Holy Church International, interview by author, 9

August 2003, Enugu, Enugu State, tape recording, Good News Theological College and Seminary, Accra.

[252] Basden, *Among the Ibos*, 117.

[253] Ibid., 119.

[254] Ibid., 118.

[255] Chinua Achebe, *Things Fall Apart* (New York: Anchor Books, Doubleday 1959) 18. Achebe mentions also, the throwing away of dead bodies to the Evil Forest of those who die during the Week of Peace at Umuafia. Ibid., 32.

[256] Ibid., 123. Information on the nature and importance of death and burial rites among the Igbos, is from Basden, *Among the Ibos*, 112-126.

[257] The creation of Evil Forests and all the beliefs associated with such forests are still prevalent among the Igbos. Narrating a horrid experience of the widowhood rites and rituals she was subjected to during the death, burial and aftermath of her deceased husband, Umejei Okafor, widow of Andrew Okafor of Ogbochie, Okpanam in Oshimiri Local Government Council of Delta State was threatened that, "Should one decline one of those (*rituals*) one would be disregarded in the community. Should one die in that state, one would not be buried; the corpse would be thrown into *ajo oshia* (evil forest) together with all one's properties." *The Sun*, 30 August 2003. (vol. 1, no. 33) 30.

[258] Achebe, *Things Fall Apart*, 148, 149. The villagers expected the missionaries and their followers to die within four days after entering the Evil Forest but none of them died.

[259] Daniel Okoh, General Superintendent of Christ Holy Church International, narrates another version of the beginning of the use of the title Odozi Obodo. He claims that calling Agnes "Odozi Obodo" was in fulfillment of a divine revelation mediated in a dream through one of her followers. The member, in a dream, heard many people calling prophetess Agnes Okoh "Odozi Obodo" repeatedly. After the member had narrated the dream during a worship service, people began calling the prophetess, Odozi Obodo. Interview by author, 26 August 2003, Asaba, Delta State, tape recording, Good News Theological College and Seminary, Accra.

[260] Peter Nlemadim DomNwachukwu, *Authentic African Christianity: an Inculturation Model for the Igbo* (New York: Peter Lang, 2000) 88.

[261] Much will be said about events that led to this name and how the Church was re-named Christ Holy Church.

[262] H. Onyema Anyanwu, "Missionaries and Women Emancipation in Igboland" *Journal of Dharma*, 26, (2001) 229.

[263] Anyanwu, *Missionaries and Women Emancipation*, 229.

[264] Ibid., 232, 233.

[265] DomNwachukwu, *Authentic African Christianity*, 42, 43.

[266] Anyanwu, *Missionaries and Women Emancipation.*, 233, 234.

[267] Rev. Samuel Ejiofor, interview by author, 9 August 2003.

[268] Daniel C. Dike, interview by author, 30 August 2003.

[269] Emmanuel Alamanjo claims that not until he had been trained by the Prophetess and commissioned to pastor a congregation, he did not know how high the economy of Nigeria was. Rev. Alamanjo, District Minister of Christ Holy Church International, Festac-Lagos District, interview by author, 30 August 2003, Lagos, Lagos State, tape recording, Good News Theological College and Seminary, Accra. Rev. Pastor Charles Obalum claims that the Prophetess fed him and 49 other pastors under training from 1971-1972. "She gave us any kind of food one would request." Charles Obalum, Pastor of Christ Holy Church International, Nteje Superintendency, interview by author, 7 August 2003, Awka-Nteje, Anambra State, tape recording, Good News Theological College and Seminary, Accra.

[270] Many other leaders of Christ Holy Church have some appellations that spur them into action.

[271] According to D. C. Dike, when difficult issues are brought before the Prophetess and her council of leaders she would say "Let us hear the voice of the Lord." The whole council will

then keep quiet for some time till some one or Mama herself speaks. She would then solve the issue authoritatively believing that the Lord had solved the problem in proxy. Daniel C. Dike, interview by author, 30 August 2003.

[272] None of her followers have a living memory of the last time River Niger dried up.

[273] There is a popular belief that in 1957 the prophetess claimed that God had asked her to throw a challenge to all spiritualists and medicine men in the Onitsha area to test her powers to ascertain if it were not from God. She, therefore, raised a platform and sat on a chair for seven days (morning till evening) asking anyone who doubted the source of her powers to come forward to challenge. It is claimed that many native doctors and spiritualists accepted the challenge and tested her with blindness, thunder, lightening, paralysis, and other spells but none succeeded.

[274] Enoch Okonkwo, "Interview with Glad News" interview by Samuel O. A. Ozomah, n.d. *Glad News*, 1, no. 2. (n.d.) 9.

[275] Cf: 1Tim. 2:11-14; 1 Cor. 14:34. The author is aware of the different interpretations of these texts and their resultant controversies surrounding the ordination of women and female leadership in the Church. The purpose of this dissertation is not to attempt an exegetical analysis of such interpretations and theological positions. This is just highlighting the belief of a prophetess who felt called by God and how God used her to make a mark on African Christianity.

[276] David O. U. Nwaizuzu, former leader of Christ Holy Church International, interview by author, 2 August 2003, Onitsha, Anambra State, tape recording, Good News Theological College and Seminary, Accra.

[277] Much will be discussed about the development of leadership in the Church in the next chapter.

[278] Lucy Harriet Harrison, founder of Church of Christ the Good Shepherd, and Theresa Effiong, founder of the Holy Chapel of Miracles (all in Nigeria), both had Catholic backgrounds. Both of them did not assume leadership of their respective churches. They entrusted leadership positions to men. Rosalind Hackett, *Women as Leaders and Participants*, 191-196.

[279] Christian Obiefuna, Superintendent Minister of Christ Holy Church International, Asaba Superintendency, interview by author, 26 August 2003, Asaba, Delta State, tape recording, Good News Theological College and Seminary, Accra.

[280] Daniel C. Dike, interview by author, 28 August 2003, Lagos, tape recording, Good News Theological College and Seminary, Accra.

[281] Enoch Okonkwo, interview by Samuel Ozomah, n.d. *Glad News*, 1, no. 2. (n.d.) 13.

[282] Enoch Okonkwo, interview by Samuel Ozomah, n.d. *Glad News*, 1. no. 2, (n.d.) 10.

[283] John Obiakor, pastor of Christ Holy Church, Ihitenansa Superintendency, interview by author, 15 August 2003, Ihitenansa, Imo State, tape recording, Good News Theological College and Seminary, Accra.

[284] Chidi Mbadiwe, elder of Christ Holy Church International, Festac-Lagos, interview by author, 28 August 2003, Lagos, Lagos State, tape recording, Good News Theological College and Seminary, Accra. Elder Mbadiwe's mother was the first Secretary to Prophetess Agnes Okoh.

[285] John Ekweoba, Assistant Superintendent Minister of Christ Holy Church International, Okigwe Superintendency, interview by author, 11 August 2003, Okigwe, Imo State, tape recording, Good News Theological College and Seminary, Accra.

[286] Emmanuel Alamanjo, interview by author, Lagos, 29 August 2003, tape recording, Good News Theological College and Seminary, Accra.

[287] Characteristics of most of these early lifestyles of the Church are still prevalent.

[288] Gabriel Chiemeka, Assistant General Superintedent and General Evangelist of Christ Holy Church International, interview by author, 27 August 2003, Nnewi, Anambra State, tape recording, Good News Theological College and Seminary, Accra.

[289] Enoch Okonkwo, interview by Samuel Ozomah, n.d. *Glad News*, 1, no. 2. (n.d.) 10.
[290] Eusebius N. Iloabuchi, acting Superintendent Minister of Nteje Superintendency, Christ Holy Church International, interview by author, 7 August 2003, Awka-Nteje, Anambra State, tape recording, Good News Theological College and Seminary, Accra.
[291] Emmanuel Alamanjo, interview by author, 31 August 2003, Lagos, Lagos State, recording, Good News Theological College and Seminary, Accra.
[292] Emmanuel Alamanjo, interview by author, 31 August 2003.
[293] Ijeoma Nwachukwu, interview by author, 18 August 2003.
[294] Claims of receiving divine directives to use streams to heal are very common in Nigerian Church history. During the influenza epidemic in 1918, Miss Sophia Odunlami, a member of the Precious Stones, claimed to have been instructed in a vision that using rain water and prayer could heal influenza patients. Many patients were reported to have been healed as a result. See Ayegboyin and Ishola, *African Indigenous Church*, 67. Joseph Babalola, one of the Christ Apostolic Church's spiritual stalwarts, too, blessed water to heal from a stream that was close to his revival ground. ibid., 74. Prophet Moses Orimolade Tunolase, who was born a cripple but later became the Baba Aladura (the Praying Father) of Cherubim and Seraphim Society, was also said to have been directed in a vision to use water from a stream for his healing. Although he was not totally healed, he was able to limp for the rest of his life. ibid., 81.
[295] The Nkissi stream can be located behind the walls of *The Church of the Holy Spirit* (a Catholic Church) at Omagba, Onitsha.
[296] Christian Obiefuna, interview by author, 5 August 2003, Ogwashi-Ukwu, Delta State, tape recording, Good News Theological College and Seminary Accra.
[297] John Obiakor, interview by author, 15 August 2003.
[298] Daniel Okoh, interview by author, 26 August 2003.
[299] Enoch Okonkwo, interview by author, 30 July 2003. There are many other pastors who claim that they were healed by the prophetess.
[300] Daniel Okoh "A Life Lived For Christ", 8 April 1995, eulogy in honor of Agnes Okoh, at Ndoni, Rivers State, (photocopy) p. 3, Official documents at the Head Office of Christ Holy Church International, Onitsha, Anambra State.
[301] Ijeoma Nwachukwu, interview by author, 18 August 2003.
[302] According to John Ekweoba, after seventeen years of marriage without children, the Prophetess prophesied to him in the middle of a conversation at Ndoni that God had answered his prayers and that his wife would give birth to a child that year. Today Rev. Ekweoba and his wife have four children. Interview by author, 11 August 2003.
[303] Gabriel Chiemeka, *Glad News*, 1, no. 2. (n.d.) 7.
[304] Gabriel Chiemeka, *Glad News* 1, no. 2 (n.d.) 7. Harvest is a terminology by West African Christians for a one day Fund Raising activities on the premises of a church.
[305] Enoch Okonkwo and Daniel Nwaizuzu, interviewed jointly by author, 30 August 2003, Onitsha, Anambra State, tape recording, Good News Theological College and Seminary, Accra.
[306] Cyril Ofoedu, evangelist of Christ Holy Church International, interview by author, 26 August 2003, Asaba, Delta State, tape recording, Good News Theological College and Seminary, Accra.
[307] Deaconess Victoria Njoku, one of the early followers and for a long time a house-help of Prophetess Agnes Okoh, interview by Emmanuel Aniago, 11 April 2003, Onitsha, Anambra State, tape recording, Headquarters of Christ Holy Church International, Onitsha. Read "Ojukwu's Message As He flees Biafra" in A. H. M. Kirk-Green, *Crisis and Conflicts in Nigeria*, 449, 450. Lt. Col. Effiong announced the Surrender of Biafra a day after Ojukwu had led Biafra to exile. In his first speech after the surrender of Biafra, Ojukwu stated that he and certain members of his cabinet left Biafra "as a result of a decision taken by that Cabinet in the interest of our people's survival." A. H. M. Kirk-Green, *Crisis and Conflict*, 453.

[308] Emmanuel Aniagor, pastor of Christ Holy Church International, interview by author, 11 August 2003, Okigwe, Imo State, tape recording, Good News Theological College, Accra.

[309] Enoch Okonkwo, interview by Samuel Ozomah, n.d. *Glad News*, 1, no. 2. (n.d.) 8.

[310] Daniel C. Okoh, *eulogy in honor of Agnes Okoh*, 8 August 1995.

[311] Daniel Okoh, interview by author, 1 August 2003.

[312] Christianah Anyanwu, midwife of Christ Holy Church International's Maternity Home, Ndoni, interview by author, 1 August 2003, Ndoni, Rivers State, tape recording, Good News Theological College and Seminary, Accra.

[313] Gabriel Okeyia, His Royal Highness, the Awo and Okpala-Ukwu of Ndoni, interview by author, 18 August 2003, Ndoni, Rivers State, tape recording, Good News Theological College and Seminary, Accra.

[314] G. I. Obikwelu, "Report on Ndoni Convention," *Good Tidings*, Third Issue, (n.d.) 12.

[315] Ibid., 13.

[316] *Glad News*, 1. no. 1, (2000) 11. An estimated crowd of one million was said to have patronized a three-day National Convention of Christ Holy Church at Ndoni from 13 to 16 February 1976. See *Good Tidings*, third Issue, (n.d.) 10, 13.

[317] Gabriel Okeyia, interview by author, 18 August 2003.

[318] Ijeoma Nwachukwu, interview by author, 18 August 2003.

[319] Clement Obiokoye, interview by author, 25 August 2003.

[320] See E. I. Alamanjo, "Rev. D. O. U. Nwaizuzu (Rtd.)" *Glad News*, 1, no. 2 (n.d.) 28.

[321] E. I. Alamanjo, "Rev. F. N. Okonkwo (Ret.)" *Glad News*, 1. no. 2, (n.d.) 28. Alamanjo states that Okonkwo and Nwaizuzu were appointed Catechists in 1954. However, when writing the life history of Nwaizuzu he states that Nwaizuzu was appointed Catechist in 1956, cf. *Glad News*, 1. no. 2, (n.d.) 30. The fact that the two men were appointed on the same day is incontrovertible. At a joint interview by author on 31 July 2003 at Onitsha, Anambra State, Okonkwo and Nwaizuzu affirmed that they were both elevated to the position of Catechists on a Friday in 1956.

[322] Ibid., 29.

[323] Ibid., 29.

[324] Emmanuel Aniago, interview by author, 31 July 2003, Onitsha, Anambra State, tape recording, Good News Theological College and Seminary, Accra.

[325] Enoch Okonkwo, interview by Samuel Ozomah, n.d. *Glad News*, 1, no. 2, (n.d.) 10. The healing of the two lame sisters occurred in 1963. See Appendix D - a picture of Rev. Okonkwo healing a lame person.

[326] Enoch Okonkwo, interview by author, 30 July 2003.

[327] E. I. Alamanjo, "Rev. D. O. U. Nwaizuzu (Ret.)" *Glad News*, 1. no. 2, (n.d.) 30.

[328] Emmanuel Aniago, interview by author, 31 July 2003.

[329] Daniel Okoh, "Focus on Rt. Rev. Marius Okoh: Foremost African Evangelist" *Glad News*, 1, no. 1, (April-June 2000) 7.

[330] The highest position of authority in the Church is *General Superintendent*. The position of Marius' mother was *General Prophetess*. Marius was the first General Superintendent of the Church. He was christened "Right Reverend."

[331] David Nwaizuzu, interview by author, 2 August 2003.

[332] Okoh, "Focus on Rt. Rev. Marius Okoh: Foremost African Evangelist" *Glad News*, 1, no. 1 (2000) 7.

[333] David Nwaizuzu, interview by author, 12 August 2003.

[334] Okoh, "Focus on Rt. Rev. Marius Okoh: Foremost African Evangelist" *Glad News*, (n.d.) 8.

[335] Ibid., 8.

[336] Ibid., 8. Other sources (Revds. Nicholas Udemba and Samuel Ejiofor) claim that Marius used

his gratuity money to buy a fleet of taxis and used the proceeds to support the activities of the church.

[337] Okoh, "Focus on Rt. Rev. Marius Okoh: Foremost African Evangelist" *Glad News*, (n.d.) 8.

[338] Okonkwo, interview by Samuel Ozomah, n.d. *Glad News*, 1. no. 2 (n.d.) 8.

[339] Okoh, "Focus on Rt. Rev. Marius Okoh: Foremost African Evangelist" *Glad News*, 1, no. 1. (2000) 8.

[340] Okonkwo and Nwaizuzu, joint interview by author, 2 August 2003, This view about Marius Okoh is shared by about 80% of the people interviewed (formally and informally). "Workers" as used in Christ Holy Church circles stands for pastors and staff of the Church.

[341] Okoh, "Focus on Rt. Rev. Marius Okoh: Foremost African Evangelist" *Glad News*, 1, no. 1, (2000) 8.

[342] Nicholas Udemba, Assistant Superintendent of Enugu Superintendency, Christ Holy Church International, interview by author, 9 August 2003, Enugu, Enugu State, tape recording, Good News Theological College and Seminary, Accra. Rev. Udemba is the General Secretary of the Church.

[343] Okoh, "Focus on Rt. Re. Marius Okoh: Foremost African Evangelist" *Glad News*, 1, no. 1, (2000) 8.

[344] Clement Obiokoye, interview by author, 25 August 2003.

[345] Isaac O. Afunwa, "Glad News Interview with Very Rev. I. O. Afunwa" interview by Samuel O . A. Ozomah, n.d. *Glad News*, 1. no. 2, (n.d.) 15.

[346] G. I. Obikwelu, "Prefactory." *Good Tidings*, third issue, (n.d.) 1.

[347] Samuel Ejiofor, interview by author, 9 August 2003. This is a miracle that is well-known among Christ Holy Church members.

[348] G. I. Obikwelu. "The Inauguration of the Christ Holy Church in Enugu and its Temporary Opening for Prayers and Worships." *Good Tidings*, third issue, (n.d.) 29.

[349] Samuel Ejiofor, interview by author, 9 August 2003.

[350] Eusebius N. Iloabuchi, interview by author, 7 August 2003.

[351] Gabriel O. Chiemeka, interview by Samuel Ozomah, n.d. *Glad News*, 1, no. 2, (n.d.) 14.

[352] Ibid., 14.

[353] Daniel Okoh, interview by author, 26 August 2003.

[354] Daniel Okoh, interview by author, 26 August 2003.

[355] Daniel Okoh, interview by author, 26 August 2003.

[356] Daniel Okoh, interview by author, 26 August 2003.

[357] Daniel Okoh, interview by author, 26, August 2003.

[358] Daniel Okoh, interview by author, 26 August 2003.

[359] Daniel Okoh, interview by author, 26 August 2003.

[360] Daniel Okoh, interview by author, 26 August 2003.

[361] The Statement of Faith will be discussed in chapter seven.

[362] The last congregation at which a person pastored before retirement is obliged to give a retirement package to the retiree at the time of retirement. This is in addition to what the Headquarters gives. At the end of every month, retired pastors are given half of the monthly allowance at the time they retired. An offering is taken for all retired pastors on the first Sunday of every June. During annual harvests, the church gives festive packages to the retirees.

[363] In 2002 the Church bought three brand new Peugeots salon cars for three former leaders of the Church - Enoch Okonkwo, David O. U. Nwaizuzu and Samuel Ejiofor. The Church, in addition, employed chauffeurs for each of the retirees and promised to give them monthly stipends for fuel. The church has built a house for Deaconess Cecilia Obi, one of the 12 members who formed the nucleus of the Prayer ministry in the late 1940s, in appreciation of her contributions to the Church.

[364] Emmanuel Alamanjo, interview by author, 29 August 2003.

[365] Emmanuel Alamanjo, interview by author, 29 August 2003.

[366] There will be more discussions on the Women's annual convention and HIV/AIDS Conferences in chapter eight.

[367] Emmanuel Asadu, Technician/audio engineer of the Nation Builders Band, the national Gospel Band. Christ Holy Church International, interview by author, 5 August 2003, Onitsah, Anambra State, tape recording, Good News Theological College and Seminary, Accra.

[368] Samuel Ejiofor, interview by author, 9 August 2003.

[369] For a detailed discussion of Western missionaries' attempt to create an indigenous Church in West Africa, see Peter Clarke, *West Africa and Christianity* (London: Edward Arnold Publishers Ltd., 1986) 47 - 85.

[370] Eusebius Iloabuchi, interview by author, 7 August 2003.

[371] Anthony Anyalebechi, evangelist of Christ Holy Church International, Ekwegbe Station, interview by author, 8 August 2003, Nssuka, Enugu State, tape recording, Good News Theological College and Seminary, Accra.

[372] Nicholas Udemba, interview by author, 9 August 2003. Udemba's home town is Umùozu, Imo State.

[373] Michael Martey Mensah, senior Evangelist of Christ Holy Church International, interview by author, 5 August 2003, Onitsha, Anambra State, tape recording, Good News Theological College and Seminary, Accra.

[374] Information of the financial practice of the Church was given by Evangelist Everest Obioma, a member of the Financial Committee of Okpoko, No. 1 congregation. Interview by author, 5 August 2003, Onitsha, Anambra State, tape recording, Good News Theological College and Seminary, Accra.

[375] Catherine Asor, interview by author, 11 August 2003.

[376] M. A. Okoh, *Christ Holy Church: Order of Services* (Onitsha: Confidence Enterprises Ltd., n.d.) 5.

[377] Ibid., 6, 7.

[378] Linda Guy, "My Africa Experience of God's People," *Glad News*, 1, no. 2, (n. d.) 18.

[379] Augustine Eboh, interview by author, 24 August 2003.

[380] The leader of the Church, the Most Rev. Daniel C. Okoh, is presently the Second Vice President of the OAIC, Nigerian Region.

[381] Michael Wells, International Director of Abiding Life Ministries International, Littleton, interview by Samuel Ozomah, 27 February 2000, Itire, Lagos State, *Glad News*, 1. no. 2 (n.d.) 19.

[382] John Obiakor, interview by author, 15 August 2003.

[383] Daniel Udema Aneso, Superintendent Minister of Nssuka Superintendency, Christ Holy Church International, Nssuka, interview by author, 8 August 2003, Nssuka, Enugu State, tape recording, Good News Theological College and Seminary, Accra.

[384] Christian Obiefuna, interview by author, 23 August 2003, Asaba, Delta State, tape recording, Good News Theological College and Seminary, Accra.

[385] Chidi Mbadiwe, interview by author, 30 August 2003, Lagos, Lagos State, tape recording, Good News Theological College and Seminary, Accra.

[386] "Crusade" as used in this work stands for outdoor evangelistic campaigns usually held in the evenings. Its use has nothing to do with the thirteenth century crusades begun by the church in Europe. The use of the term in West African Christianity was popularized by Charismatic churches and some European evangelists working in Nigeria, for example, Reinhard Bonnke, the German evangelist who ministers mainly in Africa.

[387] Daniel Okoh, "Message from the General Superintendent: Mission Statement of Christ Holy Church," *Glad News*, 1, no. 1 (2000) 5.

[388] Ibid., 5.

[389] Gabriel Chiemeka, interview by Samuel Ozomah, n.d. *Glad News* 1 no. 2, (n.d.) 7.
[390] Gabriel Chiemeka, interview by Samuel Ozomah, n.d. *Glad News* 1, no. 2 (n.d.) 7.
[391] For more details of the Second Coming of Jesus Christ, see Millard Erickson, *Christian Theology*, 1191-1200.
[392] General Superintendent, "Christ Holy Church International – Evangelism on the Move," *Glad News*, 1. no. 2 (n.d.) 32.
[393] Michael Wells, interview by Samuel Ozomah, 27 February 2000, *Glad News*, 1, no. 2 (n.d.) 19.
[394] Ugwu, *Healing in the Nigerian Church*, 109.
[395] Emmanuel Asadu, interview by author, 5 August 2003.
[396] Eugene Okere Ogbonna, Senior Catechist of Christ Holy Church International, interview by author, 9 August 2003, Enugu, Enugu State, tape recording, Good News Theological College and Seminary, Accra. Eugene Ogbonna's hometown is Ohuru, in Abia State.
[397] Emmanuel Asadu, interview by author, 5 August 2003.
[398] Daniel Okoh, "Message from the General Superintendent: Mission Statement of Christ Holy Church," *Glad News* 1 no. 1 (2000) 5.
[399] Ugwu, *Healing in the Nigerian Church*, 59.
[400] For detailed study on Witchcraft, see: E. E. Evans-Pritchard, *Witchcraft, Oracles and Magic among the Azande*. Oxford: Oxford University Press, 1937; Geoffrey Parrinder, *Witchcraft: European and African*. New York: Barnes and Noble, 1963.
[401] Kofi Asare Opoku, *West African Traditional Religion* (Accra: F E P International Private Limited, 1978) 140.
[402] Harriet Hill, "Witchcraft and the Gospel: Insights from Africa," *Missiology* 24, no 3, (1996) 334.
[403] Hill, *Witchcraft and the Gospel*, 328.
[404] Quoted in Opoku, *West African Traditional Religion*, 141. The article "The Challenge of Witchcraft" was published in *Orita* Ibadan Journal of Religious Studies, 4, no. 1, June 1970.
[405] John S. Mbiti, *African Religions & Philosophy* (New York: Praeger Publishers, 1969) 200.
[406] Ugwu, *Healing in the Nigerian Church*, 65. Ugwu footnotes the activities of the spirits thus: "Akalogeli are wandering spirits of those who died without children or wealth and consequently received no funeral rites. They wander restlessly because they are unable to reach the spirit-land. The gbnuke are spirits of those who died young. These are frustrated because they were not able to realise their aim or destiny in life. The gbnuke tend to disturb their age-grade members. The gbanye (repeaters) are believed to be a group of spirits of children who organize themselves in groups (Nd„otu) in the spirit world, and decide to be born into various homes only to die young normally before reaching puberty."
[407] Ugwu, *Healing in the Nigerian Church*, 67.
[408] Ibid., 68.
[409] M. M. Green, *Ibo Village Affairs* (New York: Frederick A. Praeger, 1964) 54.
[410] Ugwu, *Healing in the Nigerian Church*, 70.
[411] Ibid., 70.
[412] John P. Jordan, *Bishop Shanahan*, 126, 127, 128.
[413] Ugwu, *Healing in the Nigerian Church*, 71.
[414] Ibid., 71.
[415] Pobee and Ositelu, *African Initiatives*, 40.
[416] Christian Obiefuna, interview by author, 26 August 2003.
[417] The healing accounts of Ebele and Mary Dike were narrated by John Obiakor, in an interview by author, 15 August 2003, Ihitenansa, Imo State. Very Rev. Daniel C. Dike, the Superintendent Minister of Lagos Superintendency is the son of Mary Dike. His mother's healing convinced him to join the church.
[418] Cyril Ofoedu, interview by author, 26 August 2003.

[419] Emmanuel Alamanjo, interview by author, 29 August 2003.
[420] The writer is aware of the controversy over the reality or otherwise of miracles. He does not intend to make any detailed discussion in this work.
[421] Quoted in Ernst & Marie-Luise Keller, *Miracles in Dispute: A Continuing Debate* (Philadelphia: Fortress Press, 1969) 16.
[422] Samuel Ozomah, "Tribute to Very Rev. Isaac O. Afunwa: the Gallant Pull out of a Gallant Soldier," in *Glad News*, 1, no. 2, 16. The miracle might have happened in 1963. The Very Rev. Isaac O. Afunwa was retired from active ministry, though still active and robust in health, through a prophetic utterance on Feb. 23, 2001.
[423] Emmanuel Alamanjo, interview by author, 30 August 2003.
[424] Enoch Okonkwo, interview by Samuel Ozomah, *Glad News*, 1, no. 2 (n.d.) 11.
[425] Christ Holy Church International, *Sunday School Manual*, 8, July -Dec. 2003 (Lagos: Patoz Ventures, 2003) ii.
[426] Emmanuel Alamanjo, interview by author, 29 August 2003.
[427] John Ekweoba, interview by author, 11 August 2003.
[428] Peter Nlemadim DomNwachukwu, *Authentic African Christianity*, 86. See also, Hilary C. Achunike, *Dreams of Heaven: A Modern Response to Christianity in North Western Igboland, 1970-1990* (Enugu: Snaap Printing and Publishing, 1995. Isichei collaborates the growth of AIC after the war. Isichei, *A History of Christianity*, 290.
[429] Okoh, "Focus on Rt. Rev. Marius Okoh: Foremost African Evangelist" *Glad News*, 1, no. 1(2000) 8.
[430] Anderson, *African Reformation*, 96, 97.
[431] Omoyajowo, *Cherubim and Seraphim*, 65 - 70.
[432] Anderson, *African Reformation*, 107.
[433] Omoyajowo, *Cherubim and Seraphim*, 76. On page 136 Omoyajowo states: "Major A. B. Lawrence never gave a reason for breaking away from the Praying Band in 1932. We have suggested that, as a famous charismatic leader, he was impatient to take his turn at leadership after E. A. Davies and H. A. Philips. Ibid., 76.
[434] Anderson, *African Reformation*, 107.
[435] Omoyajowo, *Cherubim and Seraphim*, 65 - 85.
[436] Ayegboyin and Ishola, *African Initiatives*, 84, 87.
[437] Adogame, *Celestial Church of Christ*, 72 - 74.
[438] Anderson, *African Reformation*, 87.
[439] Ibid., 81.
[440] Quoted in Ayegboyin and Ishola, *African Initiatives*, 87.
[441] Eugene Okere Ogbonna, interview by author, 9 August 2003.
[442] Elias Amalo, Pastor of Christ Holy Church International, Okigwe Superintendency, interview by author, 11 August 2003, Okigwe, Imo State, tape recording, Good News Theological College and Seminary, Accra.
[443] Daniel C. Dike, interview by author, 30 August 2003.
[444] S. O. Obiemeka, District Pastor of Christ Holy Church International, Itire District, interview by author, 30 August 2003, Lagos, Lagos State, tape recording, Good News Theological College and Seminary, Accra.
[445] Emmanuel Alamanjo, interview by author, 30 August 2003.
[446] Eusebius Iloabuchi, interview by author, 7 August 2003.
[447] The Constitution of Christ Holy Church International, Chapter Six, 1(a).
[448] Nicholas Udemba, interview by author, 9 August 2003.
[449] DomNwachukwu, *Authentic African Christianity*. 85, 86.
[450] Ibid., 86.

[451] Enoch Okonkwo, interview by Samuel Ozomah, *Glad News*, 1, no. 2, (n.d.) 10.
[452] Ibid., 10, 11.
[453] Ibid., 11.
[454] Emmanuel Alamanjo, interview by author, 31 August 2003.
[455] Antonia Chukwura, interview by author, 31 July 2003.
[456] Antonia Chukwura, interview by author, 31 July 2003.
[457] Ndiokwere, *Prophecy and Revolution*, 77, 79.
[458] Members of the Cherubim and Seraphim related Churches, for instance, believe that the name of the Church was revealed to them by angels. Angelology is, therefore, an important doctrine in the Church. Four angels are designated as being special to the Society: Michael (Captain of the Society), Gabriel (Vice Captain of the Society), Uriel (director of the elect towards the receiving of God's grace), and Raphael (healer of the sick). Members remove their caps and fall down at the mention of Cherubim and Seraphim in a hymn. Members call upon angels for help and believe that the angels are obliged to respond to their calls. See Omoyajowo, *Cherubim and Seraphim*, 114 - 118.
[459] Morton T. Kesley, *God, Dreams, and Revelation: a Christian Interpretation of Dreams* (Minneapolis: Augsburg, 1991) 21.
[460] Ibid., 22.
[461] Ibid., 24.
[462] Okoh, *Christ Holy Church: Order of Divine Services*, 5 - 11.
[463] Aaron Chukwunyelum Eziuzor, Superintendent Minister, Christ Holy Church International, Owerri Superintendency, interview by author, 19 August 2003, Owerri, Imo State, tape recording, Good News Theological College and Seminary, Accra.
[464] Aaron Ezuizor, interview by author, 19 August 2003.
[465] John Ekweoba, interview by author, 11 August 2003.
[466] Nathan Okeke Umeh, Superintendent Minister, Christ Holy Church International, Jos Superintendency, interview by author, 20 August 2003, Jos, Bauchi State, tape recording, Good News Theological College and Seminary, Accra.
[467] Okoh, "Immersion Baptism" *Good Tidings*, third issue, (Onitsha: n.d.) 14. Capitalization not mine. He quotes Romans 6:4 and Colossians 2:12 in support of the significance of baptism by immersion.
[468] Ibid., 15. Rt. Rev. Marius Okoh quotes the following texts to support his argument: Matt. 3:2, 3; Mark 1: 15; 16:16; Acts 2:38; 8: 37. Capitalizations not mine.
[469] Ibid., 17.
[470] Ibid., 17. Capitalization not mine.
[471] Ibid., 16, 17. Capitalization not mine.
[472] Mbiti, *African Religions and Philosophy*, 170.
[473] Barnabas Otoibhi, *Help for Cultists* (Lagos: Temple Rebuilders Ministry, 1999) 30. Otoibhi quotes from page 1 of *The Post Express*, 17 July 1997.
[474] Ibid., 36. See also page 33.
[475] *The Vanguard* Newspaper reported the finding of a ritual killing site by a search party in an undeveloped bushy site of Lagos State University on August 20, 2003. The search party found a missing 34-year-old final-year student, Peters Pippen Adaba. The paper reports that one of his eyes was plucked out and "a chunk of flesh from the chest sliced away" from his decomposed body. Other human body parts were picked at the site. *Vanguard*, 21 August 2003 (Vol. 19, No. 5322) 5. On Sunday, 30 August 2003, we had a hard time convincing heavily armed policemen before they allowed me and a pastor-friend to enter the premises of Lagos State University. The policemen were guarding all entrances to the campus because some cultic members had killed a student who was taking his final exam for no apparent reason at the time.

[476] Otoibhi, *Help for Cultists*, 9, 10.

[477] Ibid., 10.

[478] Kwame Gyekye, *African Cultural Values: an Introduction*. (Accra: Sankofa Publishing Company, 1998) 78, 79.

[479] Ibid., 78.

[480] For more details about polygamy, read Mbiti, *African Religions and Philosophy*, 142 - 145.

[481] Adogame, *Celestial Church of Christ*, 170.

[482] Ayegboyin and Ishola, *African Indigenous Churches*, 95, 96.

[483] Ibid., 87.

[484] Basden, *Among the Ibos of Nigeria*, 71. Read also pages 68 - 77. For other details of Igbo marriage, read Basden, *Niger Ibos*, (London: Frank & Co. Ltd., 1966) 213 - 227 and Edmund Ilogu, *Christianity and Ibo Culture*, 28 - 30.

[485] Okoh, *Christ Holy Church: Order of Divine Services*, 20.

[486] Ibid., 20.

[487] Emmanuel Aniago, interview by author, 9 August 2003.

[488] Stephen O. Obiemeka, interview by author, 28 August 2003, Lagos, tape recording, Good News Theological College and Seminary, Accra.

[489] Christian Obiefuna, interview by author, 26 August 2003. Biblical references of Obiefuna's examples can be found in: Acts 19:11, 12; 2 Kings 5:1-15; John 2: 1-11; 5:1- 9.

[490] Afe Adogame, "Doing Things with Water: Water as a Symbol of Life and Power in the Celestial Church of Christ," *Studies in World Christianity*, 6.1, (2000) 71.

[491] Clement Obiokoye, interview by author, 25 August 2003.

[492] Mbiti, *African Religions and Philosophy*, 3.

[493] Ibid., 1.

[494] Opoku, *West African Traditional Religion*, 8.

[495] Ibid., 9, 10.

[496] B. Kesse-Amankwaa, *Indigenous Religion and Culture* (Accra: Baafour Educational Enterprise, 1980) 9.

[497] E. G. Parrinder, *West African Religion,* London: Epsworth Press, 1961. A. B. Ellis, *The Twi-speaking Peoples of the Gold Coast,* London: Chapman and Hall, 1887; S. G. Williamson, *Akan Religion and the Christian Faith,* Accra: Ghana Universities Press, 1965.

[498] For more details about the names of God in West Africa, see Opoku, *West African Traditional Religion,* 14-29.

[499] Jenkins, *The Next Christendom*, 122.

[500] Jordan, *Bishop Shanahan of Southern Nigeria,* 128.

[501] Jenkins, *The Next Christendom,* 122. Italics not mine.

[502] Solomon Amadiume, *Igbo Tradition and Philosophy,* 36.

[503] The challenge of determining what cultural and religious aspects to promote or disband in the Church will be discussed in the next chapter.

[504] The Anglican Church was for a long time officially not ordaining women into the priesthood till 1988 when the Lambeth Conference, a forum for the debate of doctrines in the Anglican Community, officially appointed a group headed by Archbishop Eames to examine the reaction of Anglicans on the issue. See The Eames Monitoring Group report. http://www.anglicancommunion.org/lambeth/report/10.html (accessed 20 February 2004).

[505] Roman Catholics observe 7 Sacraments - (1) Baptism, (2) Holy Communion, (3) Confirmation, (4) Penance (or confession/reconciliation), (5) Holy Matrimony, (6) Unction or Anointing of Oil, and (7) Ordination. For biblical support of these sacraments, read Mark A. Pearson, *Christian Healing: a Practical and Comprehensive Guide* (Grand Rapids: Chosen Books, 1995) 193 - 207.

506 See an example of the contention in Bediako, *Christianity in Africa*, 183 - 186.
507 Nicholas Udemba, interview by author, 9 August 2003.
508 Samuel Ejiofor, interview by author, 9 August 2003.
509 DomNwachukwu, *Authentic African Christianity*, 65.
510 Quoted in DomNwachukwu, ibid., 65.
511 Ndiokwere, *Prophecy and Revolution*, 101-104.
512 Quoted in Ndiokwere, ibid., 104.
513 Ibid., 105.
514 DomNwachukwu, *Authentic African Christianity*, 93.
515 Victoria Njoku, interview by Emmanuel Aniago, 4 November 2003. To do *wayo*, in this context, is equivalent to being a conman.
516 Gabriel Chiemeka, interview by Samuel Ozomah, *Glad News*, 1, no. 2 (n.d.) 9.
517 Isaac Afunwa, interview by Samuel Ozomah, n.d. *Glad News*, 1, no. 2, (n.d.) 15.
518 Mbagwu Ogbete, "Akokwa and the wider world" interview by C. B. N. Okoli, 15 -16 July 1972 and 9 January 1973, in *Igbo Worlds: An Anthology of Oral Histories and Historical Descriptions*, Elizabeth Isichei, (Philadelphia: Institute for the Study of Human Issues, 1978) 111. According to Basden, another means of slavery was by "pawning," a system where someone is handed over to a creditor, involuntarily, as a security till what is owed will be paid. Others voluntarily hand themselves over, as security, till the debt is paid. Whether voluntarily or not, another person in the family substitutes for the original debtor should the debtor die without paying the debt. Basden, *Niger Ibos*, 253 - 255.
519 Basden, *Niger Ibos*, 246.
520 Ibid., 243 - 258.
521 Ibid., 249.
522 DonNwachukwu, *Authentic African Christianity*, 25.
523 Basden, *Niger Ibos*, 257.
524 Victor E. Dike, *The Osu Caste System in Igboland: A Challenge for Nigerian Democracy* (Kearney: Morris Publishing, 2002) 4, 10, 25. Dike also claims that the system has been in existence for six centuries. See page 23. Basden adds that "To -day educated many of the civilized, educated men will not share "kola" with a man of slave descent though, in other respects, he be a friend and an equal, or even superior in wealth and employment. In some areas, it is not permissible for slaves to be buried in the same cemetery where free-born folk are laid to rest... Basden, *Niger Ibos*, 243.
525 Stephen Obiemeka, interview by author, 30 August 2003.
526 Basden, *Niger Ibos*, 244.
527 Daniel Okoh, interview by author, 26 August 2003.
528 Paul Makhubu, "Attempts to unite African Independent Churches into Associations in South Africa" in *African Independent Churches in the 80s*, 43, 44.
529 Sam Babs Mala, "African Instituted Churches in Nigeria: The Quest for Unity, Education and Identity" in *Ministry in Partnership with African Independent Churches*, 31, 33. Zaire is now known as the Democratic Republic of Congo.
530 Makhubu, *Attempts to Unite African Independent Churches*, 44.
531 Nine out of the ten colleges and seminaries are mentioned in Sam Babs Mala's article, *African Instituted Churches in Nigeria*, 32, 33. The tenth one is *Marius Okoh Memorial Seminary*, of which much will be said in this section. There may be others that are not known to the author.
532 Mala, *African Instituted Churches in Nigeria*, 33.
533 Unpublished Catalogue of Marius Okoh Memorial Seminary, (n.d.) 9.
534 Daniel Okoh, interview by author, 26 August 2003.
535 Anonymous writer, *Glad News*, 1, no. 2, (n.d.) 22.

[536] Gilliland, *How 'Christian' are African Independent Churches*, 264.
[537] Omoyajowo, *Cherubim and Seraphim*, 92.
[538] Ayegboyin & Ishola describe Cherubim and Seraphim Church as a church with "syncretistic elements." Ayegboyin & Ishola, *African Indigenous Churches*, 87.
[539] DomNwachukwu, *Authentic African Christianity*, 83.
[540] Basden, *Niger Ibos*, 161.
[541] See Amadiume, *Igbo Tradition and Philosophy*, 32, and Achebe, *Things Fall Apart*, 19.
[542] DomNwachukwu, *Authentic African Christianity*, 39.
[543] Amadiume, *Igbo Tradition and Philosophy*, 36. See Ilogu, *Christianity and Ibo Culture*, 30, 31, for variants of *Ozo* titles. Scholars differ on the spelling of the *orzo*.
[544] Ilogu, *Christianity and Ibo Culture*, 30 - 33.
[545] Quoted in Ugwu, *Healing in the Nigerian Church*, 101.
[546] Ibid., 102.
[547] Jordan, *Bishop Shanahan of Southern Nigeria*, 70.
[548] Adogame, *Celestial Church of Christ*, 37.
[549] Jenkins, *The Next Christendom*, 68.
[550] Ayegboyin and Ishola, *African Indigenous Churches*, 33.
[551] Anderson, *African Reformation*, 102, 103.
[552] Anglicans also have the position of a *Catechist*.
[553] The Muzama Disco Christo Church is known to have an administration based on the Fanti chieftaincy structure. "Appiah based his complex church organization on the traditional Fanti court and became King Jehu Akaboha I. Ibid., 78.
[554] Enoch Okonkwo, interview by Samuel Ozomah, n.d. *Glad News*, 1 no. 2, (n.d.) 12. C. A. C. is the abbreviated form of Christ Apostolic Church.
[555] Enoch Okonkwo, interview by author, 30 July 2003.
[556] Clement Obiokoye, interview by author, 25 August 2003.
[557] Christ Apostolic Church, *1971 C. A. C. Year Book* (Mushin: Remilekun Press, n.d.) 55.
[558] Clement Obiokoye, interview by author, 25 August 2003.
[559] Daniel Dike, interview by author, 28 August 2003.
[560] Daniel Okoh, interview by author, 26 August 2003.
[561] Samuel Erivwo, *A History of Christianity in Nigeria: The Urhobo, the Isoko and the Itsekiri* (Ibadan: Daystar Press, 1979) 135.
[562] Ibid., 135.
[563] Ibid., 135, 136.
[564] Ibid., 136. Deji Ayegboyin, Professor of Religions at Ibadan University, confirmed with the author, in a conversation in Lagos, 29 August 2003 that the C. A. C. adopted that style of evangelism and, thus, won many independent congregations in Eastern Nigeria. Attempts to cross-check the stand of Christ Holy Church leaders with that of Christ Apostolic Church historians proved futile since there was a fresh schism in C.A.C. at the time the author was in Nigeria doing research.
[565] See the administrative structure of Christ Apostolic Church, *1971 C.A.C. Year Book* (Mushin: Remilekun Press, n.d.) 9.
[566] Ayegboyin & Ishola, *African Indigenous Churches*, 94.
[567] DomNwachukwu, *Authentic African Christianity*, 86, 87.
[568] Daniel Okoh, interview with author, 26 August 2003.
[569] For a full discussion of the reasons, read Cyril O. Imo, *Religion and the Unity of the Nigerian Nation*, (Tyck: Reprocentralen HSC, 1995) 24 - 31. Italics not mine.

[570] Contravening the tenets of the code has some devastating punishments like amputation of limbs and even killing.

[571] Simeon Okezuo Nwobi, *Sharia Law: What a Christian Must Know,* (Owerri: Totan Publishers, 2000) 12 - 19.

[572] Ibid., 29, 30.

[573] Ibid., 31.

[574] Nathan Okeke Umeh, Superintendent Minister, Christ Holy Church International, Jos Superintendency, Jos, Plateau State, interview by author, 21 August 2003, tape recording, Good News Theological College and Seminary, Accra.

[575] CIA World Factbook, http://www.bartleby.com/151/ni.html (accessed 21 February 2004).

[576] Though the seminars were held in June and September 2003 respectively (i.e., beyond the scope of this study) I have decided to include it due to its importance to the understanding of the challenges facing the church.

[577] Daniel Okoh, "Answers to many questions." Email correspondence with author, 24 October 2003.

[578] Daniel C. Dike, interview by author, 30 August 2003.

[579] Daniel C. Dike, interview by author, 30 August 2003.

[580] Rosalind Hackett, *Women as Leaders and Participants,* 192.

[581] Ibid., 195.

[582] Isichei, *A History of Christianity,* 291.

[583] Ibid., 291.

[584] Hackett, *Women as Leaders and Participants,* 192, 194.

Bibliography

BOOKS AND ARTICLES.

Achebe, Chinua. *Things Fall Apart*. New York: Anchor Books, 1959.

Achunike, Hilary C. *Dreams of Heaven: A Modern Response To Christianity In North Western Igboland, 1970-1990*. Enugu: Snaap Printing and Publishing, 1995.

Adogame, Afeosemime U. *Celestial Church of Christ*. Berlin: Peter Lang, 1998.

_____. "Doing Things with Water: Water as a Symbol of 'Life' and 'Power' in the Celestial Church of Christ." In *Studies in World Christianity* 6.1, (2000) 59 77.

Ajayi, J. F. A. *Christian Missions in Nigeria 1841-1891: The Making of a new Elite*. London: Longmans, Green and Co. Ltd., 1965.

Alamanjo, E. I. "Rev. E. N. Okonkwo." In *Glad News*, 1, no. 2, (n.d.) 28, 29.

_____. "D. O. U. Nwaizuzu." In *Glad News*, 1. no. 2, (n.d.) 30, 31

_____. (Chairman), Christ Holy Church Int'l: Sunday School Manual. Vol. 8, July 6th to Dec. 28th, 2003.

Amadiume, Solomon. *Igbo Tradition and Philosophy*. Enugu: Aritz Communication, 1998.

Anyanwu, H. O. "Missionaries and Women Emancipation in Igboland." In *Journal of Dharma*, 26 (2001) 228-234.

Anderson, H. Allan. *African Reformation: African Initiated Christianity in the 20th Century*. Asmara: Africa World Press, 2000.

_____. *Zion and Pentecost*. Pretoria: University of South Africa Press, 2000.

_____. Types and Butterflies: African Initiated Churches and European Typologies." In *International Bulletin of Mission Research*, (July 2001) 107-113.

Anderson, Efraim. *Messianic Popular Movement in the Lower Congo*. Uppsala: Almqvist & Wiksells Boktryckeri AB, 1958

Ayegboyin, Deji & Ishola, S. Ademola. *African Indigenous Churches*. Lagos: Greater Heights Publications, 1997.

Baeta, C. G. *Prophetism in Ghana*. London: SCM Press, 1962.

Barrett, David B. *Schism and Renewal in Africa*. Nairobi: Oxford University Press, 1968.

_____. "Who's Who of African Independent Church Leaders." In *RISK*, 7, no. 3 (1971) 23 34.

_____. David B. & Padwick, T. John. *Rise Up and Walk*. Nairobi: Oxford University Press, 1989.

Basden, G. T. *Among the Ibos of Nigeria*. New York: Barnes & Noble, 1966.. *Niger Ibos*. London: Frank & Co. Ltd., 1966.

Baur, John. *2000 Years of Christianity in Africa*. Nairobi: Paulines Publications Africa, 1994.

Bediako, Kwame. *Christianity in Africa: The Renewal of a Non-Western Religion*. Edinburgh: Edinburgh University Press, 1995.

Bosch, David. *Transforming Mission: Paradigm Shifts in Theology of Mission* Maryknoll: Orbis Books, 1991.

Botchway, Frank. "The Ossamadih Church (Church of Light)." In *Journal of African Christian Thought*, 3, no. 2, (2000) 2 15.

Buhlmann, Walbert. *The Missions on Trial*. Maryknoll: Orbis Books, 1979.

Burgess, Stanley M. *The Holy Spirit: Eastern Christian Traditions*. Peabody: Hendrickson Publishers, 1989.

Christ Apostolic Church. *1971 C.A.C. Year Book*. Mushin: Remilekun Press, n.d.

Calvin, John. *Calvin's Commentary: 1 Corinthians*. Translated by John Fraser, eds. David and Thomas Torrance, Grand Rapids: Wm. Eerdmans Publishing Co., 1960.

Clarke, Peter B. *West Africa and Christianity*. London: Edward Arnold Publishers Ltd., 1986.

Debrunner, Hans. *History of Christianity in Ghana*. Accra: Waterville Publishing, 1967

Dempster, Carolyn. "Leap of Faith." In *Focus On Africa: BBC Magazine*. Jan-Mar. 2001 44 46.

Dike, Victor E. *The Osu Caste System in Igboland: A Challenge for Nigerian Democracy*. Kearney: Morris Publishing, 2002.

DomNwachukwu, Peter Nlemadim. *Authentic African Christianity: An Inculturation Model for the Igbo*. New York: Peter Lang, 2000.

Edgar, Robert R. and Sapire, Hillary. *African Apocalypse: The Story of Nontetha Nkwekwe, a Twentieth Century South African Prophet*. Johannesburg: Witastersrand University Press, 1999.

Ekechi, F. K. "The Medical Factor in Christian Conversion in Africa: Observation From Southeastern Nigeria." In *Missiology* 21, no. 3 (1993) 289 309.

Erickson, Millard. *Christian Theology*. 2nd ed. Grand Rapids: Baker Books, 2001.

Erivwo, Samuel. *A History of Christianity in Nigeria: The Urhobo, the Isoko and the Itsekiri*. Ibadan: Daystar Press, 1979.

Falola, Toyin. *Violence in Nigeria: The Crisis of Religious Politics and Secular Ideologies*. Rochester: University of Rochester Press, 1998

Forde, Daryll & Jones, G. I. *The Ibo and Ibibio-Speaking Peoples of South-Eastern Nigeria*. London: Oxford University Press, 1950.

Fulford, Ben. "An Igbo Esperanto: A History of the Union Ibo Bible 1900 150." In *The Journal of Religion in Africa*, 32.4 (2002) 457-501.

Gilliland, Dean S. "How 'Christian' are African Independent Churches?" In *Missiology* 14, no. 3 (1986) 259 - 272.

Green, M. M. *Ibo Village Affairs*. New York: Frederick A. Praeger, 1964.

Guy, Linda. "My African Experience of God's People." In *Glad News*, 1, no. 2, (n.d.) 17 - 18.

Gyekye, Kwame. *African Cultural Values: An Introduction*. Accra: Sankofa Publishing Company, 1996.

Hackett, Rosalind I. J. *New Religious Movements in Nigeria*. Lewiston: Edwin Mellen Press, 1987.

_____. "Women as Leaders and Participants in the Spiritual Churches." In *New Religious Movements in Nigeria*. Lewiston: Edwin Mellen Press, 1987, 191 208.

Haliburton, Gordon M. *The Prophet Harris: A Study of an African Prophet and his Mass Movement in the Ivory Coast and the Gold Coast 1913-1915*. London: Longman, 1971.

Hastings, Adrian. *A History of African Christianity 1950-1975*. Cambridge: Cambridge University Press, 1979.

Hill, Harriet, "Witchcraft and the Gospel: Insight from Africa." In *Missiology*, 24, no. 3 (1996) 323 344.

Idowu, E. Bolaji. *Towards An Indigenous Church*. London: Oxford University Press, 1965.

Ihejiofor, Thaddeus, et. al. *Prayer Houses and Faith Healing in Nigeria*. ed. Vincent Nwosu, Onitsha: Tabansi Press, 1971.

Ikeobi, G. C. "Catholic Response to the Challenge of 'Prayer Houses' Origin of 'Tuesday Prayer' in Onitsha." In *The Catholic Church in Onitsha*, ed. V. A. Nwosu, Onitsha: n.p., 1984.

Ilogu, Edmund. *Christianity and Ibo Culture*. Leiden: E. J. Brill, 1974. Imo, Cyril O. *Religion and the Unity of the Nigerian Nation*. Tryck: Reprocentralen HSC, 1995

Isichei, Elizabeth. *A History of Christianity in Africa*. Grand Rapids, MI: Eerdmans, 1995.

_____. *Igbo Worlds*. Philadelphia: Institute for the Study of Human Issues, 1978.

_____. *The Ibo People and the Europeans: the Genesis of a Relationship to 1906*. New York: St. Martin's Press. 1973.

Jassy, M. F. Perrin, "Women in the African Independent Churches." In *RISK*, Vol. 7, no. 3 (1971) 46-49.

Jenkins, Philip. *The New Christendom: the Coming of Global Christianity*. Oxford: Oxford University Press, 2002.

Johnstone, Patrick and Mandryk, *Operation World*. 21st Century ed. Carlisle: Paternoster Publishing, 2001.

Jordan, John P. *Bishop Shahanan of Southern Nigeria*. Dublin: Clonmore & Reynolds Ltd., 1949.

Kalu, O. U. "Color and Conversion: The White Missionary Factor in the Christianization of Igboland, 1857 1967." In *Missiology*, 18, no. 1 (1990) 61 74

_____. "Doing Mission Through the Post Office: The Naked Faith People of Igboland 1920 1960." In *Neue Zeitschrift fur Missionswissenschaft*. Separat Abdruck, 56-2000/4.

_____. "Anatomy of an Explosion." Interview by anonymous interviewer of Christian History. *Christian History*, 79, no3 (2003) 7 - 9.

Keller, Ernst & Marie-Luise. *Miracles in Dispute: A Continuing Debate*. Philadelphia: Fortress Press, 1969.

Kese-Amankwaa, B. *Indigenous Religion and Culture*. Accra: Baafour Educational Enterprise, 1980.

Kesley, Morton. *Healing & Christianity*. Minneapolis: Augsburg, 1995.

Kirk-Green, A. H. M. *Crisis And Conflict in Nigeria: A Documentary Sourcebook July 1967 January 1970*. Vol. II. London: Oxford University Press, 1971.

Loram, C. T. "The Separatists Church Movement." In *International Review of Missions*, (1926) 476-482.

Ludwig, Freider. "Elijah II: Radicalisation and Consolidation of the Garrick Braide Movement 1915 1918." In *Journal of Religion in Africa*, 23, fasc. 4 (1993) 296 317.

Makhubu, Paul. *Who Are the African Independent Churches?* Braamfontein: Skotaville Publishers, 1988.

_____. "Attempts to unite African Independent Churches into Associations in South Africa." In *African Independent Churches in the 80s*. Lagos: Gilbert, Grace and Gabriel Associates, 1983.

Mala, Sam Babs. "African Instituted Churches in Nigeria: the Quest fro Unity, Education and Identity." In *Ministry in Partnership with African Independent Churches*, ed. David Shank, Elkhart: Mennonite Board of Missions, 1991.

_____. (ed). *African Independent Churches in the 80s*. Lagos: Gilbert, Grace and Gabriel Associates, 1983.

Martin, Marie-Louise. *Kimbangu: An African and his Church*. (Oxford: Basil Blackwell, 1975.

Mbiti, John. *African Religions and Philosophy*. New York: Praeger Publishers, 1969.

Mobley, Harris. *The Ghanaian's Image of the Missionary: an analysis of the published Critiques of Christian Missionaries by Ghanaians 1897-1965*, Leiden: E. J. Brill, 1970.

Ndiokwere, Nathaniel I. *Prophecy and Revolution: the role of prophets in the Independent African churches and in biblical tradition*. London: SPCK, 1981.

Niven, Rex. *The War of Unity*. Ibadan: Evans Brothers Ltd., 1970.

Nkwoka, Anthony O. "The Role of the Bible in the Igbo Christianity of Nigeria." In *The Bible in Africa: transactions, trajectories, and trends* eds. West, Gerald Dube, Musa. Leiden: Brill, 2000.

Nwobi, Simeon Okezuo. *Sharia Law in Nigeria: What a Christian Must know*. Owerr: Totan Publishers, 2000.

Obikwelu, G. I. "The Inauguration of the Christ Holy Church in Enugu and its Temporary Opening for Prayers and Worships." In *Good Tidings*, third issue, Onitsha, (n.d.) 28 32.

_____. "Report on Ndoni Convention." In *Good Tidings*, third issue, Onitsha, (n.d.) 10 13.

_____. "Prefactory." In *Good Tidings*, third issue, Onitsha, (n.d.) 1.

Oduro, Thomas A. "The History of the Good News Training Institute." In *Ministry In Partnership with African Independent Churches*, ed. David Shank, Elkhart: Mennonite Board of Missions, 1991.

Okite, Odhiambo, "The Politics of African Church Independency." In *RISK*, 7, no. 3 (1971) 42-45.

Okoh, Daniel C. "Focus on Rt. Rev. Marius Okoh: Foremost African Evangelists." In *Glad News*, 1, no. 1, (2000) 7 9.

_____. "Message from the General Superintendent: Mission Statement of Christ Holy Church." In *Glad News*, 1, no. 1, (2000) 4 5.

Okoh, Marius. "Immersion Baptism." In *Good Tidings*, third issue, Onitsha, (n.d.) 14 18.

_____. *Christ Holy Church: Order of Divine Services*. Onitsha: Confidence Enterprises, n.d.

Olupona, Jacob K. (ed.). *Religion and Peace in Multi-Faith Nigeria*. Ile-Ife: Obafemi Awolowo University, 1992.

Omenka, Nicholas. "The Role of the Catholic mission in the development of vernacular Literature in Eastern Nigeria." In *Journal of Religion in Africa*. 16, fasc. 2 (1986) 121 137.

Omoyajowo, J. Akinyele. *Cherubim and Seraphim*. New York: NOK Publishers International Ltd., 1982.

Opoku, Kofi Asare. *West African Traditional Religion*. Accra: FEP International Private Limited, 1978.

Oraka, L. N. *The Foundations of Igbo Studies: A Short History of Igbo Language and Culture*. Onitsah: University Publishing Co., 1983.

Otoibhi, Barnabas. *Help For Cultists*. Lagos: Temple Rebuilders Ministry, 1999

Ozigboh, I. R. *Roman Catholicism in South Eastern Nigeria 1885 1931*. Onitsha: Etukokwu Publishers, 1988.

Ozomah, Samuel O. A. "Tribute to Very Rev. Isaac O. Afunwa: the Gallant Pull out of a Gallant Soldier." In *Glad News*, 1, no. 2, (n.d.) 16.

Parrinder, Geoffrey. *Witchcraft: European and African*. New York: Barnes and Noble, 1963.

_____. *West African Religion*. London: Epsworth Press, 1961.

Pearson, Mark A. *Christian Healing: a Practical and Comprehensive Guide*. Grand Rapids: Chosen Books, 1995

Pobee, John. *Toward an African Theology*. Nashville: Parthenon Press, 1979.

_____ & Ositelu, Gabriel. *African Initiatives in Christianity*. Geneva: WCC Publications, 1998

Pretorius, H. L. *Historiography and Historical Sources regarding African Independent Churches in South Africa*. Lampeter: Edwin Meles Press, 1995.

Pritchard, E. E. *Witchcraft, Oracles and Magic among the Azande*. Oxford: Oxford University Press, 1937.

Rasmussen, Ane Marie Bak, *Modern African Spirituality: The Independent Spirit Churches in East Africa, 1902-1976*. London & New York: British Academic Press, 1996.

Ratovonarivo. "The Independent Churches in Madagascar." In *African Independent Churches in the 80s*, ed. Sam Babs Mala, Lagos: Gilbert, Grace and Gabriel Associates, 1983.

Sanneh, Lamin. *West African Christianity.* Maryknoll, NY: Orbis Books, 1983.

_____. "World Christianity and the new Historiography." In *Enlarging the Story: Perspectives on Writing World Christian History,* ed. Wilbert Shenk, Maryknoll: Orbis Books, 2002.

_____. *Translating the Message: The Missionary Impact on Culture.* Maryknoll: Orbis Books, 1990.

Shank, David A. (ed). *Ministry in Partnership with African Independent Churches.* Elkhart, IN: Mennonite Board of Missions, 1991.

_____. *Prophet Harris, The Black Elijah of West Africa* Leiden: E. J. Brill, 1994.

Shenk, Wilbert R. (ed.). *Enlarging the Story.* Maryknoll: Orbis Books, 2002.

Shepherd, R. H. W. "The Separatist Churches of South Africa." In *International Review Missions,* (1937) 453-463.

Sundkler, Bengt G. M. *Bantu Prophets in South Africa.* London: Oxford University Press, 1976.

_____. & Steed, Christopher. *A History of the Church in Africa.* Cambridge: Cambridge University Press, 2000.

Tasie, G. O. M. "Christian Awakening in West Africa, 1914 1918: A Study in the Significance of Native Agency." In *The History of Christianity in West Africa,* ed. O. U. Kalu, London: Longman, 1980.

The Holy Bible: *New American Standard Bible.* Chattanooga: AMG Publishers, 1977.

Turner, Harold W. *From Temple to Meeting Place: The Phenomenology and Theology of Places of Worship.* Paris: Mouton Publishers, 1979. *

_____. *Religious Innovation in Africa.* Boston: G. K. Hall & Co; 1979.

_____. "Prophets and Politics: A Nigerian Test-case." In *Society for African Church History,* 2, no. 1 (1965) 97 118.

_____. *History of an African Independent Church: The Church of the Lord (Aladura).* Vols. 1&2. Oxford: Clarendon Press, 1967.

Ugwu, Chin nyelu Moses. *Healing in the Nigerian Church: A Pastoral-psychological Exploration.* Bern: Peter Lang, 1998.

Walker, Williston et. al. *A History of the Christian Church.* New York: Charles Scribner's Sons, 1985.

Walls, Andrew. *The Cross-Cultural Process in Christian History.* Maryknoll: Orbis Books, 2002.

_____. *The Missionary Movement in Christian History: Studies in the Transmission of Faith.* Maryknoll: Orbis Books, 1996.

_____. & Shenk, Wilbert R. (eds.) *Exploring New Religious Movements.* Elkhart, IN: Missions Focus Publications, 1990.

Weaver, Edwin & Irene. *Kuku Hill: among indigenous Churches in West Africa.* Elkhart: Institute of Mennonite Studies, 1975.

Wicker, Kathleen O'Brien. "Mami Water in African Religion and Spirituality." In *African Spirituality: Forms, Meanings and Expressions,* ed. Jacob K. Olupona, New York: Crossroad Publishing Company, 2000.

Williams, Walter. *Black Americans and the Evangelization of Africa.* Madison: The University of Wisconsin Press, 1982.

Zvanaka, Solomon. "African Independent Churches in Context." In *Missiology*, 25, no. 1, (1997) 69-75.

PUBLISHED INTERVIEWS

Afunwa, I. O. "Glad News Interview with Very Rev. I. O. Afunwa." Interview by Samuel O. A. Ozomah, n.d., *Glad News*, 1, no. 2, (n.d.) 15.

Chiemeka, Gabriel Onuorah, "Interview with Rt. Rev. Gabriel Onuorah Chiemeka," Interview by Samuel O. A. Ozomah, n.d., *Glad News*, 1, no. 2, (n.d.) 7, 9, 14.

Ogbete, Mbagwu, "Akokwa and a wider world." Interview by C. B. N. Okoli, 16 July 1972 and 9 January 1973, in *Igbo Worlds: An Anthology of Oral Histories and Historical Descriptions*, Elizabeth Isichei, editor (Philadelphia: Institute for the Study of Human Issues, 1978) 108 113.

Okonkwo, Enoch N. "Interview with Rev. Enoch N. Okonkwo (Rtd)," interview by Samuel O. A. Ozomah, n.d., *Glad News*, 1, no. 2, (n.d.) 8, 10 13, 18.

Wells, Michael. "Interview with Rev. Dr. Michael Wells." Interview by Samuel O. A. Ozomah, 27 February 2000, Itire, Lagos State, *Glad News*, 1, no. 2, (n.d.) 19, 21.

UNPUBLISHED INTERVIEWS

Alamanjo, Emmanuel. District Pastor, Christ Holy Church International, Fegge Lagos. Interview by author, 29, 30, 31 August 2003, Lagos. Tape recording. Good News Theological College and Seminary, Accra.

Amalo, Elias. Pastor, Christ Holy Church International, Okigwe Superintendency. Interview by author, 11 August 2003, Okigwe. Tape recording. Good News Theological College and Seminary, Accra.

Aneso, Daniel Udema. Superintendent Minister, Nssuka Superintendency, Christ Holy Church International, Nssuka. Interview by author, 8 August 2003, Nssuka, Enugu State. Tape recording. Good News Theological College and Seminary, Accra.

Aniago, Emmanuel. Pastor, Christ Holy Church International. Interview by author, 11 August 2003, Okigwe. Tape recording. Good News Theological College and Seminary, Accra.

Anyalebechi, Anthony. Evangelist, Christ Holy Church International, Ekwegbe Station. Interview by author, 8 August 2003, Nssuka. Tape recording, Good News Theological College and Seminary, Accra.

Anyanwu, Christianah, Midwife, Christ Holy Church Maternity Home, Ndoni. Interview by author, 18 August 2003, Ndoni. Tape recording. Good News Theological College and Seminary, Accra.

Asadu, Emmanuel. Technician/Audio Engineer, Nation Builders Gospel Band, Christ Holy Church International. Interview by author, 5 August 2003, Onitsha. Tape recording. Good News Theological College and Seminary, Accra.

Asor, Catherine. Elder, Christ Holy Church International, Okigwe congregation. Interview by author, 11 August 2003, Okigwe. Tape recording. Good News Theological College and Seminary, Accra.

Chiemeka, Gabriel Onuorah. General Evangelist and Assistant General Superintendent, CHC International, Onitsha. Interview by author, 27 August

2003, Nnewi. Tape recording. Good News Theological College and Seminary, Accra.

Chukwura, Antonia. Deaconess and Senior Midwife, Christ Holy Church International's Maternity Home, Isiokwe. Interview by author, 31 July 2003, Isiokwe, Anambra State. Tape recording. Good News Theological College and Seminary, Accra.

Dike, Daniel Chukwuenyem. Superintendent Minister, Christ Holy Church International, Lagos Superintendency, Lagos. Interview by author, 28, 30 August 2003, Lagos. Tape recording. Good News Theological College and Seminary, Accra.

Eboh, Augustine. Member, Christ Holy Church International, Aba congregation. Interview by author, 24 August 2003, Aba. Tape recording. Good News Theological College and Seminary, Accra.

Ejiofor, Samuel. Former leader, Christ Holy Church International, Onitsha. Interview by author, 30 August 2003, Enugu. Tape recording. Good News Theological College and Seminary, Accra.

Ekweoba, John. Assistant Superintendent Minister, Christ Holy Church International, Okigwe Superintendency, Okigwe. Interview by author, 11 August 2003, Okigwe. Tape recording. Good News Theological College and Seminary, Accra.

Ezuizor, Aaron Chukwunyelum. Superintendent Minister, Christ Holy Church International, Owerri Superintendency, Owerri. Interview by author, 19 August 2003. Owerri. Tape recording. Good News Theological College and Seminary, Accra.

Iloabuchi, Eusebius. Assistant Superintendent Minister, Christ Holy Church International, Nteje Superintendency, Nteje. Interview by author, 1 August 2003, Awka-Nteje. Tape recording. Good News Theological College and Seminary, Accra.

Martey, Michael Martey. Senior Evangelist, Christ Holy Church International. Interview by author, 5 August 2003, Onitsha. Tape recording Good News Theological College and Seminary, Accra.

Mbadiwe, Chidi. Elder, Christ Holy Church International, Fegge-Lagos congregation. Interview by author, 28 August 2003, Lagos. Tape recording. Good News Theological College and Seminary, Accra.

_____. Interview by author, 30 August 2003, Lagos. Tape recording. Good News Theological College and Seminary, Accra.

Njoku, Victoria. Deaconess and for a long, house-help Prophetess Agnes Okoh. Interview by Emmanuel Aniago, 4 November 2003, Onitsha. Tape recording. Headquarters of Christ Holy Church International, Onitsah.

Nwachukwu, Ijeoma. Cousin of Prophetess Agnes Okoh. Interview by author, 18 August, Ndoni. Tape recording. Good News Theological College and Seminary, Accra.

Nwaizuzu, David Ozioma U. Retired leader, Christ Holy Church International, Onitsha. Interview by author, 30 July & 2 August 2003. Onitsha. Tape recording. Good News Theological College and Seminary, Accra.

Obalum, Charles. Pastor, Christ Holy Church International, Onitsha. Interview by author, 7 August 2003 Awka-Nteje. Tape recording. Good News Theological College and Seminary, Accra.

Obiakor, John. Pastor, Christ Holy Church International, Ihitenansa. Interview by author, 15 August 2003, Ihintenansa. Tape recording. Good News Theological College and Seminary, Accra.

Obiefuna, Christian C. Assistant Superintendent, Christ Holy Church International, Asaba Superintendency. Interview by Author, 5 August 2003, Ogwashi-Ukwu. Tape recording. Good News Theological College and Seminary, Accra.

_____. Interview by author, 23 August 2003, Asaba. Tape recording. Good News Theological College and Seminary, Accra.

_____. Interview by author, 26 August 2003, Asaba. Tape recording. Good News Theological College and Seminary, Accra.

Obiemeka, Stephen O. District pastor, Christ Holy Church International, Itire District, Lagos. Interview by author, 30 August 2003, Lagos. Tape recording. Good News Theological College and Seminary, Accra.

Obiokoye, Clement. Assistant General Evangelist and Senior Superintendent, Christ Holy Church International, Aba Superintendency, Aba. Interview by author, 25 August 2003, Aba. Tape recording. Good News Theological College and Seminary, Accra.

Obioma, Everest, Financial Committee member, Okpoko # 1 congregation, Christ Holy Church International. Interview by author, 5 August 2003, Onitsha. Tape recording. Good News Theological College and Seminary, Accra.

Ofoedu, Cyril, Pastor, Christ Holy Church International, Benin City. Interview by author, 26 August 2003, Asaba. Tape recording. Good News Theological College and Seminary, Accra.

Ogbonna, Eugene Okere, Senior Catechist, Christ Holy Church International, Onitsha. Interview by author, 9 August 2003, Enugu. Tape recording. Good News Theological College and Seminary, Accra.

Okeyia, Gabriel. His Royal Highness, the Awo and Okpkala-Ukwu of Ndoni. Interview by author, 18 August 2003, Ndoni. Tape recording. Good News Theological College and Seminary, Accra.

Okoh, Daniel Chukwudumebi. General Superintendent, Christ Holy Church International, Onitsha. Interview by author, 1 August 2003, Ndoni, Rivers State. Tape recording. Good News Theological College and Seminary, Accra.

_____. Interview by author, 26 August 2003, Asaba. Tape recording. Good News Theological College and Seminary, Accra.

Okonkwo, Enoch N. Former leader, Christ Holy Church International, Onitsha. Interview by author, 30 July & 2 August 2003, Onitsha. Tape recording. Good News Theological College and Seminary, Accra.

_____ and Nwaizuzu, D. O. U. Former leaders of Christ Holy Church International, Onitsah. Interview jointly by author, 2 August 2003, Onitsha. Tape recording. Good News Theological College and Seminary, Accra.

Okpata, E. N. Pastor of Christ Holy Church, Jos Superintendency, Jos. Interview by author, 21 August 2003, Jos. Tape recording. Good News Theological College and Seminary, Accra.

Udemba, Nicholas. Assistant Superintendent, Enugu Superintendency, Christ Holy Church International, Enugu. Interview by author, 9 August 2003, Enugu. Tape recording. Good News Theological College and Seminary, Accra.

Umeh, Nathan Okeke, Superintendent Minister, Christ Holy Church International, Jos Superintendency. Interview by author, 21 August 2003, Jos. Tape recording, Good News Theological College and Seminary, Accra.

UNPUBLISHED MATERIALS

Okoh, Daniel C. "A Life Lived for Christ." Eulogy in honor of Agnes Okoh at Ndoni, Rivers State, April 8, 1995. (photocopy), p. 3. Official documents, Christ Holy Church International, National Headquarters, Onitsha, Anambra State.

INFORMALLY PUBLISHED ELECTRONIC MATERIAL

BBC NEWS/WORLD/AFRICA/COUNTRY PROFILES/Country Profile: Nigeria. http://news.bbc.co.uk/1/hi/world/africa/country-profiles/1064557.stm (accessed 16 January 2004).

CIA The World Factbook. http://www.cia.gov/cia/publications/factbook/geos/ni.html (accessed 16 January 2004).

CIA The World Factbook. http://www.bartleby.com/151/ni.html (accessed 21 February 2004).

Global Mapping Inc. *Operation World CD 2001.* (accessed 14 October 2003).

Metz, Helen Chaplin. *Nigeria: a country study* Federal Research Division, Library of Congress. http://lcweb2.loc.gov/cgi-bin/query/r?frd/cstdy:@field(DOCID+ng0028). (accessed 14 February 2004).

Motherland Nigeria: *Historical Government* http://ww.motherlandnigeria.com/govt_hist.html (accessed 10 February 2004).

The Church of Jesus Christ on Earth through the Prophet Simon Kimbangu. "Attributes of Papa Simon Kimbangu, Founder of the Kimbanguist Church." http://www.kimbanguisme.com/e-option1a.htim (accessed 20 April 2001).

The Eames Monitoring Group Report, August 1997. http://www.anglicancommunion.org/lambeth/report/10.html (accessed 20 February 2004).